A PARISH PASTORAL DIRECTORY

William Dalton

THE DIOCESE OF OSSORY

A Parish
Pastoral Directory

Edited by
William Dalton

the columba press

First published in 1995 by
the columba press
93 The Rise, Mount Merrion, Blackrock, Co Dublin, Ireland

Cover by Bill Bolger
Origination by The Columba Press
Printed in Ireland by Colour Books, Dublin

ISBN 1 85607 151 0

Contents

Foreword

Most Reverend Laurence Forristal
Bishop of Ossory

The idea of compiling a 'Pastoral Directory' for the Diocese was first mooted at a meeting of the Ossory Council of Priests in March, 1985. It arose out of deeply felt needs among priests for some form of booklet or handbook containing official Church policy and pastoral guidelines on a wide range of issues. As problems arise priests and others engaged in pastoral ministry often find themselves in the frustrating situation of knowing that precise guidelines or directives exist but not being able to locate them at short notice. This *Directory* aims at directing those with enquiring minds to the appropriate sources so that their decision-making can be rooted in sound doctrine and proven pastoral practice. The vast proliferation of official documents and pastoral letters emanating from both Rome and the different Episcopal Conferences around the world can make this exceedingly difficult. This explains the large number of references scattered throughout the *Directory*.

The Directory has had a long gestation. The decision to proceed with the project was taken at a meeting of the Council of priests in May 1986. A Steering Committee, consisting of the Bishop and a number of priests, was formed. This in turn established numerous sub-committees, each consisting of priests, religious and lay people. Each group was given a specific task and asked to report back to the Steering Committee within a specified time. Meanwhile the Steering Committee held numerous meetings discussing, amending and editing various submissions and drafts. All sections went through several different drafts and editings before arriving at their present state.

As one might expect, many of the issues addressed in this *Directory* are of a pastoral nature, and hence are of immediate concern to priests and lay people intent on living out their Christian vocation within the Church.

13

As the title suggests, it is nothing more than a *Directory*. It lays no claim to being a comprehensive textbook for the busy pastoral priest much less a compendium of pastoral theology. Its pretensions are far more modest.

It is not intended to replace or supplant conciliar or post-conciliar teaching or discipline in any way. Neither is it intended to supplement or be a kind of appendix to the 1983 *Code of Canon Law*. On the contrary it makes reference to all of these sources and many others as well in addressing the practical, pastoral issues that the average priest must face. It neither pretends nor intends to give all the answers. In other words it does not exonerate the priest from making pastoral decisions or take away his responsibility. In many instances there simply are not any universally applicable norms available. Each case must be judged on its own merits. Hence, the *Directory* sometimes stops short of giving minutely detailed norms and regulations. Good pastoral practice suggests this. Directives can, unfortunately, all too quickly become commands and even positive laws. They are not intended to be such. Directives can never replace the love and concern of a caring minister. The pastoral priest can never abdicate the more difficult tasks of evangelisation and personal decision-making. Trying to set guidelines about the levels of faith required for the reception of the different sacraments is a perfect case in point. Such judgments can only be made by the priest on the spot, guided of course by the general norms and principles as specified in Church teaching. All too often judgements about the lack of faith in these areas are based on feelings and the latter are neither the proper concern of faith nor any sort of barometer for measuring it.

The priest's decision must always be inspired by a 'compassion based on truth' (John Paul II, *Address to the Roman Rota*, January 1990). Exercising compassion therefore is always time-consuming and may even include a certain element of conflict and uncertainty. After all did not Jesus warn his disciples that the making of disciples would invariably entail an element of conflict and anxiety? It is hoped that this *Pastoral Directory* will be an aid and instrument of pastoral and spiritual renewal in the diocese and beyond.

Finally, I would like to compliment and thank all who have helped to bring this project to completion.

Preface

Ever since the Second Vatican Council the pastoral priest has been finding himself increasingly inundated by what seems like an interminable stream of official documents and decrees emanating from various sources. He knows only too well that most of these documents, or at least parts of them, are of immediate significance to his own life and ministry. But all too often he has neither the time, the appetite nor the energy to peruse them or become acquainted with them at the time of their appearing. Frequently their particular subject matter is not of immediate interest to him. Subsequently when he needs to consult them he does not know where to look, or, as is often the case, the said documents are no longer readily available or accessible to him.

Then there is the further difficulty – official documents and their directives cannot possibly cater for all circumstances and eventualities. Despite their pre-eminently pastoral thrust, day-to-day parish ministry is such that the priest is constantly encountering new situations and problems for which no concrete norms or directives exist. He must make his own informed decisions and devise his own pastoral strategy, based upon the authentic teaching of the Church and good pastoral practice. The latter must always be based upon the Church's teaching and not *vice versa*; hence, the emphasis on putting forward as briefly and succinctly as possible the Church's teaching on the different topics as they arise and then proceeding to outline some more practical, pastoral principles. It is hoped that this *Pastoral Directory* will assist the priest to understand better the Church's teaching on different issues and put it into practice as he goes about his day-to-day work.

As one might expect a considerable part of the *Directory* is devoted to the priest's pastoral, sacramental and liturgical ministry among his people. Needless to say, this particular ministry does not exhaust his priesthood. Hence, there is considerable emphasis on preparation for and celebration of the sacraments and the liturgy, and on his reaching out to people with particular needs. But the priest can reach out to people only to the extent that he himself has already experienced God's saving love in his own life.

One of the primary aims of this *Directory* is to whet the priest's appetite for further study and investigation of particular questions and issues as they arise. Hence, it incorporates many references to official Roman documents and to those of the Irish Episcopal Conference. A short bibliography is offered at the end of each chapter. In this way it is hoped that experience and learning will proceed simultaneously. Experience will create the need for study and investigation, with the latter enriching and deepening one's experience in turn.

Finally, since certain sections of this Directory are primarily of local and diocesan interest, it was decided to indicate, by adding a rule in the margin as here, those parts referring explicitly to the practice obtaining in the diocese of Ossory.

William Dalton
Editor

Official Church Documents

Apart from the *Code of Canon Law*, the official Church documents referred to most frequently throughout this *Directory* are to be found in the two volumes of conciliar and post-conciliar documents edited by Father Austin Flannery OP. Throughout the text the volumes are referred to simply as Flannery vol I or vol II respectively, with appropriate page references. The complete titles are as follows:

Flannery, A., O.P. (ed), *Vatican Council II, Vol 1, The Conciliar and Post-Conciliar Documents*, Dominican Publications, Dublin, 1975.

—*Vatican Council II, Vol II, More Post-Conciliar Documents*, Dominican Publications, Dublin, 1982.

The Code of Canon Law, Collins, London, 1983.

CHAPTER 1

The Parish

At the beginning of his pontificate, Pope Paul VI reaffirmed un-equivocally his unwavering belief in the parish structure as the primary agent of spiritual renewal in the post-conciliar Church. 'We believe', he said, 'that this old and venerable structure of the parish has an indispensable mission of great contemporary im-portance: to create the basic community of the Christian people; to initiate and gather the people in the accustomed expression of liturgical life; to conserve and renew the faith in the people of today; to serve as a school for teaching the salvific message of Christ ...' *(Discourse to the Roman Clergy, 24/6/1963: AAS 55 (1963), 674).* Some thirty years after the conclusion of the Second Vatican Council these prophetic words are more pertinent than ever. It is at the level of parish that the vast majority of people experience what it means to be Church. It is in and through the ecclesial community of the parish that the lives of people are touched by God's saving presence. In the words of Pope John Paul II the parish is the Church living in the midst of the homes of her sons and daughters *(cf The Vocation and Mission of the Laity, Christifideles Laici, 30/12/1988, n 26).* It is imperative therefore that we understand and appreciate the true significance of parish within a post-conciliar perspective.

1. The Post-Conciliar Parish

The Church's vision of parish today is very much modelled on and rooted in its own self-understanding. This new self-aware-ness finds expression in conciliar ecclesiology. The latter sees the Church primarily as a community of persons who confess and accept God's revelation in Jesus as Lord, a community united to the Father and to one another through Christ in the Spirit. The parish is the basic cell of this community; it is 'the Church placed in the neighbourhoods of humanity' *(Op cit n 27).* It is against this background that the 1983 *Code of Canon Law* defines parish:

A parish is a certain community of Christ's faithful stably

established within a particular Church, whose pastoral care, under the authority of the diocesan Bishop, is entrusted to a parish priest as its proper pastor (c 515#1).

This definition highlights the essential characteristics of parish:
- it is people-centred;
- its sole purpose is pastoral care;
- it has its own proper pastor;
- the diocesan Bishop has ultimate responsibility for it;
- it is not an autonomous entity but a cell of the larger ecclesial unit which is the diocese.

Pope John XXIII spoke of the parish as the 'village fountain' to which all have recourse in their thirst. It is a community of faith where the rights of people are primary and parish structures are secondary because 'the parish is not principally a structure, a territory or building, but rather, 'the family of God, a fellowship afire with a unifying spirit', 'familial and welcoming the 'community of the faithful' *(Op cit, n 26-27)*.

Parish and its various structures are at the service of people and not *vice versa*. It is the pastoral care of people that is all important. Hence, in the matter of the appointment of a parish priest what really matters is his suitability for the exercise of pastoral ministry in the particular parish in question (cf cs 521 #3 & 524).

2. Parish at the Service of God's People

It is within the context of the parish that Christ's faithful hear and answer their call to holiness (Mt 5:48). All parish structures and organisations are aimed at serving people in their pursuit of holiness. None of them constitute an end in themselves. It is within the context of the parish that people's experience of Church is both moulded and fashioned. It is there that the Church is seen locally. It is the *locus* in which believers live out that experience of communion and partnership which the Church is; where 'all are nourished by each one and each one is nourished by all' *(St Gregory the Great)*. It is within the context of parish that God's people exercise their rights and fulfil their obligations within the Church. The parish must endeavour to help and facilitate people in this pursuit. For the first time these rights and obligations are now listed in the *Code of Canon Law*.

By virtue of their Baptism and Confirmation Christ's faithful have the right to participate in building up God's Kingdom in the world (c 208) by bringing the Good News to their brothers and sisters (c 211) and by following their own forms of spirituality in accordance with Church tradition (c 214). Priests for their part have a corresponding duty and obligation to consult the faithful and seek their views especially in those matters which pertain to the good of the Church (c 212 #3). They do this primarily, though not exclusively, through committees, pastoral councils, parish liturgy groups and other associations within the parish and the diocese.

In addition the faithful have the right to be nourished by the Word of God and the sacraments (c 213). It should be remembered that the right to receive the sacraments is not an absolute one because the Church has both the right and duty to safeguard the sacredness of the sacraments. As a general rule the sacraments are celebrated if:

i) the recipient is properly disposed;

ii) if he/she opportunely asks for the sacrament;

iii) if the person in question is not prohibited from receiving the sacraments by reason of ecclesiastical censure (cf c 843).

In living out their Christian calling the faithful have the right to form associations which serve charitable and pious purposes or promote the Christian vocation (c 215). They have the right to a good name and reputation, and privacy (c 220) as well as the right to vindicate and defend these rights in a competent ecclesiastical forum (c 221).

If the parish is to discharge its mission properly it needs suitable financial support and resources for the purposes of worship, the support of its ministers and the works of the apostolate and charity. The faithful must ensure that the necessary resources are available (c 222 #1). Finally parents in particular have the obligation to provide Christian education for their children (c 226 #2).

Adult Religious Formation

The Irish Bishops' Conference, meeting at the Emmaus Retreat Centre in September 1986, expressed the wish the 'every parish

THE PARISH

in the country take responsibility for adult religious formation, either on its own, or in collaboration with neighbouring parishes'. Over the past decade or so Adult Religious Education Courses have been running successfully at different centres throughout the diocese. Many have participated in these courses but they still only constitute a drop in the ocean when compared with our Catholic and Churchgoing population. If one were to identify a shortcoming with regard to the said courses, it must surely be the failure of many of those who participated to become more actively involved subsequently in the life of their parishes. The time is now ripe for each parish or group of parishes to embark on a programme of Adult Religious Formation. People today find themselves living in a pluralist culture where traditionally accepted Christian values are forever being subjected to critique and analysis. Christians must anchor their faith more firmly through participating in Adult Religious Education if they are to become competent interpreters of their own tradition. Cardinal Cathal Daly reminded us of this in September 1991 on the occasion of launching the post-Confirmation programme for parishes: *Growing in the Faith:*

> The continuous increase in secular knowledge, together with the ongoing and welcome extension of access to education in our society, mean that faith is constantly being challenged by new problems and being questioned by new discoveries and new attitudes. The religious education received in one's school years was never adequate for adult living, but its inadequacy is more glaringly obvious today with every passing year (*Intercom*, February 1992, p 8).

Experience shows that people are prepared to give a commitment to short (4 nights), well organised courses, tailored to their particular needs. The mystery of suffering, pain and death are never far from day-to-day life and hence the popularity of topics dealing with bereavement and healing etc.. But perhaps the most important element of all in motivating people to participate in Adult Religious Education Programmes – one which is often forgotten – is the end or objective towards which it is leading. 'Adult Religious Education is most successful when tied in with the challenge to do something specific - faith friends, groups looking at parish needs etc ....' (Bishop Donal Murray, A.G.M. of National Association of Adult Religious Advisors, in:

Intercom, February 1990, p 15). Courses for Eucharistic Ministers are eminently successful because they are perceived by the participants as leading to a real and visible involvement in the life of the parish.

In September 1994 the Creidim Centre for Adult Religious Education opened in St Kieran's College, Kilkenny. It is a project set up for the education and formation of the people of the diocese of Ossory in the challenging circumstances of the present time. Its programmes aim at addressing topical issues touching the everyday lives of people. Brochures are circulated before each programme.

3. Parish at the Service of the Diocese and Universal Church

The parish must never see itself as an autonomous or independent unit either within the diocese or universal Church. It must always be outward-looking and intent on developing a truly 'catholic' spirit. Indeed, the Second Vatican Council urges the laity to be concerned not just for the needs of the parish but rather for the good of the diocese and the universal Church:

> The laity will continuously cultivate 'the feeling for the diocese', of which the parish is a kind of cell; they will be always ready on the invitation of their bishop to make their contribution to diocesan undertakings. Indeed they will not confine their cooperation within the limits of the parish or diocese, but will endeavour in response to the needs of the towns and rural districts, to extend it to interparochial, interdiocesan, national and international spheres (Vatican II, *Decree on the Apostolate of Lay People, Apostolicam Actuositatem*, n 10, Flannery, vol I, p 778).

i) The Parish and the Diocese:

Within the diocese there are many structures and organisations which are diocesan (if not interdiocesan) by their very nature. These rely completely on the whole-hearted support and collaboration of all the people of the diocese, e.g.

Clerical Fund Society of the Diocese of Ossory
Ossory Priests' Society
Diocesan Liturgy Committee
Diocesan Buildings and Properties Committee

Diocesan Finance Committee
Diocesan Committee for Ecumenism
Advisory Committee on Housing for the Elderly
Ossory Pastoral Group
Ossory Social Services Committee
Accord
Cura
S.O.S
Ossory Youth Services
Ossory Catechetical Centre
Adult Religious Education Committee – Creidim
Peace in Christ Retreat Centre

The smooth and effective running of these organisations requires the generous assistance of keen and competent people. To
ensure that these bodies are truly diocesan in character, priests
should periodically propose the names of suitable lay people
who might serve on these committees, and as assessors for the
appointment of primary school teachers. Finally, since these
bodies are for the most part non-self-financing, their funding depends on the generous contributions of all the people of the diocese. Priests should enthusiastically support and encourage
those collections and appeals aimed at funding these organisations.

ii) The Parish and the Universal Church:

Since the parish is the universal Church seen locally, it is by its
very nature missionary (cf Vatican II, *Decree on the Church's
Missionary Activity, Ad Gentes*, n 2, Flannery, vol I, p 814). The
Church exists for mission. It was missionary zeal that brought
the Church into existence in the very first instance and not vice
versa. It is its missionary thrust that keeps a parish vibrant and
spiritually alive. Missionary outreach is at the heart of every
parish and community.

There are many practical ways in which the parish can assist the
missions:

a) Prayer: Prayer for missionaries and their work in spreading
the gospels is the responsibility of the whole Church (*ibid* n 36).
In addition to praying for the missions at Mass, parishes might
consider organising a special service of prayer to coincide with
the departure or return of parishioners to their various missions.

It helps create and confirm a bond of human solidarity and spiritual belonging between the parish and one of its own in the mission fields.

b) *Apostolic Work Society:* There is scope within every parish for a small group of committed lay people to promote mission awareness. Some parishes already have branches of the Apostolic Work Society that make vestments and other items for the missions. Indeed, the *Decree on the Church's Missionary Activity* strongly encourages parishes to link up with a missionary counterpart so that union between the communities might be more visible and contribute to their mutual development (cf, n 37).

The Apostolic Work Society is an ideal way of promoting a keen sense of missionary awareness in the parish. It involves children, schools and parents in different local projects and normally has ongoing and direct contact with people from the parish serving on the missions. Every parish is encouraged to establish a branch of the Apostolic Work Society. A group of neighbouring parishes might consider combining for this purpose. There are already some branches in the diocese and others in the process of being established.

c) *A place of welcome for Missionaries:* The ideal parish is a place where everybody feels welcome, wanted and loved. Returning missionaries should be made particularly welcome and helped to feel part of the parish. This is all the more urgent when the person's family has moved from the parish or died. Very often this is the sole link that the missionary has with his/her roots. It is a source of great human and spiritual affirmation to the missionary to know that there is a community back home which cares.

Parishes should make a special effort to welcome the representatives of the different Missionary Institutes who visit the parish each year on mission appeal and promotion work. While recent years may have witnessed a sharp decline in missionary vocations as such, there has been a significant increase in the number of lay missionaries and volunteers who are prepared to give a few years of their life to the missions: professional people such as doctors, nurses, teachers, agricultural advisers etc.. They work side by side with the missionaries and in close collaboration with them. Priests in their preaching and through individ-

THE PARISH

ual contact might put these ideals before people who are keen and interested. Any of the Missionary Institutes will be glad to provide up-to-date information in this area.

d) Dissemination of information about the Missions: The Second Vatican Council called for the dissemination of information about the missions so that the Christian faithful might be acquainted with the present state of the Church in the world and might hear the voice of the multitudes crying 'help us' (*ibid* n 36). A practical way of doing this is through involving the children in the school in compiling a list of those from the parish currently working on the missions and the kind of work they are doing etc.. Mounting an exhibition in the parish and in the school to coincide with Mission Sunday can be a powerful way of raising people's awareness of the missions.

But perhaps the most effective way of disseminating information about the missions is through the missionaries themselves in their own native parishes. In their home parishes they command greater respect and authority than any outsider. People can identify with them because they see them as part of the fabric of their own story and heritage. Through missionaries the missions become a living reality in the lives of people. This in turn creates a sense of loyalty and obligation to particular missions.

e) Financial Support: In addition to Mission Sunday (October), on which the annual collection for the Propagation of the Faith is taken up, the parish has the opportunity to help the missions financially when a missionary visits the parish on the occasion of mission appeal. Everybody should be encouraged and given the opportunity to give whatever they can on such occasions. There is an innate generosity in people when it comes to helping the the poor and particularly the Missions.

4. The Priest in his Parish

The post-conciliar vision of parish calls for and presupposes a new way of thinking and approach to pastoral ministry. This is conveyed through the manner in which the 1983 Code integrates its treatment of 'Parishes, Pastors and Pastoral Vicars' and takes as its point of departure a definition of parish rather than a definition of pastor as had been the case in the 1917 *Code of Canon Law* (cf J. Huels, Parish Life and the New Code, in:

Concilium, n 185 (3/1986) pp 64-72). The primary role of the priest is to animate the entire Christian community by enabling it to carry out the pastoral responsibilities of the Church. He is neither expected nor encouraged to perform this pastoral ministry singlehandedly. On the contrary his task is to bring people together and seek to activate in them the graces and charisms which the Holy Spirit bestows upon each for the benefit of all (1 Cor 12:4-11). The Second Vatican Council sees parish as a partnership between priest and people. The laity's 'action within Church communities is so necessary that without it the apostolate of the pastors will frequently be unable to obtain its full effect' (*Decree on the Apostolate of Lay People, Apostolicam Actuositatem*, 18/11/1965, n 10, Flannery, vol I, p 777).

In order to remain faithful to these conciliar insights the priest '... ought to acknowledge and foster the ministries, the offices and roles of the lay faithful that find their foundation in the sacraments of Baptism and Confirmation, indeed for a good many of them in the sacrament of Matrimony' (John Paul II, *Op cit*, n 23). Representing Christ the Head, he exercises a role of leadership and discernment in organising and co-ordinating various ministries within the parish. Care must be taken to ensure that the essential difference between his own ministry, which is rooted in the sacrament of Orders, and that in which all the baptised participate is not in any way blurred or confused. The risk of this happening becomes all the more possible as the number of ordained priests decline and the laity assume more pastoral responsibilities. In the 1994 *Directory on the Life and Ministry of Priests*, the Congregation for the Clergy warns against such misunderstandings and tendencies:

> The distinction between the common and ministerial priesthood, far from creating division among the members of the Christian community, harmonises and unifies the life of the Church ...

> No community can take the place of Christ, who is the one who calls, consecrates and sends forth ministers through the legitimate Pastors, even in a situation of particular necessity, when it might consider granting itself its own priest, in ways contrary to the dispositions of the Church (n 18).

Hence, priests may confer those and only those ministries, cffices and roles on suitable lay people which are rooted in their baptismal calling. Some ministries are by their very nature 'extraordinary' and should only be instituted or invoked when there is a genuine need. It is in this light that the directives of Pope John Paul II and the recent reply of the Pontifical Commission for the Authentic Interpretation of the Code of Canon Law with regard to Special Ministers of the Eucharist must be understood.

Special Ministers of the Eucharist should not be used when:

a) the small number of communicants does not constitute a necessity;

b) when there is a sufficiency of ordinary ministers (priests and deacons) available, even though not taking part in the celebration (Reply of Pontifical Commission for the Authentic Interpretation of the Code of Canon Law, 20/2/1987, in: *Osservatore Romano* 20/8/1988).

As the representative of the Bishop, the parish priest is responsible for all pastoral initiatives undertaken within the parish. He is to work in close collaboration with the other priests of the parish and indeed of the area. Partnership between priest and people will become a reality only if built upon the more fundamental partnership between priests themselves. The latter presupposes good communication. Poor communication and secrecy begets conflict and misunderstanding. Since assistant priests are 'cooperators with the parish priest and sharers in his concern' (c 545#1), they should be thoroughly familiar with all aspects of pastoral ministry within the parish. Indeed, they should be so familiar with all aspects of parish life as to be in a position, when needed, to assume full responsibility for the parish both pastorally and administratively.

5. Pastoral Ministry in the Parish

The pastoral ministry of the priest in his parish is governed by the needs of his people. These needs will vary somewhat from parish to parish and from time to time. It is impossible to provide an exhaustive list of priestly duties and responsibilities. The new *Code of Canon Law*, relying heavily on the Second Vatican Council's *Decree on the Life and Ministry of Priests*, *Presbyterorum Ordinis*, sets forth some helpful guidelines in this regard. The duties of priests engaged in pastoral ministry may be summarised as follows:

- proclaiming the word of God;
- instructing the faithful in the truths of faith;
- promoting Catholic education ;
- educating young people in Christian values;
- seeking out those who have strayed;
- celebrating the Eucharist and sacraments:
- reaching out to the poor, the elderly and those burdened with special difficulties;
- comforting the sick and the dying;
- leading people in prayer (cf cs 528-530).

The 1994 Directory on the Ministry and Life of Priests, n 30, sets down how he will discharge his pastoral ministry:

The priest will guide the man of today in his search for the meaning of his existence, to a personal encounter with Christ … (he) will present himself as an expert in the service of humanity, a man of truth and of communion, a witness of the solicitude of the Only Shepherd for each and every member of the flock. The community will be able to count on his dedication, availability, untiring work of evangelisation and, above all, his devoted and unconditional love.

Therefore, he will exercise his spiritual mission with kindness and firmness, with humility and service, opening himself to compassion, participating in the sufferings which arise from various forms of poverty, spiritual and material, old and new. He will know how to act with humility and with mercy within the difficult and uncertain ways of the conversion of sinners, to which he will exercise the gift of truth and patience and the encouraging benevolence of the Good Shepherd, who does not reprove the lost sheep, but carries it on his shoulders and celebrates for its return to the fold (cf Lk 15:4-7).

Areas of Pastoral Ministry:

i) Pastoral Visitation:
No ministry to people can take place without contact. The priest takes special care to know his people and avail of every opportunity to make contact with them especially through the different pastoral opportunities as they present themselves.

A systematic pastoral visitation of homes is an indispensable instrument of pastoral care and is not to be equated with a mere social calling on people. This enables the priest to get to know his people and their concerns. An active ministry of presence, where the Church becomes visible by going into the homes of people including those who feel alienated and estranged, becomes the touchstone for effective ministry. The ministry of the priest in his parish is as much one of compassion as it is one of conversion. The more the Church is brought into the homes of her sons and daughters, the more likely they are to bring themselves into the house of God. It is through a ministry of compassionate presence that the more explicit proclamation of the Word becomes possible. Home visitation therefore is at the very heart of evangelisation. Every parish should have some form of regular programme for calling on parishioners or engaging in home visitation. Priests should make it a priority to visit a certain number of homes each year and if possible each week. The very vast majority of people appreciate being visited by their priest. Each priest should have a register of the people in the area of the parish assigned to him.

ii) Leading People in Prayer:

A primary function of every priest is to lead people to God in and through prayer. What people want above all of their priest is that he be a man of prayer. Prayer is his charism. He prays for his people and with them. He does this not merely through the liturgy but in a multitude of other ways also. In particular the priest tries to encourage people to come together to pray at times other than when the Eucharist is being celebrated. People learn their prayers as children but as adults they need to be taught how to pray. Serious thought should be given to helping people pray the Scriptures, and to celebrating Evening Prayer or some other devotions in the parish to mark special occasions and seasons of the year. Suitable booklets are available for Evening Prayer in the Parish.

Part IV of *The Catechism of the Catholic Church* discusses in detail the nature of Christian Prayer. This section of the *Catechism* (ns 2558-2856) has been most highly acclaimed. It could serve as a valuable aid and guide in helping people to pray.

Prayer Groups: In recent years the Church has been witnessing people's hunger for prayer and the Scriptures through the growth of prayer groups. The priest must be concerned for the welfare of these groups and do everything he can to ensure that they do not feel alienated from the Church. Different kinds of prayer and spirituality suit different people. 'There are many rooms in my Father's house' (Jn 14:2).

In 1993 on the occasion of the twenty-first anniversary of Catholic Charismatic Renewal in Ireland the Irish Bishops issued a statement applauding the work of Charismatic Renewal:

> The Irish Bishops have seen many fruits of the Charismatic Renewal during the past twenty years. Thousands have found deeper commitment to Christ, a deep love for the Holy Scriptures, an openness to the gifts of the Holy Spirit, profound gifts of prayer including spontaneous prayer, greater understanding of the Eucharist and of the Church, a fruitful love of their brothers and sisters (*Life in the Spirit*, Veritas, 1993, p 6).

While the leadership of the prayer group is usually lay, the priest has, however, a role to play. He should visit the local prayer group as often as possible. Members look to him for guidance and for the occasional input on some theological or scriptural topic. 'In the prayer group you (the priest) will find an audience that hungers and thirsts for the word. Often they look to their shepherd for food and are not fed. It is a sad fact that often the priest who is most critical of his local prayer group, who finds fault with them for their simplistic faith, their theological fundamentalism, their naïve attitude to prayer and their ignorance of modern scriptural scholarship, is the same priest who consistently refuses to share with them his own theological insights and expertise' (D. Forristal, 'The Priest and the Prayer Group', in: *Intercom*, October, 1986 pp 7-8).

Prayer for healing is an integral part of Charismatic Renewal. Healing is a complex reality coming from God himself. 'He may not always will to cure a particular sick person, but he always offers a fullness of life (Jn 10:10). Those who are involved in healing should not suggest that all sickness will be cured if only there is faith enough and prayer. There should be no suggestion that prayer can be a substitute for seeking medical help and following medical advice' (*Life in the Spirit*, pp 10-11).

THE PARISH

Scripture Groups: In today's world there is an intense hunger for the word of God among ordinary people as evidenced by the number of people joining religious sects and cults. People's brief exposure to the word of God on Sundays is often felt to be insufficient to sustain a lively faith in the complex world in which they live. The priest might take the initiative in organising or co-ordinating a Scripture-sharing group, or *lectio divina* as it is called, in his parish. Otherwise we run the risk of leaving an opening for some other group or cult to fill this void. For ages past, we have attempted to form Catholic communities around a body of theological truths or articles of faith. People today are craving for the word of God. Cardinal Martini of Milan conducts a session of *Lectio Divina* for 3,000 young people in his cathedral in Milan on the first Thursday of every month. He is convinced that it is virtually impossible to be a Christian in today's world unless one is exposed to the word of God (cf Eltin Griffin, '*Lectio Divina* in the Parish', in *Intercom*, February 1994, p 29). The great French theologian Yves Congar used to say that if in one country Mass was celebrated for thirty years without preaching and in another there was preaching for thirty years without Mass, people would be more Christian in the country where there was preaching.

A Four Night Programme during October/November and again during Lent lasting a maximum of one hour might be considered. Such a programme should be rooted in the life-experience of people – their memories, their dreams, their hopes, their strivings, their endeavours – with a view to seeing what light the Scriptures can shed on them. So often our preaching falls on deaf ears because it does not seem to relate to the concrete experience of the hearers. The difficulty with our Sunday Eucharist is that people come unprepared for the strange language of the readings. One way of meeting this challenge is through the *Lectio Divina*. To direct such a programme one does not have to be an expert in biblical exegesis. The insights of ordinary people when they come together to share and pray the Scriptures are truly remarkable. They can be invaluable for the priest when he comes to preach. In addition, the existence of a scripture group in the parish would seem to be the ideal step towards establishing 'parish cells' along the Ballinteer model of parish renewal (cf *Come and See, a New Vision of Parish Renewal*, Veritas, 1993).

The role of the priest in scripture groups is primarily that of teacher of the faith and a preserver of the authentic tradition. The Bible is God's word in human words. Hence, one must be careful to avoid the excesses of a literalist or fundamentalist approach to the Scriptures. The latter seems attractive because it relieves people of the duty to think and purports to give certainties in a time of change. In particular it provides an absolute certainty based on a belief that every word in the Bible really has been dictated word for word by the Spirit and one needs only to hold on to the literal meaning. It refuses to admit that every word in the Bible, though inspired by God, has been written by human beings who had limited capacities and resources.

The Bishops of the Province of Tuam in their 1983 Pastoral Letter, *The Cults*, provide some useful directives in this whole area:

> Random quotations from the Bible, especially when they are taken out of context, can confuse and mislead ... The Gospels didn't emerge independently of the Church. They were part of the wider preaching tradition. The point to remember is that they still are. Individual texts or passages have to be understood within the unity of all Scripture and the living tradition of the Church. To separate the scriptures from the Church is to forget their origins and distort their meaning ... today people sometimes forget, or feel that they do not need the Church. They feel that they can settle their affairs directly with God without involving the Church as an intermediary or a guide.

More recently the Pontifical Biblical Commission in its 1993 document on *The Interpretation of the Bible in the Church* identifies some of the key characteristics of the fundamentalist approach to Scripture. It had its origin at the time of the Reformation, arising out of a concern for the the literal meaning of Scripture. After the century of the Enlightenment it emerged in Protestantism as a bulwark against liberal exegesis. As the 20th century comes to an end it is winning more and more adherents, even among Catholics.

Fundamentalism places undue emphasis upon the inerrancy of certain details in the biblical texts, especially in what concerns historical events or supposedly scientific truth. It often historicises material which from the outset never claimed to be historical. Because of its literalist approach, it frequently finds itself locked into an ancient and out-of-date cosmology. In addition it often sticks rigidly to one fixed translation , whether old or present-day, failing to take into account the 'rereadings' of certain texts which are found within the Bible itself (cf *Origins* 23 (1994), 509-510). With regard to the Gospels, fundamentalism does not take into account the development of the Gospel tradition but naively confuses the final stage of this tradition (what the evangelists have written) with the initial stage (the words and deeds of the historical Jesus).

There is little point in arguing over individual biblical texts with those who advocate a literalist or fundamentalist approach to the Scriptures. The question is a much larger one touching on the nature of Christianity itself and that of the Bible. The Catholic Church professes that God has revealed himself to us through the Incarnation and continues to do so in and through his Word and the Church's Sacraments. Both word and sacrament combine human and divine elements.

The best way of meeting the challenge of Fundamentalists is by setting in motion a structure which will offer a solid and scholarly approach to the Bible which is both spiritually nourishing and intellectually satisfying.

Popular Devotions: The perceived demise of popular devotions in the aftermath of the Second Vatican Council has generated a profound vacuum in the devotional lives of many people. These devotions in their multiple forms may not have been perfect but they allowed ordinary people to sense profoundly the mercy of God and respond to it in their own personal and devotional way. People found fulfilment in them and treasured them. They afforded comfort and light in an often confused and harsh world as well as providing a suitable *locus* for catechesis and Christian formation. They were designed to foster affective religious involvement by making use of familiar prayers, hymns, music etc. (cf Donal Flanagan, 'A People in Search of Devotions', in: *The Furrow* 41 (1990) pp 490-499). Indeed, in many ways they were ideally suited for preparing people for a more full, fruitful and active participation in the Church's liturgy. This is how the Second Vatican Council views such devotions:

Popular devotions of the Christian people, provided that

they conform to the norms of the Church, are to be highly recommended, especially where they are ordered by the Apostolic See.

Devotions proper to individual churches also have a special dignity if they are undertaken by orders of the bishops according to customs or books lawfully approved. But such devotions should be drawn up so that they harmonise with the liturgical seasons, accord with the sacred liturgy, are in some way derived from it, and lead the people to it, since the liturgy by its very nature is far superior to any of them (Vatican II, The Constitution on the *Sacred Liturgy, Sacrosanctum Concilium, 4/12/1963, n 13,* Flannery, vol I, p 7).

Not to acknowledge the contribution that such devotions have made to popular religiosity in Ireland over the past one hundred and fifty years would be to ignore the story of our people (cf Michael Drumm, 'A question of Ritual', in: *The Furrow*, 45 (1994) pp 141-150). Hence, the Church actively encourages such devotions by outlining the parameters and framework for their structure and content. In concrete terms this means that consideration should be given to structuring popular devotions around the following elements:

- the Scriptures - The Second Vatican Council called for 'the treasures of the Bible to be opened up more lavishly so that a richer fare may be provided for the faithful ...' (S.C., n 51, p 17);
- the liturgical seasons and special feasts - Advent, Lent, May, October, November etc.;
- the ritual elements of the liturgy such as light, water, incense, movement, posture etc.;
- contemporary prayers and spiritual writing;
- traditional Irish prayers;
- local customs – pilgrimages, sacred places (holy wells etc.), patron's day (patterns) are all forms of popular devotions deeply embedded in our Irish culture and spirituality (cf M. Maher (ed), *Irish Spirituality*, p 135). They should be preserved and renewed.

Some Popular Devotions:

1) Exposition of the Blessed Sacrament; Benediction; Bible/Prayer Services. These are ideally suited to extended periods of eucharistic exposition. Care should be taken to ensure that peo-

ple have time for private prayer and reflection. It is never permitted to expose the Blessed Sacrament simply for the purpose of giving a blessing. Exposition must always be accompanied by a period of short or longer duration for prayer and meditation (cf Sacred Congregation for Rites, *Instruction on the Worship of the Eucharistic Mystery, Eucharisticum Mysterium,* 25/5/1967, Flannery, vol I, pp 133-135).

2) *Sacred Heart Devotions.* These have been a great source of spiritual nourishment to many generations of people and are strongly encouraged by Pope John Paul II.

3) *The Stations of the Cross.* They put people into contact with the Paschal Mystery which is at the heart of the liturgy. A scriptural meditation on each of the stations is strongly encouraged.

4) *Marian Devotions.* The Rosary is the most popular and widely used of all popular devotions. Pope John Paul II refers to it as 'my favourite prayer'. Such devotions are particularly suited to May and October. Since it is Marian by its very nature and not eucharistic, it should not be recited while the Blessed Sacrament is exposed.

5) *Devotions to the Saints/Novenas.* The cult of the saints is firmly rooted in our Christian tradition. The saints are those who have already lived out the Paschal Mystery in their lives. Individual people may have special devotion to particular saints but this does not entitle them to impose such devotions on others. Each person is free to follow his own form of spirituality, provided it is in accord with Church teaching (cf, c 214)

6) *Pilgrimages/Processions/Visits to Holy Places.* These practices are as old as Christianity itself. They express our consciousness of being a pilgrim people.

7) *Meditation.* The use of the 'Jesus Prayer' or some other Christian formula repeated over and over again can create an atmosphere of prayer and contemplation. 'Prayer around the Cross' has proved very popular with young people.

8) *Cemetery Masses* for the deceased have been growing in popularity in recent years. They should be advertised well in advance so that relatives will be able to make the necessary arrangements to be present.

9) *Triduums of Prayer* marking special occasions in the life of the parish or community.

iii) Primary Schools:

A substantial part of the priest's work has to do with schools and young people. He must be careful not to equate his school ministry to managerial and administrative matters. His role is primarily a pastoral one. All primary schools in the parish are to be visited by the priest to whom responsibility for that school has been assigned. Other priests in the parish are expected to visit the schools also. The purpose of the visit, which includes each class in turn, is to support the teachers in the religious instruction of the pupils and to guide, encourage and inspire the pupils. Irish primary teachers carry out the task of religious education with great competence, commitment and conviction. But they cannot do it alone. Ideally religious education is a work of partnership between the home and the school and the parish. However, the reality often falls far short of the ideal. 'In many situations today teachers experience a level of support from the home that is minimal or non-existent. Children miss out on the supportive home environment that is essential to their growth in faith. Teachers feel isolated and powerless at the lack of support. Often too, even those teachers who are most committed feel that they have received inadequate training and are lacking in the theological background that is necessary for their work. In such circumstances teachers look to the local clergy for support and help' (Maura Hyland, 'The Priest in the Primary School', in: Intercom, June 1990, p 4). Priests should acquaint themselves with the religious programme for the different classes and not feel intimidated in the face of the new religious education programmes and the methodologies they employ.

The priest visits the classroom not as a teacher or inspector but as a person of faith. Ideally he should be able to call each child by name. By making contact with each child individually, he can give to each a sense of his or her own value and worth. He shares in the faith-experience of the children by listening to their little stories and by helping them to articulate their joys, their hopes and their fears. He prays with the children. Prayers and prayer-services are provided in the different programmes. School and class-Masses are ideal opportunities for introducing the children to formal prayers and religious worship. Suitable times are arranged for the celebration of the Sacrament of Reconciliation, e.g. Advent, Lent, etc..

The priest will cooperate fully with the Principal and all members of the staff. In keeping with his pastoral role, he will be available to the staff and encourage and support them in the practice of their own faith and the living out of their Christian vocation (cf *Management Board Members' Handbook*, pp 11-12).

Contact with the children through the school can often provide an opening for the priest into the homes of young families within the parish. In some instances this may be the first formal contact parents have with the priest since the child was christened. Priests might make a special effort to visit the home of those children about to receive First Holy Communion and Confirmation. In consultation with the Principal and teachers the priest will arrange the pre-sacramental meetings for parents.

A priest is usually the Chairman of the Board of Management in Primary Schools. The Board must scrupulously observe the norms and regulations laid down in the *Boards of Management of National Schools* of the Department of Education and be familiar with the contents of the *Management Board Members' Handbook* (1993). It is the duty of the Board to keep accurate minutes of all meetings of the Board as well as of its financial accounts. The Patron and the Department may request to inspect these at any time. Priests should explain and stress to Boards of Management the vital importance of observing confidentiality at all times.

iv) Post-Primary Schools:

Part-time chaplains are appointed to all post-primary schools in the diocese. Their role is that of providing pastoral care and spiritual guidance within the school for pupils and staff. They work in close collaboration with the local clergy, the school authorities and the religious education teachers. The chaplain visits the school in accordance with a definite schedule and by arrangement with the Principal; meets pupils informally; develops relationships with pupils through meetings on a one-to-one basis; prays with the pupils and helps them to grow in faith. Being available to pupils at times of pain, sickness and bereavement is particularly important and much appreciated.

Prayer and participation in the liturgy are essential aspects of religious formation. It is the duty of the school to ensure that a 'sacred room' is provided for private prayer, class and school Masses, penitential services and confessions.

Daily Mass should be celebrated at special times during the year when pupils are free to choose to come. Experience proves that the opportunity to participate in daily Mass is very much appreciated during Lent and at examination time. The chaplain should involve the pupils in the preparation and celebration of the liturgy and acquaint himself with the catechetical approaches in the religious education programme. In addition, he helps organise the school retreat or days of recollection. A special Mass for Leaving Certificate pupils and their parents is a fitting climax to end the school year.

A day of recollection for the teachers, concluding with a staff Mass is recommended. It has been tried in some schools and has been widely welcomed by staff (cf M. Conlon, 'The Role of the Chaplain in the Catholic School', in: *Intercom*, April, 1991, p 17).

By involving himself in the sporting and recreational pursuits of the pupils, the priest widens his scope for greater pastoral contact with both staff and pupils.

v) Home and Hospital Visitation of the Sick and Elderly:

The priest visits regularly those parishioners who are hospitalised or house-bound. Some may wish to receive Holy Communion on a weekly or even daily basis. Special Ministers of the Eucharist, or even members of their own family, might bring them Holy Communion on a regular basis or when the priest cannot reach them. The priest enlists the help of other members of the faithful in the exercise of this caring ministry, e.g. to visit long-stay patients in hospitals or homes.

vi) Prison Visitation:

The Council for Social Welfare in its submission to the Irish Bishops (1983) recommends to priests '… to visit those of their parishioners who are in prison; to pay special attention to the needs of prisoners' families; and to offer support to discharged prisoners and their families'. Contact through the prison chaplain can be an invaluable way of making contact with the prisoner. Family and friendship mean a great deal to a prisoner. The local priest can often act as a 'go-between' in helping both the prisoner and his/her family to overcome their sense of shame and embarrassment (cf B. Kearns, 'Help for Prisoners', in: *Intercom*, July/August 1987, pp 17-18).

vii) Parish Mission/Retreat:

Since the primary purpose of parish is the spiritual well-being of its members, it is essential that every parish arrange a period of spiritual renewal in the form of a parish mission or retreat periodically. Once every five years is a useful rule of thumb to go by.

> What other pastoral event touches so many people, children going to school, old people sick in their homes, young people coming to terms with adolescence, people who have grown careless about the practice of their faith and the community at large. This is the special grace of a parish mission, it draws together all strands of a parish community … it touches young and old, rich and poor, married and single in a way that no other event does. Every mission is another sowing of the seed, another proclamation of the Good News. People are brought together in a very special way. During the week of mission an atmosphere develops which is hard to capture in words but which is palpably real to those involved. Old memories are evoked, new resolutions are made and increasingly as the days go by the mood is one of 'it is good to be here'. (D. Brennan, 'In Praise of Missions', in: *Intercom*, July/August 1989, p 10).

Unlike other spiritual exercises or devotions, a parish mission reaches out to the whole People of God, addressing their daily cares and anxieties. Priests should not be discouraged by the perceived passing efficacy of a mission. 'The mission is a moment, a special moment, a grace-filled moment in the life of a community. Like all moments it will pass, but its passing does not leave us unchanged' (*ibid.*) To ensure that maximum benefit is reaped from a mission priests might '… in the months preceding the mission pray for its success at the Sunday Masses, preach about it, talk about it in the schools, publicise it around the parish, get out a sheet with details about the mission times, etc.. Ask local groups to facilitate the mission by not scheduling meetings, matches etc. at mission time' (*ibid*, pp 10–11).

6. People within the Parish needing Special Pastoral Care

i) People with Disabilities:

Persons who suffer from a permanent mental or physical disability are in special need of pastoral care. Some have been born with disabilities, others have become subject to them through illness or accident. For some their condition is a stable one while for others it is deteriorating. Many now live in the community either alone or with their families. Others live in hospitals or residential homes. Their needs vary, depending on their degree of disability and circumstances.

Every parish has a number of people suffering from disabilities. Their presence in the Church, and their contribution to society, have in the past often been more tolerated than appreciated (cf T. O'Grady, 'Pastoral Care of the Mentally Handicapped', in: *Intercom*, June 1984, pp 4-5).

It is the duty of the priest and indeed of the whole parish community to promote their full participation in parish life. In particular the disabled person must not be forced or allowed to become the mere receiver of services but must be encouraged and helped to be a giver to the full extent of his/her ability. Hence, a workshop is an integral part of most communities catering for those with disabilities.

In ministering to those with disabilities the priest needs a special sensitivity and ability to listen attentively. He is responding not only to the disabled person but also to his/her whole family. Parents in particular need help and assistance in accepting and coming to terms with a disabled child. They need to be informed of the services available for such people. In addition, they need the occasional break from caring for those whom they love so much.

The priest must ensure that appropriate catechesis is provided on an ongoing basis either at local level or at the special schools attended. Sacramental participation (i.e. Eucharist, Reconciliation and Confirmation) should follow at an appropriate time. It is disrespectful to the person and to the family to celebrate a sacrament before there has been adequate catechesis, but it is equally disrespectful to prolong catechesis indefinitely or to avoid celebrations in the larger assembly because of fear, embarrassment or prejudice. True catechesis takes time and is often more effective after a sacramental celebration. It is for the priest in consultation with parents, teachers and those who care for the disabled to determine when this person is ready for the sacramental event. In arriving at a decision it should be remembered that religion and faith are primarily relational rather than abstract or conceptual. It is the quality of their relationships that signal their preparedness for sacraments. Relationships which are inviting and welcoming allow them to awaken gradually to the larger sacramental dimension of life.

Some disabled people because of the nature of their disability may find the actual receiving of Holy Communion difficult. If this is the case parents should talk to the priest beforehand. The priest may have the parent or person caring for him/her give Holy Communion to the disabled person. Where necessary he/she may receive from the chalice only.

The person suffering from mental disability is usually ready to receive Holy Communion earlier than the Sacrament of Reconciliation. This is a matter for the priest, parents and teachers to decide (cf Bishops' Conference of England and Wales, 'Guidelines for Priests on Mentally Handicapped People and the Reception of Holy Communion', 1983, in: *Doctrine and Life*, 33 (1983), pp 503-505).

Occasional liturgies adapted to the needs and abilities of people suffering from disabilities should be provided.

Finally, the priest should ensure that those with physical disabilities have easy access to the church and church premises.

In this diocese there are many facilities catering for those with disabilities. A complete list can be found in the *Diocesan Directory* published each year.

ii) The Elderly:

Thanks to better living-standards and advances in the field of medicine people are now living longer. Enormous resources are being invested by voluntary organisations in caring for the elderly. Care should be taken however to ensure that they are not merely recipients of pastoral care. Pope John Paul when speaking to the elderly reminded them :

> You still have a mission to fulfil, a contribution to make. According to the divine plan, each individual human being lives a life of continual growth, from the beginning of existence to the moment at which the last breath is taken *(The Vocation and Mission of the Laity, Christifideles Laici, n 48)*.

It is the task of the whole parish community to devise ways and means of helping them to put their gifts and charisms at the disposal of all. 'The gift of older people can be specifically that of being the witness to tradition in the faith both in the Church and in society (cf Ps 44:2; Ex 12:26-27),the teacher of lessons of life (cf Sir 6:34; 8:11-12), and the worker of charity' (*ibid*). Their wisdom, knowledge and experience should be called upon whenever possible. Given the phenomenon of early retirement, many are now in a position to exercise an apostolate that their work and family commitments did not permit hitherto, e.g. visiting the sick and the lonely in their homes and in hospital; praying with them; organising and running clubs and activities for the elderly in the parish. Many of them are motivated to become involved as volunteers in different organisations, contributing their time, ability and expertise. Generosity and neighbourliness towards others are the hallmarks of their ministry within the community.

Looming large in the concerns of the elderly are loneliness and the fear of becoming incapacitated and unable to fend for themselves. In response to these challenges many parishes have, in conjunction with statutory and voluntary bodies, initiated programmes of providing homes for the elderly. This is strongly encouraged for it not only enhances the quality of life for the people in question but indeed for the whole community. It enables others to minister to those in need. In some circumstances, it might be more feasible for a group of neighbouring parishes to come together in providing such accommodation. 'Meals on Wheels' are available through the Ossory Social Services for the elderly in their own homes or at designated centres. *The Diocesan Advisory Committee on Housing Elderly* shall be glad to furnish whatever advice and expertise it can in this area.

Elderly people living alone are becoming increasingly the victims of violence in our society. 'Community Alert Schemes' are strongly recommended.

iii) Youth:

The mission of bringing the message of Christ to young people presents a particular challenge for all priests. It is a ministry that cannot be ignored because as Pope John Paul II reminded us at Knock in 1979 'every generation, with its own mentality and characteristics, is like a new continent to be won for Christ'. The Irish Bishops are acutely aware of this and have expressed their concern in their 1985 Pastoral Letter, *The Young Church*.

It is the task of the parish to complement and build on the faith-foundation that young people receive in their families and schools. In order that this might begin to be achieved, priests and others must be prepared to listen to their stories, accompanying them along their particular Emmaus Road. As ministers we must be prepared to open ourselves to what they have to offer and be ready to affirm the positive qualities of their lifestyle. The goodwill, enthusiasm and vitality of young people is often misunderstood and left untapped. It should be harnessed whenever possible:

> Youth must not be considered simply as an object of pastoral concern for the Church: in fact young people are and ought to be encouraged to be active on behalf of the Church as leading characters in evangelisation and participants in the renewal of society (John Paul II, *The Vocation and Mission of the Laity, Christifideles Laici,* n 46).

Hence, their voices should be heard in pastoral councils, liturgy committees and community-based youth organisations. Their full and active participation in the celebration of the liturgy (i.e. as singers, readers and eucharistic ministers) should be encouraged and facilitated in every way possible. Because of their emphasis on experience and authenticity and thirst for justice they can indeed constitute the conscience of the whole parish community. In the words of the Irish Bishops:

> Many of them are genuinely concerned about the big issues facing humanity at the end of the twentieth century. They have a real sense of justice and often a deep generosity in wanting to heal the ills of our divided world. They have a passion for peace and a horror of war and they are angered and embittered by the scandal of so much spending on arms when so many people live in want ... They see unjust divisions in the world as a whole, but they see those divisions closer to home as well – as in Ireland, where the new wealth of the sixties has given way to the unequal opportunities of the eighties. They see their own future darkened by the shadow of unemployment and are forced to question the priorities of a society in which so many are made irrelevant or pushed aside (*The Young Church,* p 9).

Faith Development of Young People:

In recent years different programmes have been endeavouring to tackle the problems facing young people today, e.g. drug and alcohol abuse, unemployment, emigration, etc. as well as the very materialistic values being presented by the media and society in general. An essential feature of this new approach is that young people themselves act as peer ministers to one another. In short, youth ministry is 'For, With, By and To' young people. In attempting to put this form of youth ministry into practice, a number of projects and programmes have evolved throughout the country:

1) Christian Adult Education Programmes such as Discovery I & II and The Way; Faith Friends; Growing in Faith Together I & II (GIFT);

2) Formation discussion groups such as Young Christian Workers (Y.C.W. & Y.C.S.), and Christian Light Community (C.L.C.);

3) Prayer Groups, e.g. Taizé Prayer Groups;

In organising faith-development ventures, it is good to recall that from the point of view of religious affiliation young people may be divided into three broad, general categories:
- those who have developed a strong faith and are no longer satisfied with a passive role in the Church;
- those who profess a belief in God but do not see its relevance for their everyday lives;
- those who are alienated from the Church and neither see nor seek a place for themselves within its structures.

Young people who fit into each of the above categories are found in every parish and indeed in many families. They must be cared for.

The key to setting in motion any of the above programmes is a good steering committee which will recruit and train volunteer leaders to work with small groups of young people. 'The programmes offer a community dimension to the faith formation of the young, complementing what is going on in the home and the school. The leaders witness their faith through their sharing and friendship with the young. In so doing they offer the young a concrete experience of the local Church interested in, taking time to be with them' (M. Kennedy, 'Youth Ministry Programmes – Faith Friends and GIFT', in: *The Furrow 45* (1994), April, pp 235-237).

On leaving primary school many young people experience a sense of isolation from their parish, both at a physical and emotional level. Having grown up through primary school where they had close links with the parish, they now find themselves dispersed in many different directions at post-primary level. For many months of the winter they leave their local area in the dark of the morning and return in the dark of the evening. They tend to lose their connection with the local community. This dispersion coupled with the developmental changes taking place in the lives of young people affects their image of God. At this stage in their development young people need a forum where they can question and talk so that they can grow in awareness of their own spirituality and personal relationship with God.

The principal task of the parish should be to provide opportunities for young people to meet and share their life's journey. In the initial stages at least young people need to be 'consumers'. Involvement in folk-groups or in a programme such as 'Growing in Faith Together I' (published by Veritas and launched in September 1991) would seem an ideal starting point. The latter is a five-night parish-based faith development programme for young people who have been confirmed. It is facilitated by parents who will have already taken part in a training programme which enables them to lead young people in reflection and discussion (cf C. Brennan, 'Growing in Faith Together', in: *Intercom*, November, 1991, pp 24-25). This programme aims at giving young people a sense of belonging to parish and a sense of confidence when it comes to sharing their own faith-story with others. Out of this comes the desire to serve others. It is at this stage that peer-ministry programmes such as 'Faith Friends' or 'Search' might be introduced. At all stages during this process young people must be supported by adults in the community who are in touch with their own spiritual journey as well as with that of the young people.

Youth Leaders:

The ability to work with young people is not related to age or lifestyle but to a personal interest and willingness to learn. People prepared to work with young people are to be found in every parish. It might take some time to locate the right people. A Youth Leader is not the person who 'keeps order' in a club but rather an adult friend that the young person feels free to trust and confide in. The leader acts as a friend, an occasional counsellor, a link with the local community. The job makes practical demands on the person organising a good programme of activities; co-ordinating a team of helpers; ensuring a minimum amount of order and some administration. It is important that the young person sees the leader as a model as far as personal values are concerned. 'What carries most weight with them (young people) is not what they are told by 'authority' but what they believe and experience for themselves. As Pope Paul VI put it, people today are less impressed by what they are taught than by what they witness' (Pastoral Letter of Irish Bishops, *The Young Church* p 7).

When young people have grown in confidence and are made aware that they too have a voice and will be treated with equal respect to adults, they are then ready to take their place on different parish councils and committees.

A Suggested Way Forward:
Ideally every parish should have a committee which identifies the needs of their young people and which is prepared to initiate a response to those needs by involving people who are willing to work in a particular area or skill. The Ossory Youth Services will facilitate in whatever way it can in establishing such committees. It was established to provide a comprehensive range of services such as training programmes and special activities to add to, and where necessary to promote efforts to empower and enable young people. On the assumption that most young people will probably not 'buy into' something that they do not enjoy, or feel threatened by, it may not be appropriate to begin with a programme or activity that seems overtly 'religious'. Neither may it be appropriate (even if you have the necessary skills and knowledge) to begin it by yourself. You may not be able to give it the necessary time and commitment. Why not try the following approach?

1) Identify a number of adults/young adults (Ossory Youth Services can help you with this).

2) Get a six week commitment from them (one night weekly) to do a Youth Leadership Training Course (provided free of charge by the Ossory Youth Services in your parish).

3) Once training has been completed it should be possible to initiate a worthwhile and enjoyable programme of activities

for young people in your area. The programme will have been planned in detail at the training. It must be sufficiently varied to allow for:

a) participation of both boys and girls;
b) opportunities to test values and beliefs;
c) opportunities for voluntary community involvement;
d) opportunities for recreational activities, etc.;
e) opportunities to learn new and enjoyable skills.

Advantages: The above format has many benefits. It provides the community with a group of trained people who will take overall responsibility for young people. Because the programme of events is planned in detail beforehand, it allows bonding to take place between adults and young people during the initial two months, without having to worry about organisational details. Ensuring that the programme is varied from the outset (e.g. discussion groups, outings, community projects, recreational activities etc.) offers the best prospect of growth and development for all concerned. The more varied a programme is the better chance it has of surviving when some key people have to leave it.

Ossory Youth Services Support:
The existence of a youth group in the parish would enable the *Ossory Youth Services* to support more effectively youth activities with its own programmes, be they of a recreational, faith-development or community-project nature. The latter would clearly enhance the overall involvement of young people in the life of the parish and the diocese. The *Ossory Youth Services* will only be too glad to provide whatever assistance it can in helping parishes set up and co-ordinate youth ministry projects and faith-development programmes throughout the diocese.

iv) The Unemployed:

One of the greatest social evils afflicting our people right now is the scourge of high unemployment. The creation and preservation of jobs is the responsibility placed on all of us. It is a responsibility that we ourselves must confront because '… the economic development of this island can never be done for us. It can only be done by us. Neither multinationals nor the European Community can hand us a resilient, modern economy which is able to generate its own employment growth and change. Either we build that ourselves with the judiciously selected support of multinationals, foreign banks and the EC, or we still remain an economy that permanently frustrates the job aspirations of Irish People (The Irish Episcopal Conference, *Work is the Key*, n 96, p 59). The Irish Bishops have over the years in their Pastoral Letters (*The Work of Justice*, 1977 and *Work is the Key*, 1992) spoken on the jobs-crisis. In the *Work of Justice* (1977) they link the right to work with human dignity. Unemployment impoverishes not just financially but at a personal level as well.

> Work is one of man's most important means of self-fulfilment. The opportunity and the freedom to work are conditions of his dignity as a person. Work gives man that independence and that ability to provide for his own without which he can scarcely retain his self-respect ... Those who remain workless for long inevitably become marginalised in society. To remain for long out of work is damaging and hurtful to the personality. It undermines one's self-esteem. It tends to breed resentment against society.... We are saying, 'We don't need you', to thousands of young boys and girls to whom we gave a good education and in whom we thereby raised expectations of jobs corresponding to their education. Now we are letting them down. This situation is a serious reflection on our society. It should weigh on the conscience of us all. Let no-one talk of the nations's crisis being over so long as we have all these thousands unemployed (n 80).

Pope John Paul II in his encyclical letter on *Human Work, Laborem Exercens*, 1981, presents work as an integral element for promoting and enhancing human dignity:

> Work is a good thing for man – a good thing for his humanity – because through work man not only transforms nature, adapting it to his own needs, but he also achieves fulfilment as a human being and indeed, in a sense, becomes 'more a human being' (n 9).

What can be done?

The statements of the Irish Episcopal Conference, *Christian Faith in a Time of Economic Depression* (General Meeting 13-15 June, 1983) and their Pastoral Letter *Work is the Key* (1992), as well as the National Conference of Priests of Ireland (1983 A.G.M.), indicate the direction that our response at parish level might take:

1) State schemes for youth training and employment should be

THE PARISH

made known and availed of at parish level. Priests in many areas have given great leadership in this regard and others can learn from their experience. Of special significance are the various Community Schemes now available. 'While there is an evident scarcity of jobs on this island, there is no shortage of work to be done in renewing urban areas, caring for the specialised needs of vulnerable groups in the population ... conserving our environment and historical heritage' (*Work is the Key*, pp 56-57). Parishes should try to identify a range of community work that could be undertaken by the unemployed for the good of the community and the environment, e.g. social and cultural activities and recreational amenities. Funding for such projects is available from different sources.

Care must be taken to ensure that such schemes are not exploited because, as the Irish Bishops state, 'any job is not better than none' (*ibid* p 73). High unemployment must never be used as an excuse for creating more part-time, temporary and low paid jobs (cf *ibid* n 129-134, pp 73-76).

2) Some local initiatives to combat unemployment are already in place. *The Bishop Birch Training Institute* and the *Kilkenny Employment for Youth*, which was established in 1982/83. Both provide youth skills courses for early school leavers; courses for long-term unemployed people; return-to-work programmes for women over 25 years; community youth-training programmes and computer courses. What is needed above all is local leadership and initiative. The skills are there. People must be motivated to help themselves.

3) There is room for promotion of small-scale locally-based firms. In particular the parish should make available unused Church property and encourage the unemployed to establish co-operatives in the event of factory closures. Every community has persons with the competence to identify such projects and people to operate them. Individuals and groups should be given every encouragement and support for such ventures. 'Through co-operative associations, people give exceptional expression to the communal nature of their work and frequently to their links with the local community' (*ibid* n 107, p 63).

Parish pastoral councils should have a sub-committee concerning itself with the problems of the unemployed. It would identify long term and short range goals and liaise with statutory bodies charged with organising community work schemes. In addition, it might organise study-group projects at parish or inter-parish level to examine the causes of poverty and unemployment in that particular area or parish. There is much discussion-material available on this topic, cf below.

4) Priests should remind people of their moral obligation to those who are unemployed and of their duty to preserve and create jobs. The Irish Bishops underline this very strongly :

> Those who have jobs in these days of recession are a kind of privileged class. They have an obligation towards those who, through no fault of their own, have no work. In a situation where many are jobless and many more have great job insecurity, those in secure employment should consider their very security as in itself an important differential advantage and should be willing, in lieu of this advantage, to moderate their demands in other directions. A 'social partnership' between the employed and the jobless sectors of labour is just as necessary nowadays as is a social partnership between management and labour (*The Work of Justice*, n 89).

5) Priests should always have a message of hope and encouragement for the unemployed. The young must not be allowed to feel that there is no future and no job prospects for them. Many young people are still finding jobs. Many of them have the added assets of practical skills and a good education. The Christian message is always one of hope even in situations of apparent hopelessness. Apathy and defeatism are our worst enemies.

6) Despite high unemployment, people often have difficulty in obtaining the services of tradesmen for routine services and maintenance. Parishes should consider keeping registers of the services both needed and available locally. In addition a parish-based and voluntarily staffed advice centre could inform people both of their entitlements and job opportunities. The level of hardship that people experience resulting from unemployment is often unnecessarily aggravated by ignorance and misinformation.

v) The Estranged and Alienated:

Of all the groups within the parish, none is in greater need of pastoral care than those who feel lost and alienated from the Church. Jesus went out of his way to seek out the lost (cf Lk 15).

Their reasons for alienation are multiple. In some instances the ecclesial community or its representatives may have failed them, but in most cases they have voluntarily severed all visible links with the Church either because of their disenchantment with its structures or because their superficial grasp of their own faith is insufficient to sustain them in a secular environment that is more uninterested than hostile to faith (cf Michael Paul Gallagher, S.J., 'What Hope for Irish Faith?', in: *Struggles of Faith*, pp 16-23).

Priests must not feel disheartened or that they are failing in their ministry when confronted with an ever growing number of non-practising Christians. As Pope Paul VI reminds us: this phenomenon is as old as Christianity itself. What is new is its particular manner of manifestation today.

> In the history of Christianity the problem of the non-practising Christians is of long standing: it arises from a certain natural weakness and inherent inconstancy which, alas, is deeply rooted in the minds of men. But in our day it presents certain new features and this may often be explained by the fact, which is characteristic of our time, that men are so to speak, without roots. As a result of this, Christians associate a great deal with non-believers and are constantly being influenced by those who have no religion. Furthermore, our contemporaries who do not practise any religion are much more eager than in other days to explain their attitude and to justify it as a form of internal religion based on their own laws and standards of authenticity (*Apostolic Exhortation, Evangelisation in the Modern World, Evangelii Nuntiandi*, n 56, Flannery, vol II, p 737).

In order to reach out to these people the Church must seek constantly the right approach and suitable language. On the one hand this involves standing firmly on the side of truth and on the other using all of one's skills to help the estranged to come to see and accept this truth in his or her life.

> The preacher of the gospel is, therefore, a man who forgetful of himself, and even at the cost of great personal sacrifice, is always seeking out the truth to hand it on to others. He must never falsify it, never conceal it in the desire to please men, to astonish or shock, to show originality or to attract attention. He must never reject the truth nor allow it to be obscured by his lethargy in seeking it out neither for his own advantage

nor from motives of fear ... As we are pastors of the faithful our ministry makes it incumbent on us to protect, defend and communicate the truth without regard for any loss or suffering it may involve (*ibid* n 78, p 754).

In practice this means helping them to come to a realisation of where they are in the faith-journey and encouraging them to gradually integrate the gifts of God and the demands of his definite and absolute love in their entire personal and social life. 'Therefore an educational growth process is necessary, in order that individual believers, families and peoples, even civilisation itself, by beginning from what they have already received of the mystery of Christ, may patiently be led forward, arriving at a richer understanding and a fuller integration of this mystery in their lives' (John Paul II, *The Christian Family in the Modern World, Familiaris Consortio*, 22/11/1981, n 9, Flannery, vol II, p 821).

A suitably adapted programme, based on the Rite of Christian Initiation of Adults (RCIA), is used widely and effectively in many countries and cultures today in reaching out to baptised non-believers. Its principal value resides in the fact that it recognises the gradualness of conversion and doesn't rush people into sacraments before they are ready for them. In addition it places strong emphasis on moral and spiritual conversion rather than purely intellectual knowledge of the faith. Finally, the whole programme is very much parish-based and is celebrated in and through the liturgy. But an adapted version of the RCIA Programme is not necessarily the only option. Other alternatives may be possible.

> Such alienation can perhaps best be met by many forms of small-group renewal within the large Church .... Translating this into the situation of Irish Catholicism, there is an urgent need for church cells larger than the family but smaller than the parish (Michael Paul Gallagher S.J., Op cit p 21).

How to approach the alienated:

What is of paramount importance is the manner in which we approach the alienated. Great skill and tact is called for if we are not to 'crush the bruised reed and quench the wavering flame'.

1) Personal Contact: There is no substitute for personal and individual contact with the alienated. By visiting them in their homes the priest demonstrates that the Church is still interested in them even though they may long since have lost interest in it.

2) Manner of Contact: Both experience and statistics demonstrate that the manner of communication is much more significant than the content when it comes to conveying a message. 55% of communication happens by visual means or appearances. The eyes, we are told, are the doorways to the soul. 38% of communication occurs through the tone of one's voice and only 7% happens through the actual content of the message itself. It is good to be aware of the potential for misunderstanding and harm through the wrong type of communication.

3) Occasions for Contact: The Church's mission to people in the ups-and-downs of life presents many ideal opportunities for reaching out and touching those who are only lukewarm in the faith. Sacramental occasions in particular should be availed of to reach out not just to those immediately involved but to the wider congregation as such. Family celebrations such as weddings, anniversaries and funerals are special times of grace and faith-strengthening not just for the immediate family but for all who are present. For some it may be the only occasions when they are exposed to the signs of faith in the liturgy. Informal contact with people on these occasions can prove very beneficial and fruitful. Other occasions that should not be missed out on are First Confession, First Communion and Confirmation of children. They are times for rekindling faith and commitment to religious practice. Experience shows that parents are more open to evangelisation at the First Communion of their children than at any other time.

4) The Church is for People: There are several church axioms which if kept in mind will help the priest deal kindly and compassionately with people. 'The sacraments are for people' *(Sacramenta sunt propter homines)* and not *vice versa.* If, having applied all the relevant pastoral norms and directives concerning the admission of a person to a particular sacrament an insoluble doubt remains, the benefit of the doubt goes to the person. The sole exception to this rule pertains to the bond of marriage where the institution of marriage enjoys the favour of the law (cf c 1060).

Church law stands by this approach when it states in one of its axioms: 'favours are to be multiplied; burdens are to be restricted'. The *Code of Canon Law* warns against arbitrary use or even misuse of its laws in pastoral situations. 'Laws which prescribe a penalty, or restrict the free exercise of rights, or contain an exception to the law, are to be interpreted strictly' (c 18).

5) *Avoid Defensiveness:* Many of those who come seeking the sacraments, e.g. baptism for their children, marriage in church etc. will hold values or follow practices contrary to Church teaching. This can trigger off negative reactions in the priest if he views their values as personal attacks on him and what he represents. Such defensiveness causes inner anguish to the priest and reduces his pastoral effectiveness. The priest should try to refrain from making judgements about the individual's culpability in these matters. He must always remember that the Good News both summons us and empowers us to repent and believe in it. If a person's beliefs and values are at variance with what the Church teaches perhaps it is because he/she does not yet 'believe' the Good News!

6) *Be Positive and Flexible:* People who approach the priest seeking sacraments or other services do so with openness and good will. There may be other complicating factors, e.g. an irregular marriage situation, infrequent attendance at Sunday Mass, etc., but these should not be allowed to colour the reception they receive. To welcome them warmly and explain with enthusiasm what the Church has to offer starts the encounter off in the right atmosphere and direction. One should not expect too much too quickly.

7. Parish Structures at the Service of Parish

Every parish needs certain structures to help it realise its mission. But structures as such are always at the service of the parish and must never be seen as an end in themselves. Obsolete structures must not be allowed to impede the parish in the pursuit of its mission. Their purpose is to give expression to a vision of parish, and hence are in need of constant reappraisal and renewal. Articulating a common vision of parish does not come easily. Usually needs are met on an *ad hoc* basis by small groups pursuing particular goals. As groups develop and multiply, the need for co-ordination of effort and resources becomes evident. Fragmentation of efforts and overlapping of resources must be minimised if all pastoral needs are to be addressed. One structure that can ensure coordination of efforts and energy is a parish pastoral council (cf Rosetta Grey, 'A Vision of Parish', in: *Intercom*, September 1993, pp 15-16).

THE PARISH

i) Parish Pastoral Council:

The Emmaus Meeting of the Irish Bishops (September 1986) strongly urged the establishing of pastoral councils in every parish. These councils provide a very suitable and practical way for involving the laity in 'examining and solving pastoral problems by general discussion' (John Paul II, *The Vocation and Mission of the Laity*, n 27).

This council is a representative body of the faithful, working in close collaboration with the priest(s) of the parish, with a view to furthering the mission of Christ in its entirety in this particular area of the Lord's vineyard. Its concerns are the whole range of pastoral tasks within the parish:

- proclaiming the word of God;
- celebrating the Eucharist and the sacraments;
- instructing the faithful;
- educating the young in Christian values;
- promoting social justice;
- reaching out to the poor and elderly;
- comforting the sick and dying;
- leading people into communion with God through prayer and example (cf cs 528-530).

Its purpose, therefore, is to study and research the needs of the parish; to recommend and help implement policies and programmes which will enable the parish to live out the demands of the gospel in its day-to-day life.

1) Its position *vis-à-vis* the Finance Committee:
The parish pastoral council is not a finance committee (cf cs 536 & 537). The pastoral council takes precedence over all other church-related committees within the parish. This is because the purpose of parish is pastoral ministry as such. The finance committee on the other hand is a group of lay people who advise the priest in the material administration of the parish – preparing budgets, overseeing property maintenance and fund-raising, etc.. It is for the pastoral council to determine policy and priorities within the the parish.

2) Its position *vis-à-vis* the priest:
'The parish pastoral council has only a consultative vote' (c 536 #2). It is advisory to the priest in all areas of pastoral concern in

the parish. Though the priest is not bound to follow the advice of the council, even if it is unanimous, nevertheless, without what is in his judgement an overriding reason, he is not to act against it, especially if it is unanimous (c 127 #2, 2). The priest is the President of the council. There can be no meeting of the council without the priest.

3) Establishing a Parish Pastoral Council:
Setting up a parish pastoral council should not be rushed into. It is something that should evolve 'from below' rather than be 'appointed from above'. The need for it should grow out of the desire of existing groups and bodies functioning within the parish to co-ordinate and structure their efforts and resources. It is a futile exercise establishing a pastoral council and then wondering what it should do. Something should already be happening in the parish which is in need of co-ordination and evaluation before one contemplates setting up a pastoral council. The parish should be alive. Merely going through the motions of voting and nominating members to a pastoral council is no guarantee that the council will ever function. Indeed, it might even be more a hindrance than a help in promoting the mission of the parish.

The success of a pastoral council presupposes the common vision and full participation of all the priests of the parish, where there is more than one priest. Successful pastoral councils are an extension and confirmation of the partnership and collaboration already existing among the priests of the parish.

A pastoral council (or what might more accurately be described as a 'pastoral group') can be set up in different ways:

Parish Assembly Model: Neighbourhood Masses are arranged throughout the parish and are followed by a discussion of pastoral needs with a view to working out a pastoral plan. Each neighbourhood is then invited to elect two or more people to represent them at a parish assembly day. Meanwhile the priest in his Sunday homilies explains the idea of a pastoral group who will assist him in all areas of pastoral ministry in the parish. The parish assembly day is directed by a skilled facilitator and at the end of it representatives are elected or selected to form a pastoral group within the parish. Other members are nominated directly by the priest(s). All are formally commissioned at a parish liturgy to which the whole parish is invited. At the commissioning ceremony the representatives commit themselves to undertaking the course of preparation and ongoing formation, as well as discharging their duties to the best of their abilities. In due course this group will evolve into the parish pastoral council.

Nomination/Election Model: In almost every parish today there is a core group of people exercising various ministries on behalf of the community, e.g. eucharistic ministers, readers, organists, musicians, youth leaders, St Vincent de Paul, adult religious education leaders, etc.. These different groups are asked to nominate one or two members who will form a steering committee to monitor what is already happening in the parish by way of pastoral activity and to plan future directions. Part of their brief would be to tap new resources and identify those pastoral areas currently being overlooked. In the process of doing this the steering committee seeks nominations of people representative of different geographical areas within the parish, age groups and social classes. If the said nominees are willing to be involved, their names will appear on a ballot paper for that area of the parish. Elections of members to serve on a parish pastoral group are then held. The priest is free to nominate some further members to it. In due course the parish pastoral group undertakes an appropriate course of preparation and spiritual formation. At a later stage, perhaps a year later, they are constituted into a pastoral council.

Rural Parish Model: Some parishes within the diocese are made up of two or more small communities. Since the full pastoral mission of the Church must be exercised in each of these areas, it is advisable that each should have a pastoral group to assist the priest. Ideally, these pastoral groups should come together to form a single parish pastoral council.

The first task of the priest in his particular area is to identify the various organisations functioning within that area of the parish and the needs they are serving. He arranges a meeting of those already involved in serving the different pastoral needs and of other potential members with a view to identifying areas of ministry currently being neglected. At the meeting he floats the idea of forming a pastoral group. Somebody who already has some experience of working in a pastoral council provides some input and facilitates the meeting. Those present are broken up into small discussion groups of 3-4 people each and are asked to identify the pastoral needs of their community as well as indicating the areas of ministry they would like to exercise if requested. Feedback is taken by the facilitator and in due course the most pressing areas of pastoral ministry are identified and the names of those willing to help out in each area. These names are balloted on and two people for each area of ministry are elected. Together with the priest they form a pastoral group which in due course will join with the pastoral groups of the other areas of the parish and evolve into a pastoral council.

4) Guidelines for selecting/electing Members
of the Pastoral Pastoral Council:

No effort should be spared to ensure that the right kind of people are elected and selected to serve on the parish pastoral council. The following criteria and qualifications should be kept in mind:
- they should be interested in promoting the overall pastoral mission of the Church;
- they should accept the teachings of the Second Vatican Council;
- they should be capable of grasping the meaning and mission of the Church;
- they should be believing and praying Christians;
- they should be baptised members of the Catholic Church;
- they should be willing to undertake a course of preparation and ongoing formation ;
- they should be prepared to devote considerable time and effort to homework, committee meetings etc.;
- they should be able to work with other people;
- generally speaking they should be 18 years or over.

5) Constitution:

The Code of Canon Law requires that the parish pastoral council be 'regulated by norms laid down by the diocesan bishop' (c 536 #1). The norms of this constitution should be as simple as possible. A copy of a Draft Constitution for Parish Pastoral Councils will be found in an Appendix II at the end of this Directory.

ii) Parish Finance Committee:
'In each parish there is to be a finance committee to help the parish priest in the administration of the goods of the parish ...' (c 537).

This committee is distinct from the Parish Pastoral Council, having its own proper structure and area of concern. It is a new juridical structure introduced by the 1983 *Code of Canon Law*. In Ossory Diocese there is to be one finance committee only in each parish. It is distinct from any exclusively fundraising committee, even of a permanent nature, which may be in the parish.

The Parish Priest and Curate(s) are *ex officio* members, with the Parish Priest or his designate being chairman of the committee. In addition there must be at least four lay people, two of whom must be women. The work of the finance committee entails the following:

- assisting the priest to draw up an accurate inventory of parish property and equipment;
- assisting the priest to draw up an annual parish budget of income and expenditure;
- assisting the priest in preparing the parish account books;
- advising the priest on matters pertaining to insurance and safeguarding parish property and assets.

(cf Appendix II of this Directory for Norms for Parish Finance Committees in Ossory).

iii) Parish Liturgy Committee:

In addition to parish pastoral councils, the Irish Bishops at their Emmaus Meeting (September 1986) recommended the setting up of a liturgy group or committee in every parish. This is necessary because the task of celebrating the liturgy pertains to the whole people of God, priest and people alike. The liturgy is not something the priest does for the people but rather something that they celebrate together.

1) The Role of the Parish Liturgy Committee:

Its overall purpose is to promote a more worthy, fruitful and prayerful celebration of the Church's liturgy in the parish. It does this by encouraging and facilitating a more full and active participation by all in the celebration of the liturgy. The Committee sets about achieving these aims through a variety of ways:

Sunday Eucharist: Vital to any particular celebration is proper planning and preparation. Since the Sunday Eucharist is the very core of the Church's liturgical celebration, the liturgy committee should be instrumental in planning its celebration. (cf The Celebration of Sunday in this *Directory*, pp 170ff).

Privileged Seasons: No parish or community can afford to be without an active and efficient liturgy committee if it is to celebrate the liturgy of Advent, Christmas, Lent and Easter with proper dignity and solemnity. The preparation of these liturgies should begin in good time. A study of the recent document from the Congregation for Divine Worship, 28/2/1988, *Celebrating Easter* (Veritas: Dublin, 1988) is essential reading for every Liturgy Committee.

Co-ordination of Ministries: The liturgy is by its very nature the celebration of God's people hierarchically ordered. In concrete terms this means that there are particular tasks or ministries that belong by right to different people. Nobody should usurp these these ministries, much less accumulate them to himself/herself. Insofar as possible the different ministries should be exercised by different people - readers, cantors, choir, organist, eucharistic minister, commentator, collector, altar server, usher, etc. (cf *General Instruction on Roman Missal*, 26/3/1970, nn 65-73, Flannery, vol I, pp 182-183). It is the task of the liturgy committee under the leadership of the priest to co-ordinate and train people to exercise these different ministries in a competent and dignified manner. The Diocesan Liturgy Committee will give whatever assistance it can in training people for different ministries. However, this must not be seen as a substitute for the more effective training which takes place on an ongoing basis at parish level. This latter form of training pertains to the Parish Liturgy Committee.

Other Celebrations: Apart from the Sunday Eucharist there are many other liturgical celebrations where an effective liturgy committee can render invaluable assistance to the priest in both planning and celebrating, e.g. Baptism, Confirmation, First Confession and First Holy Communion, penitential services, weddings, ordinations, centenaries, funerals, cemetery liturgies etc.).

Para-liturgies: The past few decades have witnessed the demise of many of the 'old' devotions without their being replaced by any new forms. The liturgy committee should work for the celebration of services other than Mass so that the Mass is restored to its proper place in a great cycle of prayer and praise. In particular the possibility of celebrating Evening Prayer in the parish might be usefully explored.

THE PARISH

2) Setting up a Parish Liturgy Committee:

There should be a liturgy committee in each parish and a liturgy group for each church where the liturgy is celebrated on a regular basis. Normally the liturgy committee will be represented on the parish pastoral council.

Members of the Liturgy Committee should be selected on the basis of their expertise and competence and readiness to be involved in leading people to a fuller and more fruitful celebration of the liturgy. The committee shall have the priest as its chairman or president and one or more people representing the different ministries:

- lay readers;
- special ministers of the Eucharist;
- music ministry – choir-director, organist, etc.;
- sacristan, etc.;
- people interested in the liturgical environment.

There should above all be an element of flexibility about membership. The youth of the parish should be encouraged to take an active role in the celebration of the liturgy and should be represented on the committee. Indeed, the involvement of the sixth class children in primary school in preparing and celebrating the liturgy might well be a point of departure in the process of establishing a parish liturgy group (cf B. Hoban, 'Parish Liturgy Group', in: *Intercom*, April, 1987, pp 24-25).

3) Formation and Training:

The liturgical and spiritual formation of its members is among the principal tasks of every Liturgy Committee. This training takes place on an ongoing basis rather than by a brief course at the outset. It is achieved above all by doing. In our Christian tradition the liturgy itself has always been seen as a medium for both teaching and learning. A liturgy group might begin with a series of meetings lasting one hour, with half devoted to instruction on some particular area of the liturgy and the remainder given over to preparing specific liturgies (cf *ibid* p 24). There are many resources available by way of books, videos etc. from the bookshop of the Irish Institute of Pastoral Liturgy, Carlow. Finally, members of the Committee should be encouraged to attend lectures and seminars dealing with matters of special interest to them. Since the liturgy is 'the source and summit of the

Church's life' (S.C. n 10) and in a certain way a barometer of the spiritual well-being of the parish, it follows that those who are intimately involved in its planning and celebration should prepare themselves spiritually for this task. Part of each meeting should be given over to prayer and reflection. A vigil or evening of prayer should be organised occasionally, perhaps in conjunction with other groups from the parish or from neighbouring parishes.

Recommended Reading:
John Paul II, *The Vocation and Mission of the Laity, Christifideles Laici,* 30/12/1988, Veritas, Dublin, 1988.
John Paul II, *This is the Laity, Simplification of Christifideles Laici,* Grail, Leominster, Hereford, 1989.
Centesimus Annus, CTS/Veritas, 1991.
Catechism of the Catholic Church, Veritas, 1994, Parts III & IV.
Irish Bishops' Conference, *The Works of Justice,* Veritas, Dublin, 1977; *The Young Church,* Veritas, Dublin, 1985, *Work is the Key,* Veritas, Dublin, 1993, *Life in the Spirit,* Pastoral Guidance on the Catholic Charismatic Renewal, Veritas, Dublin, 1993.
Gallagher, M.P, S.J., *Struggles of Faith,* The Columba Press, Dublin, 1990.
Bausch, W.J., *The Christian Parish,* Twenty-Third Publications, Mystic, Connecticut, 1980.
Bausch, W.J., *Hands-On Parish,* Twenty-Third Publications, Mystic, Connecticut, 1989.
Lyons, E., *Partnership in Parish,* The Columba Press, Dublin, 1987.
Sweetser, T., S.J., & Holden, C., Wisniewski, *Leadership in a Successful Parish,* Harper & Row, San Francisco, 1987.
Champlin, J.M., *The Marginal Catholic,* Ave Maria Press, Notre Dame, Indiana, 1989.
Dalton, W., *Parish Pastoral Councils,* The Columba Press, Dublin, 1993.
Joyce, J., *The Laity: Help or Hindrance?,* Mercier Press, Cork, 1994.
Earley, C., & McKenna, G., *Actions Speak Louder,* The Columba Press, 1987.
Maher, M., (ed), *Irish Spirituality,* Veritas, Dublin, 1981.
Magee, J., 'The Diocesan Bishop and Mission Awareness', *Intercom,* October, 1988, 5-6.

Hoban, B., 'Parish Liturgy Group', *Intercom*, April, 1987, 24-25.

Homer, C., 'The Forming of a Children's Liturgy Group', *Intercom*, July/August, 1986, 5-6.

Brennan, C., 'Growing in Faith Together', *Intercom*, November, 1991, 24-25.

Daly, C., 'Winds of Change', *Intercom*, February, 1992, 6-9.

Barrett, M., 'Emotional Attitudes and Adolescent Faith', *Intercom*, February, 1992, 17.

Morley, M., 'A Faith Experience for Young Adults', *Intercom*, February, 1992, 18-19.

Forristal, D., 'The Priest and the Prayer Group', *Intercom*, October, 1986, 7-8.

Kearns, B., 'Help for Prisoners', *Intercom*, July/August, 1987, 17-18.

Conlon, M. 'The Role of the Chaplain in the Catholic School', *Intercom*, April, 1991, 16-17.

Hyland, M., 'The Priest in the Primary School', *Intercom*, June, 1990, 4-5.

Gallagher, S., 'Youth Ministry at Teach Bride', *Intercom*, June, 1993, 28-29.

Drumm, M., 'A Ritual Question', *The Furrow 45* (1994), March, 141-150.

Grey, R., 'A Vision of Parish', *Intercom*, September, 1993, 15-16.

McGaughey, A., 'Parish Ministry', *Intercom*, September, 1993, 17-18.

CHAPTER 2

Infant Baptism and Christian Initiation of Adults

1. Introduction

Baptism is the first of the sacraments of the New Law and the gateway to the rest of the sacraments. It is the sacrament by which men and women are incorporated into the Church and become sharers in his life as his adopted children. They are freed from all stain of sin, original and personal (cf *General Introduction to Christian Initiation*, 24/6/1973, nn 3-5, Flannery, vol II, pp 22-23).

It is through Baptism that new Christians join the existing faith-community, i.e. the parish. Hence, Baptism is a communal rather than an individual affair. No effort should be spared in doing away with any semblance of private Baptism and in promoting a more communal understanding and approach to it. The underlying reason for the 'privatisation' of this sacrament in the past was due to its being perceived in the popular mind as essentially concerned with freeing the child from original sin. Ignored or relegated into a poor second place were its other central effects such as entry into the community of the Church, participation in the Paschal Mystery and receiving the gift of the Holy Spirit. Today the Church aims at keeping all aspects of the sacrament in focus.

2. Preparation

Like all of the other sacraments Baptism is a sacrament of faith by which men and women, enlightened by the grace of the Holy Spirit, respond to the gospel of Christ. For the Church therefore there is nothing more important than to awaken in all - catechumens, parents and sponsors - an active and living faith enabling them to participate fruitfully and worthily in this sacrament. 'Baptism is the sacrament of faith. But faith needs the community of believers. It is only within the faith of the Church that each of the faithful can believe. The faith required for

BAPTISM

Baptism is not a perfect and mature faith, but a beginning that is called to develop' (*Catechism of the Catholic Church*, n 1253). Hence it is merely the first step in that faith-journey that makes a person a Christian and a member of Christ's Church. The overall objective of a preparation programme is to communicate the conviction that Baptism is a process rather than a once-off event (cf Michael & Terri Quinn, 'Baptism: Should Preparation be Obligatory?', in *Intercom*, March 1987, pp 4-5). Ideally, the parish community must take responsibility for those baptised into it. Catechising and sacramentalising must always go hand-in-hand. It is not enough to baptise in the hope that somebody else will do the catechising. 'If we refuse to face the question of faith at Baptism then we will reap a harvest of indifference and ignorance when it comes to marriage. Once we baptise people then they have a right to marriage in the Church and one cannot demand the same level or type of faith for marriage as one can for Baptism' (M. Drumm, Infant Baptism and Adult Faith', in: *The Furrow* 44 (1993), p 138). It is for these very reasons that Church law today requires that both parents and sponsors be suitably instructed about the meaning of Baptism and their duties arising from it (c 851, 2). It is the responsibility of the parish priest to ensure that such preparation is given. Preparation may take different forms.

i) Pre-Baptismal Catechesis:

Ideally preparation for infant baptism should consist of one or more pre-baptismal meetings or instructions about the meaning of Baptism and the obligations arising from it. Sponsors should be encouraged to attend while not obliging them to do so. These meetings may take place before or after the birth of the child but always before the Baptism is celebrated. They might take the form of a few families coming together at a suitable time and venue or of the priest or some members of the parish baptismal team visiting the families in their homes. The latter seems to be the more successful. The 'home visitation' approach puts emphasis on the Church reaching out to families in their homes while the 'baptismal meeting' approach stresses the public and communal nature of the sacrament (cf Archdiocese of Dublin, *Pastoral Guidelines on Infant Baptism*, 1993). Both approaches combine social, prayer and instructional elements. There is a wide variety of video and other suitable resource material available to help the priest and those involved in baptismal ministry in the parish (cf end of this chapter). The question often arises as to when pre-baptismal preparation should begin! Parents are often reluctant to participate in any concrete planning or preparation before the child is born for fear it might be stillborn. However, experience shows that most expectant mothers welcome and appreciate a blessing from the priest. Preparation for Baptism might begin with an invitation to all expectant parents (fathers included) to come to the presbytery or church for a blessing in the months prior to the birth. When the child is born the parents will normally approach the priest in order to arrange for the Baptism. This is the opportunity for the priest to explain to them that either he himself or some members of the parish baptismal team (or both) will visit them in the near future in connection with the Baptism of their child.

Getting parents to come to a particular venue at a designated time for a pre-baptismal preparation class can prove difficult and awkward for them. By visiting them in their home the priest will have an opportunity to make concrete, pastoral contact with the family - perhaps for the first time. The members of the pre-baptismal team could then concentrate on preparing the liturgy of Baptism with the family, praying with them and discussing parenting skills. This approach guarantees a maximum flexibility in that the particular needs and circumstances of each couple can be taken into account. Obviously, the birth of the first child is always a special event in the life of the family but it must not be allowed to take from the importance of the birth of subsequent children. Every child is special and precious in the eyes of God and must be welcomed in the same way.

ii) Pre-Baptismal Preparation Team:

It is recommended that each parish should have a small group of people who will assist the priest in preparing people for the Baptism of their children and godchildren. Ideally such a group would consist of four to six people (a married couple and if possible a religious and some others) appropriately trained for this ministry (cf Rosetta Grey, 'A Vision of Parish', in: *Intercom*, Sept 1993, pp 15-16). Larger parishes, depending on the number of baptisms each year, might need more people. In preparing people for this ministry a number of smaller parishes might consider combining in hosting and organising a course of training. The purpose of the course is to update and deepen the team members' understanding and appreciation of Baptism so that they will be better equipped to share their faith and experience with parents and sponsors.

The course should include items such as:
- the Church's current understanding of Baptism as found in the *General Introduction to Christian Initiation*, 24/6/1973 (Flannery, vol II, pp 22-28) and the *Introduction to the Rite of Infant Baptism*, 24/6/1973 (Flannery, Vol II, pp 29-32);
- the Rite of Infant Baptism itself;
- the impact of the newly born child on the home and family etc.;
- parenting skills and the task of handing on the faith in the home;
- a prayer/spiritual dimension.

The baptismal group works at all times in close collaboration with the priest. It is for the priest and the group to determine the manner and format of the pre-baptismal preparation, taking into account individual cases and particular circumstances. It should be remembered that baptismal teams themselves need to be nourished on an ongoing basis. Otherwise they will simply disintegrate and die. It is strongly recommended that team members meet frequently to review their ministry and make a day's retreat once a year. Having prepared families for the baptism they should endeavour to keep up the pastoral contact afterwards by inviting parents to special eucharistic celebrations of thanksgiving and blessing of children. The latter might take place at three monthly intervals.

iii) Sponsors:

C 874 lists what is required of a sponsor if he/she is to undertake this role validly. The person must have reached the age of sixteen years, have received all three sacraments of initiation and intend discharging one's duties as sponsor, i.e. being a living example of faith to the child and helping him/her grow in faith especially if the parents are neglecting their role as Christian parents. There is no longer any prohibition on a religious or cleric being a sponsor. The Bishop or parish priest can for a just reason permit a person under 16 years to be sponsor.

A non-Catholic may be a Christian witness at a Catholic Baptism and *vice versa*, the other person being the sponsor. To underpin the essential relationship between Baptism and Confirmation it is desirable that the sponsor chosen at Baptism undertake this role at Confirmation also (c 893 # 2).

It should be noted that there is nothing to prevent an older brother or sister being a sponsor provided the above requirements are fulfilled.

3. Celebration

1) Since Baptism is primarily initiation into the Christian community, it should be celebrated in a communal setting and in the parish where the parents are living. Permission of one's own proper priest is required if the Baptism is to take place elsewhere. Every effort should be made to make Baptism a parish celebration. Welcoming a new member into the community should be presented as a significant event in the life of the parish. Parents should be discouraged from requesting to have their child baptised other than in the parish where they are living.

2) In order to make for a more ordered and dignified celebration and to highlight the importance of this sacrament each parish should have fixed days and times for Baptism, in the same way as it has fixed times for the Eucharist. This information should be displayed in the church porch and published in the parish bulletin. To highlight its paschal and community dimensions, Baptism should be celebrated at least occasionally during the principal Mass on Sundays, e.g. the Feast of the Baptism of the Lord, the Easter Vigil, Pentecost Sunday. Except in case of necessity, it is liturgically inappropriate to celebrate Baptism during Advent or Lent. Traditionally these were seasons of preparation for Baptism. With regard to the celebration of Baptism during the Easter Vigil or during Mass the minister should familiarise himself with the directives concerning those parts of the rite to be included or omitted as the case may be (*cf Rite of Baptism for Children, Introduction, ns 28-29*).

3) As in all other areas of liturgical celebration, every effort should be made by the celebrant to promote active participation and involvement of those taking part in the liturgy, e.g. readings, intercessions, singing, etc.. In the interests of dignity and decorum it might be good to limit the number of children to be baptised in any one ceremony.

BAPTISM

4) The Rite of Baptism is rich in symbolism and ritual – word, water, oil, baptismal robe, light, gesture, sound and touch – and as such demands much from the celebrant. There should be a noble simplicity about the objects used. Above all they should be clean and dignified. The baptismal font should always be used. It should be located in a prominent place in the Church, permitting maximum visibility and access. It should be remembered that signs cannot be 'sacred' signs unless they are truly signs in the first place, i.e. they must be authentic. Water flows, vessels contain and clothing drapes. Water should be heard and seen to flow; oil that is immediately wiped off is a counter-sign. If the child arrives already dressed in its baptismal robe, its symbolism is enfeebled and diminished. Some parishes have found it more convenient and meaningful to have the parents bring along a white blanket in which the child is wrapped at the stage of 'clothing with the white garment'. Superimposed commentary and explanation during the baptismal liturgy itself is often more a hindrance than a help. It obstructs the ritual flow and rhythm rather than enhancing it. The proper place for such commentary and explanation is during the pre-baptismal catechesis.

5) The liturgical environment should be properly heated and lighted and equipped with a baptismal font worthy of the event being celebrated. Anything less undermines the whole basis of pre-baptismal catechesis.

4. Adult Initiation

i) Christian Initiation of Unbaptised Adults:

What used to be referred to as 'receiving converts into the Church' is now called 'Christian Initiation of Adults'. The Second Vatican Council decreed the restoration of the catechumenate (cf *The Constitution on The Sacred Liturgy, Sacrosanctum Concilium*, n 64, Flannery, vol I, p 21) as the ordinary way for both preparing and admitting adults into the Church. In January 1972 the Congregation for Divine Worship promulgated an interim version of the *Rite of Christian Initiation for Adults* (RCIA). The final text (1986) has now been published, complete with commentary.

It is the mind of the Church that this rite or a suitably adapted form of it should become the norm for preparing and admitting new members into the Catholic Church and for the preparation of uncatechised for Confirmation and Eucharist. The rite itself makes provision for all the different types of circumstances and people the priest is likely to encounter in this area, e.g. unbaptised adults, unbaptised children of school-going age, baptised but unacatechised children and adults, those baptised into another Christian denomination etc..

The strengths of the RCIA Programme are that it sees conversion as a process, a faith-journey rather than an event. It also recognises different stages in this faith-journey and celebrates them liturgically. The candidate is helped and encouraged along this faith-journey by a sponsor or faith-friend and indeed by the whole Christian community. The different liturgical celebrations are to be found in the RCIA itself and in the Roman Missal, pp 752-755. The period of enquiry, catechumenate and enlightenment may extend over a full year, or longer if desired. The final stage of the catechumenate should coincide with the season of Lent. It is most fitting and appropriate that the catechumens be received into the Church during the Easter Vigil. All three sacraments of initiation are conferred in one and the same celebration by the priest admitting them (cf c 883, 2).

The RCIA does not contain material for the instruction of the candidates as such. Suitable material may be found in some of the catechetical books used both in primary and post-primary schools. The assistance of a competent lay person might be enlisted to help in the instruction and preparation of candidates.

ii) Christian Initiation of Adults in Exceptional Circumstances:

In exceptional circumstances, when it is deemed that a candidate either because of serious illness, advanced age or change of residence, etc. cannot go through all the stages of the RCIA the local Ordinary may permit initiation without delay. In such cases an abbreviated form of the RCIA is used (RCIA, 1986, Part II, Ch 2). A similar procedure may be followed in cases where the local Ordinary judges that the candidate is sincere in his conversion to Christianity and has arrived at a sufficient level of religious maturity. The full rite of Christian initiation is carried out in one and the same celebration. It is preferable, however, that some other elements from the RCIA be included also (cf RCIA, n 307).

In all cases, however, before receiving the sacraments of initiation the candidate chooses a sponsor or faith-friend who will

BAPTISM

help him/her prepare. Suitable instruction is given over a period of time and as far as possible the celebration of Christian initiation takes place on a Sunday with the active participation of the local worshipping community or at least in the company of the candidate's relatives and friends. The Easter Vigil is indeed the most appropriate time for such a celebration. Receiving a person into the Christian community is a formal and public act and should be seen to be such. Private and secret admission of candidates does not do justice either to what the Church is or to Christian initiation as such.

iii) Christian Initiation of Children of School-going Age:

Children who were not baptised as infants and who are now part of the First Communion or Confirmation Class are becoming more numerous. Frequently they may be children of parents who have returned from abroad or who have come to live in Ireland or of parents who have simply lapsed in the practice of the faith. These children cannot be treated as adults for they are still dependent on their parents or guardians. Yet if they have reached the use of reason they are capable of presenting themselves, with their parents' permission, for the sacraments. What must the priest do in these circumstances?

There are different options open to him:

1) Admit the child together with his/her parents and other members of the family wishing to receive Christian Initiation to a regular RCIA programme, making the necessary adaptations (cf RCIA, Part II, Ch 1);

2) Adapt the RCIA programme to meet the needs and spiritual progress of the child in question (n 243). Find a sponsor or faith-friend for the child to help him/her prepare for Baptism. If necessary this preparation might extend over a longer period. The child must not be rushed into the sacraments before he/she is ready for them. Whichever approach is adopted, adequate catechesis and pre-sacramental preparation must be ensured.

iv) Reception of Baptised Christians
into Full Communion with the Catholic Church:

The discipline concerning the admission of baptised Christians into full communion of the Catholic Church has changed considerably as a result of the Church's teaching on ecumenism.

This discipline together with its corresponding rite are to be found in the RCIA (Part II, Ch 5). It is also available in a special booklet entitled *Rite of Reception of Baptised Christians into Full Communion with the Catholic Church* (CTS, London, 1980).

The following issues should be borne in mind:

1) The baptised Christian is to receive appropriate doctrinal and spiritual preparation and to participate in worship in accordance with the provisions of the *Directory on Ecumenism*, 14/5/1967 (cf *RCIA* n 391).

2) The sacrament of Baptism is not repeated and conditional Baptism is not given indiscriminately but only as a last resort, i.e. when an insoluble doubt arises either about the fact of Baptism or the validity of the rite used (cf c 869).

3) The rite of reception normally takes place within Mass, though not necessarily. For ecumenical reasons, it may be more appropriate to celebrate the Mass with only a few relatives or friends present (cf *RCIA* n 389). Likewise it may not be appropriate to celebrate this rite during the Easter Vigil.

4) Since the admission of adults into full communion with the Catholic Church necessarily entails reception of Holy Communion, those who are barred from it may not be admitted into full communion until the reason preventing them from receiving the Eucharist has been removed, e.g. an irregular marriage union (cf *Congregation for the Doctrine of the Faith.* Private Reply, 11/7/1983 in: *Roman Replies*, pp 2-3). This teaching dates back to the time of Hippolytus (215). He enunciates it in his *Apostolic Tradition*, n 16.

5) In the case of Eastern Orthodox Christians no liturgical celebration is required but simply a profession of Catholic faith (cf *RCIA*, n 388).

6) Before being received into the Church, the candidate should receive the sacrament of Reconciliation (cf *RCIA* n 395).

7) The priest receiving the candidate into full communion must be mandated by the Bishop to celebrate the sacrament of Confirmation (cf *RCIA* n 394 & c 863).

5.Particular Problems and Related Issues

i) Baptism of Children of non-Practising Parents:

While insisting on the necessity of baptism for salvation, the Church is forever conscious of her obligation to safeguard and protect the integrity and meaning of this sacrament, especially when it is being conferred on infants. Sometimes the level of faith-commitment on the part of parents may be so low as to call into question the very integrity and authenticity of what is being celebrated. With regard to infant Baptism it has been the practice of the Catholic Church from time immemorial to insist that there be a 'well-founded hope' that the child be brought up as a Christian. (cf c 868 #1, 2).

In its *Instruction on Infant Baptism*, 20/10/1980 (Flannery, vol II, pp 103-117) the Congregation for the Doctrine of the Faith addresses itself directly to the issue of discerning and evaluating when this 'well-founded hope' might be deemed to be present. In Part III of the document the Congregation proposes some pastoral guidelines to help priests in the more difficult situations. These guidelines may be summarised as follows:

1) In circumstances where there is genuine doubt about the sufficiency of the faith-commitment on the part of parents, the priest should be careful to avoid the two extremes, namely: the blanket refusal of Baptism because of weak or non-existent faith, and the indiscriminate celebration of Baptism irrespective of the level of faith-commitment of the parents.

2) In doubtful cases 'assurances must be given that the gift thus granted can grow by an authentic education in the faith and Christian life, in order to fulfil the true meaning of the sacrament. As a rule, these assurances are to be given by the parents or close relatives although various substitutions are possible within the Christian community. But if these assurances are not really serious there can be grounds for delaying the sacrament; and if they are certainly non-existent the sacrament should even be refused' (n 28).

Thus, if the assurances are deemed inadequate, the priest has no option but to postpone Baptism and invite the parents to participate in a course of pre-baptismal catechesis. Great care should be taken to explain to the parents that Baptism is not being refused but merely delayed until their level of faith-commitment makes the celebration of the sacrament more authentic and meaningful. The deferral of Baptism should be seen as an 'educ-ational delay ... aimed at helping the family grow in faith or be-come more aware of its responsibilities' (n 31).

If the parents refuse the invitation to participate in pre-bap-tismal catechesis, and if the required assurances cannot be given by somebody else, the priest may have no option but to post-pone Baptism indefinitely and enrol the child for a future cate-chumenate. 'Enrolment for a future catechumenate should not be accompanied by a specially created rite which would easily be taken as an equivalent of the sacrament itself' (*ibid*).

Evaluating these 'assurances':

1) It is the task of the priest, taking into account all the circum-stances, to evaluate these assurances and the sincerity with which they are given. The marital status of the parents must never be a factor in evaluating these assurances.

2) Any pledge giving a well-founded hope for the Christian up-bringing of the children in the Catholic tradition deserves to be considered as sufficient.

3) These assurances may be given by parents or by godparents who promise to take sincere care of the child.

4) Regular attendance at Sunday Eucharist by the parents must not constitute the sole criterion when evaluating these assur-ances. In fact the *Instruction on Infant Baptism* does not mention Mass attendance by parents as a pre-requisite for the Baptism of their children. In the whole of Church tradition the issue has al-ways been a 'well-founded hope of Christian upbringing for the child' rather than attendance at Sunday Eucharist. If one makes Mass attendance by parents the principal criterion for admitting children to Baptism, there is the risk that parents may well re-spond (sometimes with resentment) by participating in the Eucharist for a few weeks in order to satisfy the demands im-posed. But as soon as the Baptism is over, they may well return to former patterns. This obviously defeats the whole purpose of the exercise. In this rather difficult and delicate area the Church is more intent on sowing the seeds of faith or nourishing the lit-tle faith there is by an ongoing catechesis of the parents. The priest of course must always teach the ideal, i.e. regular atten-dance at Sunday Eucharist and a more active participation in the parish life. This may not always be realisable.

BAPTISM

5) In assessing these assurances the priest should keep in mind the principle of gradualness as enunciated by Pope John Paul II in his Apostolic Exhortation, *The Christian Family in the Modern World, Familiaris Consortio* (Flannery, vol II, p 821). Conversion is not something instantaneous but 'is brought about concretely in steps that lead us ever forward'. Some people advance more slowly than others along the road of conversion. Great sensitivity is called for on the part of the priest when dealing with people in these circumstances. The priest might take the encounter between Jesus and the woman at the well (Jn 4) as his model and guide. He ministered to her despite her repeated attempts to evade the deeper issues facing her. He reached out to her as he found her. Her tangled domestic situation did not constitute an obstacle. Great care should be taken to ensure that one does not crush the bruised reed or quench the smouldering flame.

6) The marital status of the parent(s) does not impede the giving of these assurances.

ii) Baptismal Registration of non-Marital Children:

C 877 #2 deals with this issue but in practice more complex situations may arise than those envisaged by the legislator of universal law. In deciding how a particular baptismal entry should be made in the register the priest must be guided by the following principles:

- the principal purpose of the baptismal register is to record the fact of Baptism and not to make a statement about the child's lineage;
- the baptismal record should avoid all danger of defamation of character and the risk of libel;
- to avoid subsequent confusion and embarrassment, any discrepancy or disharmony between birth and baptismal records should be eliminated i.e. the child should have the same name in both registers.

The child of an unmarried mother: In accordance with c 877 #2 the mother's name is entered, with the child taking the mother's surname. The father's name is not entered unless:

- his paternity is established by a public document, e.g. civil birth certificate; maintenance order, etc. – this is the preferable option; or
- he declares before a priest and two witnesses, either orally or

in writing, that he is the natural father of the child and wishes this fact to be recorded. A mere written request to the priest by either or both parties regarding the name the child should be given does not suffice. Should the father's name be entered on the basis of either of the above reasons, the appropriate reason is mentioned in the register and a record of it is kept. In this instance the child may assume the father's surname, if the parents so wish.

The child of parents in a non-canonical marriage: Children born to Catholics whose marriage is not recognised canonically are registered in accordance with the principles outlined above. An entry to the effect that the parents are married civilly only is made in the appropriate column.

The child of a married woman, her husband not being the father: In this situation certain legal presumptions come into play. According to canon law children born 180 days or more after the date of the marriage and within 300 days of the dissolution of conjugal life are presumed legitimate (c 1138 #2) and should be registered accordingly. The husband is presumed to be the natural father. But this presumption may be rebutted by contrary proof. Such proof would require:
    - the husband denying paternity under oath;
    - the natural father accepting paternity under oath;
    - the mother swearing to the truth of these facts;
    - the circumstances concurring.

In the event of the above proofs being made available, the name of the natural father may be entered in the baptismal register with the child taking his surname. The mother's name is her married name, not her maiden name. Reference is made to the basis of the entry in the appropriate space.

A similar entry might be made on production of a civil certificate of birth. Like its canonical counterpart, civil law presumes that the father of a child born to a married woman is her husband. However, a Dublin High Court decision, before Judge O'Hanlon, December 1982, directed the Registrar General that a child be registered in the name of its natural father when the husband, wife, natural father and circumstances all concurred that the latter was in fact the natural father.

BAPTISM

The child of a couple married ecclesiastically only: The registration is made in the normal way in accordance with c 877 #1. Every effort should be made to ensure harmony between birth and baptismal registration.

iii) Altering the Birth and Baptismal Registration of a Child:

Changing the child's surname on Civil Birth Certificate: In accordance with the 1931 Legitimacy Act ' ... an illegitimate person is legitimated upon the subsequent marriage of the parents, provided the father is domiciled in this country at the time of such marriage, and both he and the mother could have been lawfully married to each other at the time of the birth or at some time during the period of ten months preceding the birth' (A. Shatter, *Family Law in the Republic of Ireland*, Wolfhound Press, Dublin, 1977, pp 154-155). The parents can apply to have the child re-registered in the surname of the father by completing the appropriate 'Re-Registration' form obtainable from the local Registrar's Office.

Changing the child's surname in the Baptismal Register: To ensure harmony between registration of birth and baptism it is advisable to defer all alterations in the baptismal entry until the desired changes have first been completed civilly. The latter (a public document) may then be used as the basis for the alteration in the baptismal entry.

The 1956 Maynooth Statutes required the written permission of the local Ordinary before altering a baptismal entry. It should be remembered that any alteration is made by adding to what is already there rather than by deletion. Deletion is never permitted. The basis for the alteration should also be noted.

Cancellation of the baptismal entry: A baptised person may lapse from the practice of the faith or even formally defect from the Church by joining some other denomination or sect, but he cannot renounce his baptismal status. Since the the baptismal entry is primarily a record of same, it may not be cancelled or destroyed. However, a record of his/her formal defection from the Catholic faith should be noted in the observation column of the register as this might well indicate the validity or otherwise of a subsequent civil marriage which the party might enter (cf c 1117).

iv) Baptism and Registration of an Adopted Child:

The Irish Episcopal Conference decreed at its Meeting in November 1980 that a central baptismal register for all adopted children be kept in each diocese. In this register are entered all details of adoption and Baptism as supplied by the Adoption Board. All future entries, (e.g. Confirmation, Marriage, Sacred Orders, Religious Profession, etc.) will be made only in this register and no certificate is issued except from it. This is in the interests of preserving confidentiality. Normally this register is kept at the Diocesan Offices or in the particular parish designated for this purpose.

Hence, once a child has been adopted, no further communication will be made with the place of Baptism and no reference to the fact of adoption is made in the baptismal register. Records of Baptism are issued from the Diocesan Offices from the special Register.

Should a child who has already been adopted be presented for Baptism in a particular parish, the priest, having celebrated the Baptism does not enter anything in the local baptismal register but forwards all details to the Diocesan Offices for recording in the special register. All other details will be supplied directly to the Diocesan Offices by the Adoption Board (cf *Canon Law Digest*, vol XI, pp 195-196). As regards adopted children already registered in their respective parishes, directive n 157 of the Maynooth Statues still applies:

- when issuing a certificate of Baptism for an adopted child the shorter form is to be used, i.e. the form which makes no reference whatever to the names of parents or sponsors;
- if for any reason a more detailed certificate of Baptism is required, the priest having custody of the baptismal register shall forward the said certificate to the person requesting it through the Diocesan Offices of the place where the person resides. Under no circumstances shall such a certificate be transmitted through the person in question or anybody else.

v) Rite of Bringing a Baptised Child to the Church:

What used to be referred to as 'supplying the ceremonies' for children baptised in emergency is now called the Rite of Bringing a Baptised Child to the Church. Provision for this liturgical celebration is made in a special chapter in the *Rite of Baptism for Children* (Veritas, 1992) pp 116-125. It is very similar

BAPTISM

to the regular Rite of Baptism itself except that those parts pertaining directly to the liturgy of the sacrament are omitted.

The appropriate additions are made in the baptismal register, i.e. names of sponsors, date of celebration, etc..

vi) Baptism in Danger of Death:

An adult in danger of death may be baptised if he has some knowledge of the principal truths of faith and has in some manner manifested his intention to receive Baptism and observe the requirements of the Christian life (c 865 #2).

'An infant of Catholic parents, indeed even of non-Catholic parents, may in danger of death be baptised even if the parents are opposed to it' (c 868 #2). The thinking behind this provision - which on the surface appears to be in conflict with the Church's teaching on religious freedom and the rights of parents over their children - upholds the view that the child's right to Baptism and salvation takes precedence over all other rights.

'When a person is at the point of death or when time is pressing because death is imminent, the minister, omitting everything else, pours natural water (even if not blessed) on the head of the sick person, while saying the usual sacramental form' (*Pastoral Care of the Sick*, n 277). 'The intention required is to will to do what the Church does when she baptises, and to apply the Trinitarian baptismal formula' (*The Catechism of the Catholic Church*, n 1256). Hospital sisters, doctors, midwives and nurses should be instructed with regard to baptising infants in danger of death and ensuring that the Baptism is properly recorded.

An abbreviated form of Christian Initiation is to be found in a special chapter of the *Pastoral Care of the Sick*, pp 231-243.

vii) Stillbirth:

During the course of their ministry most priests will occasionally encounter the tragedy of stillbirth. By stillbirth is meant a pregnancy loss occurring when the woman is five or more months pregnant; a pregnancy loss earlier than five months is referred to as a miscarriage or spontaneous abortion. The pastoral care of bereaved parents calls for a special degree of sensitivity on the part of the priest. The mother especially experiences feelings of bewilderment, disorientation and depression. Often there is a sense of guilt arising from a conviction of failing to take proper care of herself during the pregnancy. Not infrequently these guilt feelings are linked to a certain sense of shame. This shame is associated with the sense of having failed as a woman in the feminine function of bearing a living child. Consequently there tends to be a well-meaning conspiracy of silence. Bereaved women can feel isolated and are often discharged as soon as possible from hospital.

The Role of the Priest:

Much of the anxiety and bewilderment that parents feel on the occasion of stillbirths (or cot-deaths before Baptism) derive from concern for the child's eternal salvation and the necessity of baptism for same. While the Church has always insisted on the necessity of Baptism for salvation, it has always accepted the sufficiency of Baptism of desire (i.e., the desire to have their child baptised thus becoming an adopted child of God) in the case of children who die before Baptism. Priests, medical personnel and social workers should endeavour to dispel any misconceptions parents may have with regard to this issue and reassure them that God is a loving Father. It is incomprehensible and totally incompatible with the idea of a loving God that an unbaptised infant should suffer any loss or discrimination in his sight. The most recent teaching on this issue is to be found in the 1980 *Instruction on Infant Baptism*, (Congregation for the Doctrine of the Faith) and reiterated in the Catechism: 'As for children who die without baptism, the Church can only entrust them to God's mercy, as she does in the funeral rite provided for them' (n 13, Flannery, vol II, p 106). It is worth noting that neither this *Instruction* nor the *Introduction to the Rite of Infant Baptism* make any reference to Limbo as such. Rather it now seems fairly well established that the teaching on Limbo was never part of the Church's teaching as such but rather the postulate of theologians in discussing a variety of matters. 'The pastor can and should tell the Christian parents of children who have died without baptism that there is no definite doctrine of faith regarding the fate of such children, and that consequently they can entrust the final lot of their child to the mysterious but infinitely kind and powerful love of God, to whose grace no limit is set by the earthly circumstances which he in his providence has allowed to come about' (Peter Gumpel, 'Limbo', in: *Encyclopedia of Theology, Concise Sacramentum Mundi*, p 851).

A request by the parents, especially the mother, to have the still-

BAPTISM

born child baptised will usually provide the opening and opportunity for the priest or medical person to explain the meaning and purpose of Baptism. 'Aborted foetuses, if they are alive, are to be baptised, insofar as this is possible' (c 871). Only a living person is capable of receiving a sacrament. However, there is a world of difference between saying 'I cannot baptise your child' and saying 'the Church has special prayers for this situation'. The priest should pray with the parents, helping them to work through their grief and loss rather than suppressing it. The gospel story of the raising of the widow's son at Nain would seem particularly apt in these circumstances (Lk 7:11-17). *The Order of Christian Funerals* provides suitable prayers for baptised children and for those who died before Baptism.

Both parents should, if they wish, be allowed to see the dead child, and encouraged to give it a name. Hospital personnel can be of great assistance to the priest in this matter. A Liturgy of the Word may be celebrated in the hospital, in the child's home, or perhaps more often at the graveside. This is followed by Christian burial in a marked family grave (cf cs 1180 & 1183 #3). As a general rule the priest should not tell the parents what to do but rather make suggestions to them with regard to the different options available. The funeral liturgy fulfils both a therapeutic and religious role. Consequently it should never be omitted. Do not encourage parents to rush the funeral. This can be hurtful to them. It could be interpreted as saying to them that the baby was not a real person. To dispel any such misconceptions a Civil Register for Stillbirths has now been introduced in Ireland. In all probability the parents will need some additional counselling over a more protracted period of time. The attendant grief and sense of loss is shared by both parents. Visit the parents afterwards and listen to their story, their questions, their anger and reassure them that these feelings are perfectly normal. Neither does it help to try to explain their loss in terms of its being 'God's will' or 'you will have an angel in heaven' (especially if the child was born with some serious disability). Parents prefer to have their baby here on earth. The words of a mother who has been through the trauma of losing her own child at birth are particularly helpful:

> It is important to acknowledge the pain of families who experience the death of an infant. Allow them to feel their grief is legitimate and needs to be felt and lived through. Allow

them time to grieve and show their sadness. Show sympathy, attempt to understand, but above all listen with an open heart. I think it is often enough to be with people in their grief, to be open to their pain. We cannot remove pain and grief with sympathetic words; we often try to dismiss a person's pain by comparison with greater tragedies (J. McKenna, 'A Quiet Sadness', in: *Intercom*, May 1992, p 19).

viii) Baptism of a Child of a Mixed Marriage:

The Baptism of a child born to a couple who belong to differing Christian Churches can often be problematic. Parents may sometimes request that the child be baptised into both Churches. This is not possible since Baptism is understood to entail initiation into, and membership of a specific believing community, namely the Catholic Church (cf Pontifical Council for Promoting Christian Unity, *Directory for the Application of Principles and Norms on Ecumenism*, 1993, n 97).

While acknowledging at all times the joint responsibility of Christian parents with regard to the education and upbringing of their children 'the suggestion of dual-membership' or 'double belonging' and joint registration in both Churches is to be avoided (Archdiocese of Dublin 1993, *Pastoral Guidelines on Infant Baptism*, p 8). The reasoning behind this is linked to our understanding of 'Church'. 'Church' is not merely an abstract title given to all who believe in Christ. Rather, it is a visible community which gathers regularly for worship, and proposes certain beliefs and values to its members. Through Baptism a child is received into that visible community. 'Where both parents are active and committed members of different churches it is very likely that their children will be involved in both, but it is necessary for them to belong to one or the other' (Bishops' Conference of England and Wales, *Mixed Marriages*, 1990, p 16).

ix) Baptism of Travelling People and their Children:

This matter is best left to the personal parish priest for travelling people or whoever has pastoral responsibility for them.

BAPTISM

Some Baptismal Resources

Videos
a) *Our Child's Baptism* by Raymond Topley (Veritas), £35.
A 50-minute video comprising several sections that can be used for the training of baptismal teams and parents presenting their child for baptism. It contains the Rite of Baptism in full, plus interviews with Archbishop Joseph Cassidy and different couples.
b) *A Vision of Parish* (Veritas), £30.
Contains a section on the Faith Friends approach to baptismal preparation as pioneered in the parish of St Michael's, Inchicore, Dublin.
c) *Sacrament of Welcome* (American - Franciscan Communications) Available from Veritas. Video 1 - Faith Journey; Video 2 - Symbols and the Rite of Baptism; Video 3 - Christian Parenting.

Audios:
Baptism: *A New Creation* by Raymond Topley.
A 60-minute audio tape dealing with the history of baptism, the RCIA, and the Rite of Baptism for Children from the point of view of celebration and preparation for the parents.

Books:
a) *The Ministry of Baptism* by Sr Briege O'Hare, £2.50.
The 'Faith Friends' approach to baptismal preparation.
b) *Your Baby's Baptism* (Redemptorists), £1.56.
Attractively produced colour book for parents.
Pamphlets:
a) *Baptism* by Fr Oliver Crilly (Veritas), 50p.
b) *Baptism* by Joseph Martos (Ligouri), 67p.

Manuals:
Parish Baptism Team Manual by Raymond Topley
Deals in a practical way with all aspects of baptismal preparation of parents in the light of ten years experience of working with parish baptism teams in Dublin Diocese.

Recommended Reading:
Congregation for Divine Worship, *Rite of Baptism for Children*, Dublin: Veritas, 1992; *Christian Initiation: General Introduction*, 24/6/1973, Flannery, vol II, 22-28; *Introduction to the Rite of Infant Baptism*, 24/6/1973, Flannery, vol II, 29-34.

Congregation for the Doctrine of the Faith, *Instruction on Infant Baptism*, 20/10/1980, Flannery, vol II, 103-117.

Archdiocese of Dublin, *Pastoral Guidelines on Infant Baptism*, 1993.

Neunheuser, B., *Baptism and Confirmation*, Burns & Oates, London, 1964.

Swayne, S., *The Sacraments, A Pastoral Directory*, Veritas, Dublin, 1976, 9-38.

Huck, G., *Baptism in the Parish: Understanding the Rite, Liturgy Training Publication*, Archdiocese of Chicago, 1980.

Searle, M., *Christening, the Making of Christians*, The Liturgical Press, Collegeville, 1980.

Kavanagh, A., *The Shape of Baptism, the Rite of Christian Initiation*, Pueblo, New York, 1978.

Marsh, T.A., *Gift of Community: Baptism and Confirmation*, Glazier, Wilmington, Delaware, 1984.

Champlin, J.M., *The Marginal Catholic*, Ave Maria Press, Notre Dame, Indiana, 1989.

Quinlan, J., *Loved and Lost: The Journey through Dying, Death and Bereavement*, The Columba Press, Dublin, 1996.

Drumm, M., 'Infant Baptism and Adult Faith', *The Furrow* 44 (1993) 131-139.

McKenna, J., 'A Quiet Sadness', *Intercom*, May 1992, 17-19.

Quinn, M. & T., 'Baptism: Should Preparation be Obligatory', *Intercom*, March 1987, 4-5.

CHAPTER 3

Confirmation

1. Introduction

Through the sacrament of Confirmation, Christians continue on the path of Christian initiation. They receive the gift of the Holy Spirit and become witnesses of Christ in the work of building up his Kingdom on earth. In order that they may properly appreciate this gift and mandate, they must be suitably prepared. In accordance with the enunciated policy of the Irish Episcopal Conference, 'the sacrament of Confirmation (shall) be conferred on the faithful not "at about the age of discretion" but rather towards the end of the primary-school curriculum, i.e. at the age of 11 or 12 years' (Decrees of the Irish Episcopal Conference', n 11, in *Intercom*, December 1987/January 1988, p 9). As a general rule therefore Confirmation is conferred on children of Sixth Class in Primary School. In parishes where Fifth and Sixth Classes are combined for teaching purposes, Confirmation is celebrated every alternate year with the children of both classes being eligible.

2. Preparation

i) Candidates:

Priests and people are jointly obliged to ensure that the faithful are properly instructed for Confirmation and come to it at an opportune time (c 890). This instruction is effected both through catechesis and the liturgy. The priests of the parish should visit the schools frequently and involve themselves actively in the catechetical and liturgical preparation of the children. In particular they should make themselves familiar with the Church's understanding of this sacrament as contained both in the catechetical programme and in the rite itself. Priests should work in close collaboration with teachers, encouraging, assisting and supporting them whenever possible. Use of the 'Faith Friends' programme is strongly recommended. 'Preparation for Confirmation ... should strive to awaken a sense of belonging to the Church of Jesus Christ, the universal Church as well as the parish community' (*Catechism*, n 1309). It entails helping them celebrate the sacrament of Reconciliation in a manner consistent with their age and maturity.

ii) Parents and Sponsors:

In every parish there should be one or more pre-Confirmation meetings for parents and sponsors. The first of these takes place some months prior to Confirmation so as to enable both parents and sponsors to become involved in the work of preparation. Topics such as the role of the Spirit in the life of the Christian, the meaning of Confirmation and its intimate connection with Baptism might be discussed. Questions about who should be sponsors and the Confirmation pledge might also be raised at this meeting. The method used in adult education is most suited to this type of occasion, i.e. twenty minutes of input followed by twenty minutes of discussion in small groups and concluding with feedback, further questions and discussion, etc.. To help them in this task priests might enlist the assistance of teachers and others skilled in the area of adult religious education and facilitating group discussion. People who have attended the Diploma Course in Adult Religious Education might be able to help out here.

Shortly before the celebration of Confirmation priests should arrange a special liturgy or paraliturgy for parents, sponsors and children. Parents, teachers, children and the parish liturgy team might combine in preparing this special liturgy. *The Teacher's Book for Sixth Class* (Veritas, 1987), pp 454-457 and a small booklet entitled the *Rite of Confirmation* (Veritas, 1983), provides a ready-made 'Paraliturgy in Preparation for Confirmation' (pp 18-24). Parents and sponsors should be afforded the opportunity to receive the sacrament of Reconciliation either at this celebration or later.

iii) Who may be Sponsors:

Insofar as possible the person to be confirmed should have a sponsor. Ideally '... the sponsor chosen (should) be the one who undertook this role at Baptism' (c 893 #2) but this may not always be feasible, keeping in mind the criteria set down in c 874

concerning sponsors. Having the same sponsor for both sacraments brings out more clearly the essential relationship between
Baptism and Confirmation.

The question is often raised 'may a parent be a sponsor to
his/her child'? *The Introduction to the Rite of Confirmation*, n 5 (cf
Roman Pontifical p 64) seems to permit it while the *Code of Canon
Law* explicitly excludes it (c 874 #1.2). This discrepancy was noted
in a report to the Code Commission. The Commission held that
the exclusion of parents from sponsorship was appropriate
'since the function (of sponsorship) is adjunctive and quasi-
suppletory, namely to assist the parents in the Christian up-
bringing of their children'. The report went on to add however
that 'parents may certainly present their children (for
Confirmation), but then it must be said that sponsors are lacking, for it is proper that parents name the sponsors' (Corriden,
Green, Heintschel, *The Code of Canon Law*, A text and
Commentary, 1985, pp 641-642). Thus, the mind of the Code
Commission is clear: parents may present their child to the
Bishop for Confirmation but this does not make them sponsors
as such. There is nothing to prevent an older brother or sister
acting as sponsor provided they meet the requirements of c 874.

3. Celebration

1) Confirmation in Ossory Diocese is celebrated within Mass,
which, fittingly, is concelebrated by the Bishop and priests of the
parish and other priests who are involved in the liturgy, e.g. relatives of children being confirmed.

2) The liturgy begins with the entrance procession and incensation of the altar. The thurifer leads the procession and the entrance hymn continues until the incensation has been completed.
The incense may be put in the thurible before leaving the sacristy.

3) The children should be taught and reminded to join in the responses for the people at Mass, i.e. from the 'Amen' at the Sign
of the Cross at the beginning to the 'Thanks be to God' at the
very end. Particular attention should be given to the 'Amen' responses during the solemn blessing at the end.

4) The pre-Gospel readings should be done by parents, sponsors
or teachers. Priests should read only the Gospel. Some of the
newly confirmed may join parents, sponsors or teachers in the
Prayer of the Faithful and Offertory Procession.

5) Candidates' names are called out individually, if this would not prolong the celebration unduly. Where there are more than 70 children for Confirmation the names are not read out.

6) Candidates kneel before the Bishop in pairs for the anointing with chrism.

7) On kneeling before the Bishop the child will clearly tell him, his/her names, first the Christian or baptismal name and then the Confirmation name. The latter should always be a saint of the Church.

8) The person presenting the child puts his/her right hand on the right shoulder of the candidate. The Rite of Confirmation takes place in front of the altar, in an area permitting maximum visibility to all in the church. A chair for the Bishop is located in a suitable place in front of the altar. He wears his mitre during the anointing with chrism.

9) Rehearsals should be arranged so that the children and others involved in the liturgy know what to do.

10) Ordinarily there should be a sponsor for each child to be confirmed. While it is desirable that it be the same person who undertook this role at Baptism, provided he/she is available and suitable; nonetheless, the choice of a special sponsor for Confirmation is not excluded. Teachers, parents, and children should be made aware of the options available. Sponsors must not be under the age of sixteen years.

11) Even though Confirmation cards are not used in the actual ceremony, they must however, be completed in the normal way to facilitate the registration of Confirmation afterwards.

12) To create a proper setting and environment for prayer, those who come to the ambo for the Prayer of the Faithful should remain there until the Bishop has concluded the Prayer of the Faithful. Likewise those designated to take part in the Offertory Procession should remain in their places until after the Prayer of the Faithful has been concluded.

13) During the Mass the 'Lord, Have Mercy', the 'Holy, Holy' and 'Lamb of God' should be sung. However, care should be taken to ensure that the congregation is not wearied by an inordinate amount of singing. Hymns to Our Lady are not sung during Mass. The congregation should be prepared and encouraged to take an active part in the singing and music during the celebration.

CONFIRMATION

14) There should be hymns, prayers and reflection during the anointing with chrism and distribution of Holy Communion. Prayerful, reflective silences should also be observed so that the actual rite of Confirmation can be seen and heard.

15) The Bishop holds the pastoral staff during the reading of the Gospel and wears the mitre for the actual rite of Confirmation. He wears the mitre for the final blessing, and the pastoral staff after the third invocation of the final blessing.

16) After the Post-Communion Prayer and before the final blessing the Confirmation Pledge is given to the children who wish to make it. All children remain seated and those wishing to make the Confirmation Pledge are invited by the Bishop to recite silently the following prayer:

> Lord God, for love of you and through concern for my family, my friends and my future happiness, and out of my wish to serve Christ, your Divine Son, more generously, I promise with your help, not to take alcoholic drink until I am eighteen years of age.

During the course of preparing for Confirmation priests and teachers should explain the importance of the Confirmation Pledge. The fact that the pledge is made silently does not take from its seriousness and solemnity.

17) Before he leaves the parish the Bishop requests that he be given in writing the number of boys and girls actually confirmed.

18) A child in the Confirmation class who happens to have been confirmed already is presented to the Bishop in the normal way and the Bishop is reminded of this fact. The child need not necessarily be kept until last in the line.

19) The text of the Mass is the ritual Mass of Confirmation as given in the Roman Missal except for the Sundays of Advent, Lent, Easter and Solemnities when one is obliged to follow the Mass of the day. 'The vestments for the Mass are red or white or of some other festive colour' (*Ceremonial of Bishops*, 1989, n 459).

20) The readings, unless otherwise specified, are taken from the readings for Confirmation (*Lectionary* vol III pp 86-108).

On the Sundays of Advent, Lent, Easter and Solemnities, one is obliged to follow the readings of the day for the most part but 'one of the readings may be taken from those provided in the Lectionary for Mass for the ritual Mass for Confirmation'

(*Ceremonial* ..., *ibid*). On other Sundays and feasts the ritual Mass of Confirmation with its proper readings are used.

21) After the ceremony, the Bishop meets the principal teachers and the teachers of the Confirmation Classes. He may meet briefly the members of the Boards of Management of the Schools. He will then meet the children and their families for the usual photographs.

22) Before leaving the parish, the Bishop, with the priests of the parish, will inspect the current parish Registers of Baptism, Confirmation and Marriage.

4. Particular problems and related issues

i) Confirmation of Adults Baptised in Infancy:

Occasionally the priest will come across an adult who has not been confirmed. This may only become known when the person presents himself/herself for marriage. 'Sometimes the preparation of a baptised adult for Confirmation is part of his preparation for marriage. In such cases, if it is foreseen that the conditions for a fruitful reception of Confirmation cannot be satisfied, the local Ordinary will judge whether it is better to defer Confirmation until after the marriage' (Introduction to the *Rite of Confirmation*, 22/8/1971, n 12). It is recommended that the *Rite of Christian Initiation for Adults* be suitably adapted and used in preparing the person for Confirmation (*ibid*, n 3).

When the person has been suitably prepared to receive the sacrament worthily and fruitfully, the priest should consult the Bishop with regard to the celebration of the sacrament. He may decide to celebrate it himself at a special ceremony or make some alternative arrangement (cf c 884 #1).

ii) Confirmation in Danger of Death:

'If a Christian is in danger of death, any priest should give him Confirmation. Indeed the Church desires that none of her children, even the youngest, should depart this world without having been perfected by the Holy Spirit with the gift of Christ's fullness' (*Catechism*, n 1314).

Confirmation in these circumstances should if possible be celebrated in the context of Mass at which the family and friends are present. The Rite of Confirmation is to be found in the *Pastoral*

Care of the Sick, 1983, pp 231-243, omitting those parts which pertain to Baptism as such.

In the case of a sick child, he/she may also receive Holy Communion provided he/she can distinguish the Body of Christ from ordinary food and receive it with reverence (c 913 #2).

iii) Confirmation of People with Disabilities:

Developmentally disabled persons may live at home or in a residential facility. They may be able to speak or may be nonverbal. While not being capable of abstract conceptual thought such people have their own ways of relating to others and to the world. Since grace is primarily relational and faith is neither fundamentally abstract nor conceptual, people with disabilities are capable of growing in faith and benefiting from the grace of the sacraments. Hence, they are admitted to the sacraments. This approach contrasts starkly with the older attitude that such people needed only the sacrament of Baptism in order to go to heaven. The canonical requirement that a person have reached 'the age of reason' before receiving the other sacraments was interpreted strictly along conceptual lines. Today that criterion has been broadened to embrace the relational aspect as well. In preparing developmentally disabled people for the sacraments what is important is the quality of their relationships. 'Relationships which are inviting and welcoming, and which foster insight and assent, allow them to awaken gradually to the larger sacramental dimension of life. This active spiritual nourishment is a far cry from the days when parents took their children from one parish to another with the hope that someday someone would give their children Communion' (Archdiocese of Chicago, *Access to the Sacraments of Initiation and Reconciliation for Developmentally Disabled Persons*, Pastoral Guidelines, 1985, p 3).

Preparation of disabled persons for the sacrament of Confirmation and indeed the other sacraments as well is best done in the context of a group rather than on a one to one basis. It is disrespectful to the person and to the family to celebrate a sacrament before there has been adequate catechesis, but it is equally disrespectful to prolong catechesis indefinitely or to avoid celebrations in the larger assembly because of fear, embarrassment or prejudice. With regard to the nature and content of the preparation two extremes must be avoided: to treat the disabled as 'holy innocents' on the one hand, and therefore needing no pre-sacramental preparation, and to attempt to impart the type of preparation befitting a child of average intelligence and ability (cf D. Wilson, 'The Church, the Eucharist, and the Mentally Handicapped', in: *The Clergy Review* 60 (1975), p 83). It pertains to the family and those who care for the disabled person to make the prudential judgment that a person is ready for the sacramental event. True catechesis takes time, but is often more effective after a sacramental celebration, when even greater meaning is discovered, based on common lived experience.

Insofar as possible when celebrating Confirmation, the person's age is to be respected. Developmentally disabled adults ordinarily should be confirmed with other adults.

iv) Confirmation of Children Attending non-Catholic and non-Denominational Schools:

The same criteria apply here as to children attending Catholic schools. Priests and parents are jointly obliged to ensure that such children receive proper instruction and spiritual preparation, and that they receive the sacrament at an opportune time. How this is best accomplished is a matter for the priest and parents to decide. The process already used to prepare these children for First Confession and First Communion might profitably be used for Confirmation also.

v) Confirmation for Travelling People and their Children:

This matter should be referred to the personal pastor for travelling people or whoever is entrusted with this responsibility. A special booklet, *First Communion and Penance, and Confirmation* (published by Parish of the Travelling People, Dublin, 1994) is now available.

Recommended reading:

Paul VI, *Apostolic Constitution, Introducing the Rite of Confirmation*, 15/8/1971, *Instructions on the Revised Roman Rites, Collins*, London, 1979, pp 53-59.
Congregation for Divine Worship, *Introduction to Rite of Confirmation*, 22/8/1971, *Instructions on the Revised Roman Rites*, pp 60-67.
Catechism of the Catholic Church, Veritas, Dublin, 1994.

Kavanagh, A., *Confirmation: Origins and Reform*, Pueblo, New York, 1988.

Marsh, T.A., *Gift of Community, Baptism and Confirmation*, Glazier, Wilmington, Delaware, 1984.

Marsh, 'Confirmation', *Intercom*, June 1991, pp 14-15

Neunheuser, B., *Baptism and Confirmation*, Burns & Oates, London, 1964.

Osborne, K., *The Christian Sacraments of Initiation: Baptism, Confirmation, Eucharist*, Paulist, Mahwah, New York, 1987.

Rahner, K., *Meditations on the Sacraments*, Burns & Oates, London, 1977.

Swayne, S., *The Sacraments, A Pastoral Directory*, Veritas, Dublin, 1976, pp 38-47

Dalton, W., 'Confirmation: Earlier or Later', *The Furrow* 40, 1990, pp 149-155.

Hyland, M., 'Reflections on Confirmation', *Intercom*, April 1993, pp 18-19.

CHAPTER 4

Reconciliation and Peace

1. Introduction

The entire life and ministry of Jesus may be summed up in the single word 'reconciliation'. In the words of St Paul 'God in Christ was reconciling the world to himself ... and has entrusted to us the news that we are reconciled' (2 Cor 5:19). The Church proclaims and professes God's mercy in this truth, as it has been handed down to us by Divine Revelation. All people are charged with communicating to others God's mercy and forgiveness. By virtue of their calling and ordination, priests are commissioned and empowered in a very special way to be instruments of God's mercy and ministers of his reconciliation (Jn 20:21-23). 'Priests, then, by the will of Christ are the only ministers of the sacrament of Reconciliation' (cf Congregation for the Clergy, *Directory on the Life and Ministry of Priests*, 1994, n 51). They must not only preach peace and forgiveness to others, but they must offer themselves as ones who have experienced these realities in their own lives. They must themselves be witnesses of the realities of which they speak *(ibid,* n 53). This is because 'modern man listens more willingly to witnesses than to teachers; if he is to listen to teachers it is because they are also witnesses' (Paul VI, *Evangelisation in the Modern World, Evangelii Nuntiandi,* 8/12/1975, n 41, Flannery, vol II, p 728).

Shift in emphasis:

In the past this sacrament was spoken of almost exclusively in terms of 'confession', i.e. confession of sins. This particular characterisation placed emphasis on the enumeration of sins, the listing of one's faults and failures and the confiding of one's mistakes to the priest as God's representative. The priest in turn absolved the penitent from his/her wrong-doing, declared the Lord's forgiveness and imposed a salutary penance. In time the sacrament came to be viewed almost exclusively in juridical rather

RECONCILIATION

RECONCILIATION

than in spiritual terms. The confessional itself was frequently referred to as the 'sacred tribunal', with the priest presiding as a kind of judge. This was long way from the medieval tradition which viewed the priest as befriending the penitent along the road of conversion. They were co-penitents. The priest prayed, wept and did penance together with the sinner. He was personally involved in the conversion of the sinner and the celebration of God's mercy (cf David Power, 'The Sacramentalisation of Penance', in: *Worship: Culture and Theology*, 1990, pp 216-217). The Church draws attention once again to this aspect of the sacrament.'The confessor is not the master of God's forgiveness, but its servant. He should have ... respect and sensitivity towards the one who has fallen; he must love the truth, be faithful to the Magisterium of the Church, and lead the penitent with patience towards healing and full maturity. He must pray and do penance for his penitent, entrusting him to the Lord's mercy' (*Catechism*, n 1466).

While confession of sins is indeed an integral element of this sacrament both from a theological and psychological viewpoint, it must never be equated with it. The sacrament entails more than simply confessing one's guilt and receiving absolution from an authorised minister. It includes acts of penance and reaching out to those from whom we have been alienated through sin. We cannot be reconciled to God without first being reconciled to our neighbour (cf Mt 5:23-25). The one who refuses to forgive others burns the bridge over which he himself must pass.

The Church today favours the terms 'penance' and 'reconciliation' when referring to this sacrament. Indeed, this is the very terminology that Pope John Paul II uses in the title of his 1984 Apostolic Exhortation, *Reconciliation and Penance*, on this subject. This terminology highlights the change of heart that is necessary and the ongoing nature of the reconciliation process.

Reconciliation both presupposes and announces conversion. The journey of conversion has already begun ever before the penitent approaches the priest for this sacrament. The sacrament itself is a unique moment in this journey but not the only one. Like the other sacraments, Reconciliation is primarily a process rather than an event. Hence, Reconciliation must not be seen as limited to its sacramental expression. There are times when the priest will be called upon to mediate in disputes between families or individuals. This too is part of his ministry of reconciliation.

Since this sacrament celebrates conversion, it has much in common with Baptism, particularly with adult Baptism. The process of conversion in each case is supported and nourished by prayerful listening to the word of God.

Decline in the practice of going to Confession:

Over the past fifteen years there has been a marked decline in the number of people going to Confession regularly. Some are even asking if we are witnessing the demise of the sacrament of Penance itself! It should be remembered that frequent Confession (i.e. monthly or even weekly) only became the norm in this century, peaking in the 1950s. It flourished under the influence of Pope Pius X encouraging frequent Communion, and the commonly held belief that one had to go to Confession before receiving Holy Communion (cf Bill Cosgrave, 'The Decline of Confessions: Disaster or Return to Normal', in *The Furrow* 45 (1994), March, p 159).

Priests today are often concerned about the decline in the number of people coming to the sacrament of Reconciliation and the increase in those receiving Holy Communion regularly. What should be remembered is that the Eucharist itself is essentially the celebration of togetherness, of unity and of reconciliation. The penitential rite at the beginning of Mass reminds us of this. Through the eucharistic celebration 'a fragile, dismembered community comes together and is strengthened and reconstituted by the word and presence of God. Unfree people taste freedom. Strangers become friends. Sinners drink the cup of salvation. That this should take place at a table seems particularly fitting since the table as a piece of furniture provides the opportunity for persons to look at each other, eye to eye, and to disclose themselves to one another. This happens most often in the context of a meal when food and drink provide the fuel for revelation and intimacy uncommon in other settings. At least temporarily, a bonding takes place among guests, nurtured by the host/hostess who planned, prepared and served the meal. No ordinary bonding, the Eucharist effects a *koinonia* among persons flawed by sin, divided not only against each other but conflicted even within themselves (Rom 7:15-23).' (D. Donnelly, 'Eucharist and Reconciliation', in: *The New Dictionary of Sacramental Worship*, P. E. Fink, ed., p 391).

Relating the sacrament of Reconciliation to people's lives:

Many people have lost faith in the sacrament of Reconciliation because it fails to lift them up when they feel broken and bruised by the slings and arrows of life. People today are painfully aware of their brokenness, so much so that they scarcely need to be reminded of it. What they need above all is an experience of healing. One way of making Reconciliation more meaningful to people is by emphasising more the healing aspect of this sacrament. In the scriptures the forgiveness of sins and healing, both spiritual and physical, are intimately related. This is so in many of the healing miracles worked by Jesus. In the past greater emphasis was placed on the confession of sins – the juridical aspect of the sacrament – than on the experience of being healed. Penitential services should focus more on a celebration of the Lord's healing power rather than on a listing of one's faults and failings. People are already painfully aware of their shortcomings. What they need assurance about is the Lord's healing presence in their lives.

2. Preparation

Like all of the other sacraments, Reconciliation is pre-eminently a sacrament of faith. It presupposes faith, it strengthens it and nourishes it. It announces and celebrates that aspect of faith called conversion, i.e. our response to God's invitation in the changing circumstances of our life. Conversion is itself a faith-journey admitting of varying degrees and stages. In the words of John Paul II '... conversion ... is brought about concretely in steps which lead us ever forward' (*Familiaris Consortio*, n 9, cf Flannery, vol II, p 821). Clearly it is not something instantaneous which is over and finished with in a moment. Rather, it is a dynamic process allowing for the gradual and progressive integration of God's gifts and the demands of his absolute love in our entire social and personal life.

The very nature of conversion shapes and determines the manner in which this sacrament is prepared for and celebrated. Conversion is effected through acts of penitence, e.g. prayer, fasting, almsgiving and other acts of practical charity. The sacrament of Reconciliation must never be presented as a quick and repeatable way for remitting sins or an easy substitute for doing penance. A proper catechesis on this sacrament is essential if people are to be helped to approach it in a more adult and fulfilling way. Such catechesis should be undertaken regularly in preaching and teaching, and should together with works of practical charity constitute an integral part of preparation for the sacramental celebration of Reconciliation. Priests are encouraged to make use of the liturgical seasons of Lent and Advent as times of preparation for and the celebration of this sacrament. In particular, they might in consultation with the Parish Liturgy Group consider organising and celebrating at the beginning of the season a non-sacramental penitential celebration as recommended in the *Ordo Paenitentiae*, 1974, n 36. Such services are designed to dispose individuals and congregations to a better and deeper penitence and ultimately a more fruitful use of the sacrament.

Care should be taken that the faithful do not confuse these celebrations with the celebration of the sacrament of Penance. Penitential celebrations are helpful in promoting conversion of life and purification of heart. It is desirable to arrange such services especially for these purposes:
- to foster the spirit of penance within the Christian community;
- to help the faithful prepare for Confession which can be made individually later at a convenient time;
- to help children gradually to form their conscience about sin in human life and about freedom from sin through Christ;
- to help catechumens during their conversion (*ibid*, n 37, cf Flannery, vol II, pp 48-49).

The celebration of these services do not necessarily require the presence of a priest. Their structure is similar to that proposed in the *Rite of Reconciliation of a Number of Penitents*. Such celebrations will help the faithful to make a more adult confession. An isolated sacramental act without the context of inner repentance, mutual good works and fraternal love can be meaningless. It runs the risk of lacking what St Thomas called the *veritas sacramenti* or sacramental authenticity.

The role of the priest with regard to reconciliation must not be seen to be limited to the confessional. He and indeed every

Christian are called upon to be both agents of reconciliation and peace in situations of disharmony and conflict. Such conflict can arise between family members, between neighbouring families, between communities or in the context of trade disputes between employer and employees. While always remaining absolutely impartial the priest must be seen to be at the vanguard working to restore peace and harmony. 'Blessed are the peacemakers, they shall be called sons of God' (Mt 5:9).

3. Celebration

i) The Different Forms:

The *Ordo Paenitentiae*, 1974, provides three different rites or options for the celebration of the sacrament of Reconciliation:

Rite I: Reconciliation of Individual Penitents

This is the regular manner of celebrating this sacrament. The priest greets the penitent in a friendly manner, inviting him or her to have confidence in God. The priest or penitent reads some text from Sacred Scripture, helping the penitent to discern his or her sinful condition and God's call to repentance. This may also be done beforehand by the penitent by way of preparation for the sacrament. The confessor helps the penitent make an integral confession but without having recourse to an inquisitorial procedure. The confessor then counsels the penitent and imposes a suitable penance which should be thought of not so much in terms of expiation for past sins but as a remedy for weakness and a help for amendment of life. Hence, the penance should not be such that it can be discharged momentarily but should if at all possible be linked to service of neighbour and works of charity, thereby reflecting the social nature of sin and its remission. The confessor then gives the penitent sacramental absolution.

Rite II: Reconciliation of a Number of Penitents with Individual Confession and Absolution

This form of Reconciliation, which brings out best the communal and ecclesial nature of sin and reconciliation should be celebrated regularly, especially during the season of Advent and Lent, and also in preparation for First Confession, First Holy Communion and Confirmation. Of particular interest is what some refer to as a variant of this rite, i.e. after communal preparation the penitent approaches the priest and makes a generic confession of sins by mentioning some major faults. This form of the sacrament is perfectly lawful and acceptable provided the penitent is aware that he/she is expected to mention all those grave faults of which he/she is conscious and which have not already been submitted to the sacramental seal. The faithful should be encouraged to confess venial sins but are not obliged to do so (cf c 981 #2). Hence, when celebrating this form the priest should encourage the faithful to mention specifically all the grave sins for which they are seeking pardon. In addition penitents should be encouraged to remain for the conclusion of the liturgical celebration, rather than departing after they have made their confession.

Rite III: Reconciliation of Penitents with Communal Confession and Absolution

'It can happen that, because of a particular combination of circumstances, absolution may be, or even ought to be, given to a number of people together, without individual confession of sins' (ibid n 31, cf Flannery, vol II, p 46).

This rite is intended for use in only very exceptional circumstances – the kind of circumstances which would hardly ever be verified in the Irish context. The conditions governing this rite are laid down in c 961 of the 1983 Code of Canon Law and are even more restrictive than the original norms issued by the *Congregation for the Doctrine of the Faith* in June 1972 and subsequently incorporated into the *Ordo Paenitentiae*, 1974, ns 31-35. It now pertains to the diocesan Bishop to judge what constitutes a case of 'grave necessity', warranting the use of this rite. Finally, such episcopal approval must have been obtained in advance (cf c 961).

The 1994 *Directory on the Ministry and Life of Priests* remind priests of their duty and obligation to '… follow the ecclesial norm which defends and promotes the value of individual and personal confession … reserving the use of general confession and absolution to only extraordinary cases which fulfil the required conditions, in accordance with existing norms' (n 52).

ii) Faculties to hear Confessions:

In order to hear confessions validly and lawfully confessors need the requisite faculties (c 966 #1). The granting of such faculties belongs to the local Ordinary (c 969 #1). Any priest who has habitual faculties to hear confessions can by virtue of the law exercise that faculty everywhere in the world unless a particular Ordinary has decided otherwise (c 967 #2). In the event of 'common error' the Church supplies jurisdiction or 'executive power of governance', as it is now called (cf c 144).

Religious and missionary priests receive their ministerial faculties from the Bishop of the diocese where the House to which they are attached is located, i.e. their domicile (cf c 103). In the event of their changing domicile they must seek ministerial faculties anew from the Bishop of the diocese in which the House to which they have been transferred is located.

iii) Satisfaction and Penance:

'True conversion is completed by acts of penance or satisfaction ... The kind and extent of the satisfaction should be suited to the personal condition of each penitent ...' (*Ordo Paenitentiae*, n 6c). Confessors should keep these directives in mind and avoid giving penances which are momentarily discharged, e.g. three Hail Marys, etc.. The latter cheapens and devalues the very notion of conversion and ultimately leads to confusion and disillusionment on the penitent's part. The sacrament of Reconciliation is pre-eminently a rite of passage or transition from a state of alienation from God and neighbour to a mending of those relationships that have been ruptured. This process takes time and effort. The penance that priests give should take cognisance of this fact. Hence, priests should acquaint themselves and their people with the divine law obligation to do penance as explained in the Apostolic Constitution, *Paenitemini*, 17/2/1966, cf Flannery, vol II, pp 1-12; Decree n 14 of the Irish Episcopal Conference concerning Friday Penance, in: *Intercom*, Jan/Feb 1988, p 11. *The Catechism* discusses the different forms of penance that a Christian might embark upon (cf n 1434 -1439).

iv) Formula of Absolution:

The formula of absolution as given in the 1974 *Ordo Paenitentiae* and reiterated in the Catechism of the Catholic Church, n 1449, should be used: 'God the Father of mercies ...'. The integrity of the sacrament requires that the entire form of absolution including the words: 'I absolve you ...' be used.

v) Place of Reconciliation:

Reconciliation should be celebrated in a Church or oratory or other suitable place. Care should be taken to ensure that the environment is conducive to prayer and reflection, e.g. adequate heating, lighting space, etc.. A poor liturgical environment does nothing for the sacrament.

Every effort must be made to ensure that the penitent has the option of confessing face to face with the priest or anonymously if he/she should so wish. Reconciliation rooms/confessionals allowing for this option must be provided in all new churches and suitable space adapted for this purpose in older ones.

vi) Time of Reconciliation:

The sacrament of Reconciliation may be celebrated at any time of the day, but it is desirable that fixed times be set in each parish. These times should be well publicised. In addition to these fixed times priests might be sensitive to the needs and wishes of people to approach this sacrament on the occasion of funerals and weddings.

As it is impossible to participate fully in two different liturgical celebrations taking place simultaneously, priests should not hear confessions while Mass is in progress in the same church.

> The faithful are to be constantly encouraged to accustom themselves to going to confession outside the celebration of Mass, and especially at the prescribed times. In this way the sacrament of Penance will be administered calmly and with genuine profit, and will not interfere with participation in the Mass (Sacred Congregation for Rites, *Instruction on the Worship of the Eucharistic Mystery, Eucharisticum Mysterium,* 25/5/1967, Ch II, Sect. E, cf Flannery, vol I, p 123).

Of particular significance in this regard is the liturgy of the *Sacred Triduum.* It is intended to be celebrated by all, i.e. by both priests and people together. Confessions, therefore, must not be heard while the liturgy is in progress in the same church. Under no circumstances must the liturgies be seen as punctuating the ministry of reconciliation during these days. As a general rule the hearing of confessions should cease about fifteen minutes prior to the commencement of the particular liturgy in question.

RECONCILIATION

4. Particular problems and related issues

i) Children's Confessions:

Priests should be familiar with the manner in which reconciliation is presented in the catechetical programme in the school. The priest's role is to confirm and consolidate this programme. The format for the celebration of the sacrament is also given. This should be followed so as not to confuse the children. First Confession should be prepared for and arranged along the lines suggested in *Unit 4 of Show us the Father (First Class/Primary 3 Teacher's Book).*

Parents too should be helped to understand and participate in their children's preparation for this sacrament. At least two meetings for parents should be held prior to First Confession. Those who do not attend these meetings should be visited by the priest so that they too may be prepared for their children's confession and be encouraged to celebrate the sacrament together with their children.

At least two months should elapse between First Confession and First Communion. This is to allow the child to differentiate between these sacraments and to facilitate the teaching and learning of the different prayers for the respective sacraments.

Having received First Confession, children should be encouraged to cultivate the habit of receiving this sacrament regularly. In the weeks prior to Christmas and Easter priests of the parish, and school chaplains in post-primary schools, should ensure that all children have the opportunity to receive the sacrament of Reconciliation.

ii) First Confession before First Communion:

The 1973 *Declaration on First Confession and First Communion* of the Congregation for the Clergy and the Congregation for the Discipline of the Sacraments, (cf Flannery, vol I, p 241) stipulates that First Confession should precede First Communion. C 914 is in broad general agreement with this policy but in a less forthright way.

iii) Reconciliation of those living in Irregular Unions:

In his Apostolic Exhortations, *The Christian Family in the Modern*

World, Familiaris Consortio, 22/11/1981 and *Reconciliation and Penance,* 2/12/1984, Pope John Paul II, addresses himself directly to this issue:

> Reconciliation in the sacrament of Penance, which would open the way to the Eucharist, can only be granted to those who, repenting of having broken the sign of the Covenant and of fidelity to Christ, are sincerely ready to undertake a way of life that is no longer in contradiction to the indissolubility of marriage. This means, in practice, that when for serious reasons such as for example the children's upbringing, a man and woman cannot satisfy the obligation to separate, they take on themselves the duty to live in complete continence, that is by abstinence from the acts proper to married couples (*The Christian Family* ..., n 84, Flannery, vol II, p 889).

People in this situation, who cannot receive the sacrament of Reconciliation 'should be encouraged to listen to the word of God, to attend the sacrifice of the Mass, to persevere in prayer, to contribute to works of charity and community efforts in favour of justice, to bring up their children in the Christian faith, to cultivate the practice and spirit of penance and thus implore, day by day God's grace. Let the Church pray for them, encourage them and show herself a merciful mother, and thus sustain them in faith and hope' (*ibid*).

The Pope explains the Church's position in this very delicate area. On the one hand the Church must present herself as the mediator of God's compassion and mercy, while on the other she must remain faithful to the principle of 'truth and consistency, whereby she does not agree to call good evil and evil good. Basing herself on these two complementary principles, the Church can only invite her children who find themselves in these painful situations to approach the divine mercy by other ways, not however through the sacraments of Penance and Eucharist, until such time as they have attained the required dispositions' (*Reconciliation and Penance,* n 34). For a more detailed discussion of this, see pp 163-168 of this *Directory.*

iv) Reserved Sins:

The *1983 Code of Canon Law* abolished reserved sins but not reserved censures. The latter still exist, though greatly simplified and reduced in number.

RECONCILIATION

v) Censures:

A censure is a penalty imposed by the Church on a person for committing certain crimes or offences, e.g. excommunication resulting from apostasy and abortion (cs 1364 #1 & 1398). Normally, the censure bars a person from receiving the sacraments, including Reconciliation. Hence, a person under censure must first have the censure remitted by a priest who has the requisite faculties before he can receive forgiveness for the sin in question.

When a confessor comes across what appears to be a censure he must:

a) Decide if in fact any censure has been incurred. There are many mitigating factors and excusing circumstances, e.g. age, ignorance, freedom, deliberation, etc.. If the penitent is unaware that a censure is attached to the crime in question, no censure has been incurred. This will be the situation in most instances.

b) Set about remitting the censure if he deems that one has been incurred. If danger of death threatens, then any confessor can validly and licitly remit all censures, even those reserved to the Holy See (c 976). In most instances the priest is authorised by virtue of his confessional faculties to remit those censures reserved to the Ordinary (e.g. abortion and apostasy). Should a particular confessor not be so authorised, or encounter a censure reserved to the Holy See, e.g. direct violation of the sacramental seal (c 1388 #1); desecration of the sacred species (c 1367), attempting to absolve sacramentally one's accomplice in a sin against the Sixth Commandment of the Decalogue (c 1378 #1), he is exhorted to make use of the the provisions of c 1357 #1, i.e. remit the censure and forgive the sin, and ask the penitent to return at a later date to receive the instructions or *mandata* (i.e. a particular act of penance) from the competent authority. The confessor, while concealing the identity of the penitent, makes recourse to the Bishop on the penitent's behalf. The Bishop will either deal with the matter himself, if he is competent to do so, or make recourse to the Sacred Penitentiary. In due course he will communicate back to the confessor who will in turn pass on the appropriate instructions to the penitent.

In its Letter, *Pro Memoria*, of 24/10/1993, the Apostolic Penitentiary explains in detail how recourse is made and lists the different instances when such recourse might be necessary:

1. Profanation of the Most Holy Species (c 1367).

2. Absolution of an accomplice in a sin of dishonour (cs 1378 & 977).

3. Direct violation of the sacramental seal (c 1388).

4. Irregularity contracted by a priest because of the crime of abortion (c 1041, 4).

5. Omission of the burden of Masses by a priest.

(cf *Canon Law Digest*, 1991, vol XI, pp 49-52)

Recommended Reading:

Congregation for Divine Worship, *Rite of Penance* (1974), Veritas, Dublin, 1976.

Ordo Paenitentiae, 1974, *Introduction to the New Order of Penance*, Flannery, vol II, 35-52.

Paul VI, *Apostolic Constitution, Paenitemini*, 17/2/1966, Flannery, vol II, 1-12.

John Paul II, *Reconciliation and Penance, Post-Synodal Apostolic Exhortation*, 2/12/1984 (CTS, Do 562).

Catechism of the Catholic Church, Veritas, Dublin, 1994.

Swayne, S., *The Sacraments, a Pastoral Directory*, Veritas, Dublin, 1976, 96-104.

Hellwig, M., *Sign of Reconciliation and Conversion, the Sacrament of Penance for our Times, Message of the Sacraments*, vol IV, Glazier, Delaware, 1982.

Bausch, W.J., *A New Look at the Sacraments*, Twenty-Third Publications, Mystic, Connecticut, revised 1983.

Cosgrave, W., 'The Decline of Confessions', *The Furrow 45* (1994), March, 158-162.

CHAPTER 5

Ministry to the Sick and Dying

1. Introduction

The healing ministry of Jesus was central to his proclamation of the kingdom of God. When sending out the seventy-two disciples he said to them: 'Cure those who are sick and say, the kingdom of God is very near to you' (Lk 10:9). From the earliest of times the Church has been faithul to this mandate of healing. The reforms of the Second Vatican Council reinstated the title 'Anointing of the Sick' for that sacrament which had come to be called 'Last Anointing'. With this change came a shift in emphasis reversing a history that had seen this sacrament relegated to those at the point of death. The section of the Roman Ritual entitled *Pastoral Care of the Sick* locates the sacramental act of anointing within the larger context of pastoral care and presents a wide variety of prayers and scripture readings to be used on visits to the sick, at Communion for the sick, for the actual anointing of the sick and for those already dead before the priest arrives.

The Second Vatican Council also re-ordered the sequence of the sacraments with regard to those who are dying. Viaticum is restored as the last sacrament for the dying. The *Catechism of the Catholic Church* reminds us that 'the Eucharist should always be the last sacrament of the earthly journey, the 'viaticum' for 'passing over' to eternal life' (n 1517).

Another significant change that the Second Vatican Council introduced with regard to all of the sacraments is the notion of 'process'. Nowhere is this more evident than in the *Pastoral Care of the Sick* (1983). The entire ministry of caring for the sick and dying is sacramental in the broad sense of the word, with the Sacrament of the Sick being its culmination and high point. The older understanding of this sacrament saw it very much in terms of an isolated event, placing a high premium on the priest arriving as close as possible to moment of death. Today the sacrament is very much the Sacrament of the Sick and equally important is the pastoral care that precedes and follows the actual sacrament.

2. The Ministry of Healing

Healing and curing are not synonomous. Healing is the reversal of the process of personal dissolution and disintegration resulting from illness while curing tends to focus on repairing the mechanism that has been damaged. Healing concentrates on reintegrating the relational world of the sick person. Sickness affects the sick person's immediate circle of family and friends. The other spouse faces the prospect of life with a dependent partner or perhaps with none at all. The mother of the sick child sees vanishing before her eyes all those hopes and dreams she had for the child. The child loses an identity and authority figure. The wider family circle and local commumnity are forced to reorganise their life and work schedule, temporarily or even permanently around the vacuum left by the sick person. Sickness is not something that affects the individual person only. Every sick person has many co-sufferers. Healing addresses itself to repairing and restoring those relationships that have been ruptured and strained because of the illness. While a cure is certainly important to the sick and their immediate family, it is never more than a partial goal to be undone by subsequent illness and death. Healing occurs when the sick person and the immediate family come to terms with their pain and loss by reordering their lives and relationships accordingly. Even where a cure is impossible, as in the case of terminal illness, healing is often requested and received. In a word, the person who has experienced healing no longer feels the need to be cured.

3. Visiting the Sick

At the heart of any relationship with the sick is the belief that the visitor has time to spend listening to him/her, time to share stories from the past and fears for the future, and, time to pray. Visiting sick people is healing them. They are being re-assured that they are not alone or abandoned. A hurried interchange before or after receiving Holy Communion on a First Friday is hardly adequate. Consequently, the pastoral activity of a parish should be so arranged as to facilitate a regular and systematic visitation of those parishioners who are sick at home or in hospital.

i) Identifying the Sick and their needs:

The needs of the sick and the practical skills required to minister to them will vary with their age and condition. Is the person young or old? Is the illness critical? Is it terminal or transient? Consideration of the following categories may be helpful:

1) Children with terminal illness;
2) Children with severe physical and/or mental disability;
3) Young chronic sick, house or hospital-bound with severe paralysing diseases, e.g. multiple sclerosis;
4) Young terminally ill, people under fifty years of age who may have a spouse and children to worry about;
5) Sick who live alone;
6) Addicts: alcoholics, gamblers and chemical dependants;
7) People with AIDS;
8) Geriatric patients at home, in homes or in hospitals;
9) Psychiatric patients;
10) Acutely ill of all ages, probably in hospital in the pre-(serious) operation category.

In all cases the priest should seek the advice and support of medical staff, social workers, hospital chaplain and others concerned with the care of the sick person. In this way a more effective and comprehensive pastoral strategy can be adopted.

All who deal with the sick, particularly with the terminally ill, must understand the various phases a patient goes through when he/she realises that the illness is serious. There is an initial period of silence where the sick person is emotionally taken up with the illness. In the next stage of anger or aggression family, friends, medical staff, God and the Church, may be rejected. Those close to the sick person should not take this reaction as a personal affront, but rather as a cry for help and understanding. A period of depression and rebirth usually follows in which the sick person begins to take stock of the situation. Finally, there is a stage of acceptance or negation in which the illness is either endured with serenity or met with contempt and revolt (cf Charles W. Gusmer, *And You Visited Me: Sacramental Ministry to the Sick and Dying*, Pueblo, 1984, p 140). Those who minister to the sick must be able to offer support at every stage of the way.

THE SICK AND DYING

Sensitivity to the needs of the family of the sick person is very important. This is particularly true when the person is seriously ill, an addict, or is suffering from AIDS. In the case of death, visiting and support must continue to help with the trauma of bereavement. A group often neglected is the parents of stillborn babies or of babies who die soon after birth (cf Section dealing with Stillbirth in this *Directory*, pp 78-81).

ii) The Ministry of the Community:

Ministry to the sick is the task of the whole Christian community, not just that of the priest alone. All Christians by virtue of their Baptism participate in this ministry 'by doing all that they can to help the sick return to health, by showing love for the sick, and by celebrating the sacraments with them' (*Pastoral Care of the Sick*, n 33).

The primary purpose of this ministry is to strengthen the sick person by the reassurance of his/her faith in the Gospel of Jesus Christ and in his triumph over suffering and death. While always fighting against sickness and seeking the blessings of good health, the Christian must never lose sight of the redemptive value of suffering which is embraced in Jesus' name.

It should always be pointed out that sickness cannot be regarded as a punishment inflicted on each individual for personal sin (Jn 9:3). Why some people suffer physical or mental illness must remain a mystery to us.

iii) The Specific Role of the Priest:

While all who visit and care for the sick are concerned for the whole person, physical, spiritual and emotional, the priest's role has a specific focus. Firstly, he represents the caring sacramental Church in a unique and personal way. He gets to know the sick or disabled person within the family setting. He does this through routine visitation of the home. Many parents of disabled persons feel hurt by the absence of a visit from the priest and the opportunity to clarify their own feelings and personal faith. Parents welcome attention being focussed on the sick or disabled member of the household. It boosts the self-image of all concerned. Time spent with the sick and disabled is time well-spent. It makes a healing impact on the whole family. It lays the foundation for a more deeply-rooted, personal relationship be-

THE SICK AND DYING

tween the priest, the sick or disabled person and the family (cf T. O'Grady, 'Pastoral Care of the Mentally Handicapped', in: *Intercom*, June 1984, pp 4-5).

Secondly, the priest is called to encourage and support the community's ministry to the sick. This can be achieved both by the priest's own example and by fostering and encouraging the efforts of individuals and groups in caring for the many needs of the sick within the community, e.g. having a group in the parish whose specific role is visiting old and long-stay patients in hospitals and nursing homes. Their efforts, either 'spiritual' or 'temporal', should be seen as ministries of the community, side-by-side with other ministries.

The priest should pray with the sick person. Prayer is something that the sick person finds difficult. The interruption in life-style that sickness causes interferes with our accustomed ways of praying. Hence, rites entitled 'Visits to the Sick' and 'Visits to a Sick Child' in *Pastoral Care of the Sick* include readings from Scripture and special prayers to support the sick person and those looking after him/her. The latter should be invited to join in selecting and offering the prayers for the sick person. Before leaving the sick person the priest should always impart a blessing.

The priest also has the duty of praying for the sick in his care, both in private prayer and in commending them to the prayer of the parish community in the Prayer of the Faithful at the Sunday Eucharist and at other celebrations.

During each visit the priest should prepare the sick person to receive the Eucharist or the Sacrament of the Sick at a subsequent visit. Should the sick person express a wish to do so, the Sacrament of Reconciliation should be celebrated.

4. Communion of the Sick

Priests with pastoral responsibilities should see to it that the sick or aged, even tbough not seriously ill or in danger of death, are given every opportunity to receive the Eucharist frequently, even daily, especially during the Easter Season (*Pastoral Care of the Sick*, n 72).

Through preaching and the celebration of the liturgy the priest should highlight the link between the community's celebration of the Eucharist and Communion of the Sick. It is interesting to note that one of the original purposes of reserving the Blessed Sacrament in the tabernacle was to nourish the sick with the Body and Blood of the risen Lord. It is strongly recommended that Special Ministers of the Eucharist bring Holy Communion to the sick and house-bound from the Sunday celebration of the Eucharist.

To provide frequent Communion for the sick, the community must have a sufficient number of Special Ministers of the Eucharist. They should be familiar with the rites of Communion in Ordinary Circumstances and Communion in a Hosptial or Institution as outlined in *The Pastoral Care of the Sick*. Special hand-books for Ministers of the Eucharist are available.

When the Eucharist is brought to the sick, it should be carried in a pyx. Those caring for the sick person should be asked to make the appropriate preparation (white table-cloth, candles, holy water) and to join in the prayers so that the occasion is both a dignified and joyful community celebration.

Sick people who are unable to receive Communion under the form of bread may receive it under the form of wine alone (*Pastoral Care of the Sick*, n 74). Care should be taken in storing the precious blood in the tabernacle and in carrying it to the sick.

When possible the priest should make it his special care to cele-brate the Eucharist for the family of a sick person who is chroni-cally ill and housebound.

5. The Sacrament of the Sick

In the Sacrament of the Sick, the Church commends to the suf-fering and glorified Lord, the faithful who are dangerously ill so that he can support and save them.

i) Preparation:

The Sacrament of the Sick ought to be seen not as an isolated event, but as a privileged moment in the overall pastoral care of the sick. It is, in fact, the ritual high-point of this care. It is not a sacrament for those who are on the point of death, as the older name 'extreme unction' might suggest (*Vatican II, The Constitution on the Sacred Liturgy, Sacrosanctum Concilium*, n. 73, Flannery, vol I, p 22). It should be celebrated at the beginning of a serious illness. The practice of delaying the reception of the sacrament until the last moment betrays a mistaken understanding of the meaning and purpose of the sacrament (cf *Pastoral Care of the Sick*, n 13). Such an attitude should be addressed in preaching and in counselling the sick and their families. Priests should take the opportunity from time to time in their preaching to remind people of the Church's understanding of this sacrament today. It will take much time and patience to wean people off the older understanding and to change attitudes, especially when the latter were rooted in centuries old tradition. This tradition has now changed.

ii) Celebration:

Since all sacraments are an expression of the faith of the Christian community, and since the Sacrament of the Sick seeks to redress the personal fragmentation and isolation from others brought about by illness, it is most fittingly celebrated when those who care for the daily needs of the sick person can be present and actively involved in selecting appropriate prayers and readings, etc.. The sick person suffers from physical separation through confinement to bed, etc.. This is indicative of a deeper separation, that of loneliness and inabilty to relate to others. The Sacrament of the Sick seeks to address these realities. The believing community through the ministry of the priest re-assures the sick person of its loving care and concern both for him/her and for all who have been affected though his/her illness. The priest mediates both the healing power of God and the concern of the community. In addition he brings spiritual consolation to the sick person.

> What the sacrament of Anointing attempts to deal with specifically is the feeling and experience of distance from God that the sick have because they no longer have their accustomed relationship with themselves and others. Gone is a sense of self-reliance which may have been a strong factor in their faith. Also gone are the supports of family, friends, peers, employees, students or whatever that make up the structure of their lives when they are healthy. Their ordinary life context has disappeared and has been replaced by so many alienating components. For many this makes it

quite difficult to maintain communication with God because just as there had been an accustomed way of living so there had been an accustomed way of praying. Both are dissolved together. Many people cannot transfer their life of prayer from one context to another and so become convinced that they cannot pray (J. L. Empereur, *Prophetic Anointing*, p 148).

The rite of anointing as found in *Pastoral Care of the Sick* must be used. Here, the rite is arranged for various situations: Anointing outside Mass, Anointing in a Hospital or Institution and a Continuous Rite of Penance, Anointing, and Viaticum to be used in exceptional circumstances.

A communal celebration of the sacrament whereby a number of people are to be anointed may be held in accordance with the regulation of the diocesan Bishop (c 1002). In the Diocese of Ossory, this is highly recommended, especially during the *Diocesan Lourdes Pilgrimage* and at other times of the year. It is also highly desirable that it be celebrated in this manner in homes for the elderly and in institutions and hospitals catering for people with long-term illness and disability. Since the sacrament highlights our participation in Christ's triumph over suffering and death, a communal celebration during the Easter Season would be particularly appropriate (cf *Pastoral Care of the Sick*, n 108).

In the case of a sudden illness, an accident, or when a person is in immediate danger of death, the rites for exceptional circumstances may then, and only then, be used. While these rites are intended to be celebrated integrally, the priest should judge, in the light of the particular circumstances, how much time remains before death and how much of the rite is possible. Conditions may also prevent the normal anointing on the forehead and hands. In such a case, a single anointing on another suitable part of the body is sufficient, while the whole sacramental form is said.

iii) Who should be Anointed?

'The anointing of the sick can be administered to any member of the faithful who, having reached the use of reason, begins to be in danger of death by reason of illness or old age' (c 1004 #1). In deciding who should be admitted to the sacrament, the minister must prudently judge the seriousness of an illness. The Pastoral

Care of the Sick suggests that the following should be admitted:
- a sick person before surgery (n 10);
- elderly people who have become notably weakened, even though no serious illness is present (n 11);
- sick people who, although they have lost consciousness or the use of reason, would probably have asked for it were they in control of their faculties.
- sick children may be anointed if they have sufficient use of reason to be strengthened by this sacrament (n 12).

Recent perspectives on sickness suggest that it cannot be defined in medical terms only. As well as bodily pain and psychic depression, it also includes isolation and despair, hardness of heart and spiritual distress. When one of these creates a crisis situation in someone's life then anointing is appropriate. If in doubt as to the severity of the illness the sacrament is to be administered (cf c 1005).

The sacrament may be repeated if the sick person recovers after being anointed and then falls ill again, or if, during the same illness, the person's condition deteriorates. If, a short time after an initial anointing, the patient's condition deteriorates considerably, the reception of the Eucharist as Viaticum is preferable to a further anointing.

The Sacrament of the Sick is not to be administered to a person who is already dead. In this case the *Prayers for the Dead* (cf *Pastoral Care of the Sick*, nn 226-231) are used instead. However, priests should be very sensitive to the faith and expectations of people in such circumstances. It takes a whole generation to wean people off what they have been accustomed to. Hence, rather than saying that he cannot anoint a person who is already dead, it is preferable to explain that the Church has special prayers and blessings specifically designed for such circumstances.

6. Ministry to the Dying

Few areas of pastoral concern are as much appreciated as the priest's compassionate presence to the dying and their families. When everything else has been forgotten people will still remember and remark upon the kindness of a particular priest to their dying relative or friend. This is all the more so if the death is brought about by a terminal illness.

On receiving the news of terminal illness people often experience a crisis of faith concerning the reason for their sickness and God's role in it. In the initial stages of the illness however, they are usually sufficiently strong and composed to grapple with the crisis now confronting them. The preparation for the sacraments of Reconciliation, Holy Communion and Anointing of the Sick and their celebration can be a source of great consolation and strength to all concerned.

As the illness progresses the priest may find himself being taken more and more into the confidence of the sick person and those who care for him/her. Disagreement among family members as to what is best for the patient is not unusual. The family may sometimes turn to the priest for his advice with regard to the medical procedures being proposed. The dignity of human life requires that everything possible be done to preserve life while not prolonging suffering unnecessarily.

When the patient has come to accept the inevitability of the death he/she may broach the issue of the funeral liturgy by suggesting readings and music. The priest should not shy away from the task. The funeral liturgy itself acts as a kind of bridge or transition point from this life to the next.

As the moment of death approaches the sick person tends to leave the past behind and live each day as it comes. He/she often retreats more and more into silence. This should not be interpreted as rejection by those who are caring for the sick person. During the final days or hours of a person's life the priest can offer valuable support and companionship. It is not a question of many words but rather of quiet presence around the bed of the dying person. By suggesting to the family that they hold the hand of their loved one or moisten parched lips or wipe a perspiring forhead, or by saying a short simple prayer or by inviting those present to make the sign of the cross on the forehead of the dying person, can ease the pain and sense of separation that is taking place. Common-sense, straightforward gestures will speak more eloquently than multiplied prayers and repeated rituals (cf G. J. Calhoun, 'Ministry at the time of death', in: *The New Dictionary of Sacramental Worship*, p 322).

7. Particular Problems and Related Issues

i) Anointing People with Disabilities:

In ministering to those with disabilities one should never lose sight of the great ministry of the disabled themselves. They are transparent signs of our own vulnerability and state of dependence: we are not creators of our own destiny but creatures dependent upon our Creator who gave us life and lovingly maintains us in being (cf Kate Rackham, 'Handicapped People and Ministry', in: *The Way* 25 (1985), p 137).

'It is very important to make clear that Christians who live in situations of illness, pain and old age are called by God not only to unite their suffering to Christ's Passion but also to receive in themselves now, and to transmit to others, the power of renewal and joy of the risen Christ' (John Paul II, *The Vocation and Mission of the Laity, Christifideles Laici*, n 53).

While people with disabilities may not be actually ill, they can nevertheless be included within the more extensive category of sickness as such. In many cases anointing can help the disabled person overcome the fragmentation of personality caused by mental or physical disability.

Indiscriminate anointing of those with disabilities is to be avoided. One cannot and should not be anointed simply because one is disabled. But whenever a disability presents an obstacle to human and spiritual growth then the Sacrament of the Sick should be celebrated. A communal celebration of the sacrament is particularly meaningful in this case. This allows the disabled person to experience the affirmation and acceptance of the Christian community when they feel they have been abandoned by others, and helps other members of the community to accept those with disabilities and overcome any uncomfortable feelings.

ii) Sacrament of the Sick and non-Catholics:

Occasionally during the course of hospital ministry priests may be approached by non-Catholics wishing to receive the Sacrament of the Sick. In this regard the conditions as specified in the *Directory on Ecumenism*, 14/5/1967 apply. The priest may anoint a non-Catholic when:

    i) danger of death threatens;
    ii) the person cannot approach his/her minister;

iii) the person spontaneously asks for the sacrament;
iv) the person is properly disposed and manifests a
faith in the sacrament consistent with that of the Church (cf
n 55, Flannery vol I, p 499).

iii) Ministry to AIDS Sufferers:

In recent years society has been grappling with a new killer disease called AIDS. As with all other diseases, AIDS is a human illness to which we must respond in a manner consistent with the best medical and scientific information available. As Christians we must follow the example of Jesus who placed no limits on his love and concern for those alienated from society in their day because of their illness and brokenness. Our response to people suffering from this disease must be one of compassion rather than judgement. As priests we must try to disseminate this attitude among our people.

For Christians, then, stories of persons with AIDS must not become occasions for stereotyping or prejudice, for anger or recrimination, for rejection or isolation, for injustice or condemnation. They provide us with an opportunity to walk with those who are suffering, to be compassionate towards those whom we might otherwise fear, to bring strength and courage both to those who face the prospect of dying as well as their loved ones (United States Catholic Conference Administrative Board, 'The Many Faces of AIDS: A Gospel Response', in: *Origins* 17 (1987) p 484).

In order to be effective in his own ministry to AIDS sufferers and help others in their ministry, priests must first of all dispel irrational fears that people may have of being contaminated by the AIDS virus. According to medical expertise and research one cannot be infected with the AIDS virus by casual contact. The disease itself is contracted primarily through:
- the use of contaminated intravenous needles or other drug paraphernalia infected with the AIDS virus;
- intimate sexual contact with a person already carrying the AIDS virus;
- by coming into contact with tainted blood either through blood transfusion or otherwise;
- pregnancy, if the mother is already infected by the AIDS virus.

Persons with AIDS, their families and their friends need solidarity, comfort and support. As with others facing imminent death, they may experience anger toward and alienation from God and the Church as they face the inevitability of dying. It is important that somebody stand with them in their pain and help them, in accord with religious tradition, to discover meaning in what appears to be meaningless (*ibid* p 487).

The priest must be an anchor of Christian hope for people submerged in a sea of despair. As one whose vocation it is to be a model and paradigm of ministry to the broken and the wounded, it is his special responsibility to care for the sick, to show them that they are loved and to ensure that they are treated with dignity and respect (cf California's Bishops, *A Pastoral Letter on Aids*, *Origins* 16 (1987) p 788). In ministering to AIDS patients and their families the priest works in close collaboration with medical and health care workers. Should there be any need to take special precautions, the latter will be able to advise him accordingly.

Finally, the priest should remember that the diagnosis of AIDS may precipitate other information about the victim's lifestyle coming to light. The priest is called to lend his practical, emotional and spiritual support to families in these circumstances. Since the identity of people with AIDS is confidential, every precaution should be taken to maintain that confidentiality.

iv) Those living in Irregular Unions:

Occasionally the priest will be called to the scene of an accident or sick-bed of a person who is known to be living in an irregular union. May the Sacrament of the Sick be celebrated in such circumstances?

Canon law would not seem to bar people living in irregular unions from receiving this sacrament. In fact the only people precluded by canon law are 'those who obstinately persist in a manifestly grave sin' (c 1007). Sin is ultimately an internal condition of soul, a rupture of one's personal relationship with God. Hence, it is a subjective matter and so cannot be determined by one's external or visible status within the ecclesial community. People obstinately persist in serious sin when they stubbornly reject the teachings and laws of the Church and continue in some sinful situation from which they are morally (emotionally and spiritually) and physically capable of removing themselves. It cannot be said that a person living in an irregular union is always obstinately persisting in a situation of manifestly grave sin.

v) The terminally ill

Pastoral care for the terminally-ill raises the delicate, ethical issue of how much the patient actually knows or should be told concerning his/her condition. The dignity of the human person would seem to suggest that patients have the right to be told the nature of their illness, the purpose of the treatment to be given and its possible consequences. Medical personnel sometimes appear to opt for shielding the terminally-ill from the real facts of their condition. However, it can be assumed that most terminally-ill patients have a strong suspicion of the seriousness of their condition even though they may refrain from speaking openly of it for fear of upsetting family members and friends. They may acknowledge their condition indirectly by what they say and do or enquire if they are expected to recover their health.

While respecting the patient's right to know the truth, what is of vital importance is the manner in which this truth is communicated. 'It is the right of the patient to decide whether, and to what extent, to be informed of his condition. This requires great sensitivity and judgment on the part of the medical team. Such decisions can only be made against the background of some personal knowldege of the patient .... The middle way between truth and the witholding of truth is to bring terminally-ill persons gradually to an awareness of their condition. The way in which this is done, and the speed with which it is done, will vary from person to person in accordance with each unique personality. The truth of their condition should not be forced on patients but gradually revealed, always allowing the patient to set the pace' (A. Larkin, 'Truth-telling to the Terminally-ill', in: *Intercom*, December/January 1987, p 6).

Recommended Reading:

Pastoral Care of the Sick, Apostolic Constitution, Sacrament of Anointing of the Sick (Paul VI), General Introduction, Veritas, Dublin, 1983.

Gusmer, C.W., *And You Visited Me: Sacramental Ministry to the Sick and the Dying*, Pueblo, New York, 1984.

Various Authors 'Handicapped People in the Church', *The Way*, 25 (1985), 122-140.

Kübler-Ross, E., *On Death and Dying*, Macmillan, New York, 1969.

— *Living with Death and Dying*, Macmillan, New York, 1981.

Nilkas, G.R. and Stefanics, Ch., *Ministry to the Sick*, Alba House, New York, 1982.

Fink, P. E., (ed) *Anointing of the Sick*, Liturgical Press, Collegeville, 1987.

Empereur, J. L., *Prophetic Anointing, Message of the Sacraments 7*, Michael Glazier, Delaware, 1982.

Calhoun, G. J., 'Ministry at the time of Death', *The New Dictionary of Sacramental Worship*, (ed P. E. Fink, SJ), Gill & Macmillan, Dublin, 1990, 319-324.

THE SICK AND DYING

CHAPTER 6

Priesthood

1) The Priest in the Post-Conciliar Church

The Second Vatican Council tells us that 'through the sacred ordination and mission which they receive from the bishops priests are promoted to the service of Christ the teacher, priest, and king; they are given a share in his ministry, through which the church here on earth is being ceaselessly built up into the People of God, Christ's Body and the temple of the Spirit' *(Decree on the Ministry and Life of Priests, Presbyterorum Ordinis*, n 1, Flannery vol I, p 863). Later on in the same document priests are reminded that 'in the name of the bishop (they) gather the family of God as a brotherhood endowed with the spirit of unity and lead it in Christ through the Spirit to God the Father' (n 6, p 872). The priest in the parish 'takes the place of the bishop' *(Constitution on the Sacred Liturgy, Sacrosanctum Concilium*, n 42, Flannery, vol 1, p 14) and hence is seen as a leader in the Church, a leader of the community which is the church in a particular locality.

Throughout the Church's history and tradition the priest has always been seen as a leader and shepherd of his people after the example of Christ the Good Shepherd (Jn 10). Indeed, the New Testament Priesthood makes sense only in the context of ministry to God's people. What has changed since the Second Vatican Council is the manner and style in which this ministry is exercised. In his 1987 'Holy Thursday Letter to Priests', Pope John Paul II situates the identity and mission of the priest within the framework of conciliar ecclesiology:

> The Second Vatican Council presents the life of the Church as a pilgrimage of faith (cf *L.G.*, ns 48ff). Each one of us dear brothers, by reason of our priestly vocation and ordination, has a special part in this pilgrimage. We are called to go forward guiding others, helping them along their way as ministers of the Good Shepherd (n 13)

The priest then is a fellow-pilgrim with his people in their journey of faith. He is a partner with his people, leading them to holiness and animating them in the exercise of their mission in the Church. He needs them as much as they need him for he too needs to be encouraged, to be nourished and to be consoled. Like every other Christian, he is subject to the physical and psychological ills to which the flesh is heir. He will have to make personal, moral decisions about his lifestyle - honesty, money, sexual behaviour, ambition, anger, and a host of other issues. He will discover that time and circumstances will throw aspects of his faith into confusion and uncertainty. But in such moments he knows that he is not alone in his faith-journey. He is accompanied above all by his brother priests and by his people.

In his own personal life the priest should pursue a simple way of life, 'voluntarily embracing poverty to follow Christ more closely. In all aspects (living quarters, means of transportation, vacations, etc.) the priest must eliminate any kind of affectation and luxury (Congregation for the Clergy, *Directory on the Ministry and Life of Priests*, 1994, n 67).

i) The Priest as Builder of Community:

The primary way in which a priest serves his people is by building community. 'In a divided world the priest is called to be in the service of communion, gathering his people in the unity of one faith nourished by God's word and in charity renewed through the grace of the sacraments, especially the Eucharist. This service demands a witness to compassion, mercy, pardon and reconciliation' (*The Formation of Priests in the Circumstances of the Present Day, Lineamenta, Veritas*, 1989, n 13). In order that he might build community the priest must first know his people. 'He is therefore to visit their families, sharing in their cares and anxieties and, in a special way, their sorrows, comforting them in the Lord. If in certain matters they are found wanting, he is prudently to correct them. He is to help the sick and especially the dying .... He is to be especially diligent in seeking out the poor, the suffering, the lonely, those who are exiled from their homeland, and those burdened with special difficulties' (c 529 #1).

Building community is not the exclusive responsibility of the priest. Every community is endowed with a wide variety of different ministries which are intended for its well-being. The priest therefore is not expected to discharge the entire mission of the Church singlehandedly but in collaboration with others. This of course makes serious demands on the priest in terms of time and skills. It is invariably easier to do something oneself than to engage and involve others in discharging that same task. But conciliar ecclesiology very definitely opts for the latter. Pope John Paul II reaffirms this in his 1988 Apostolic Exhortation concerning the role of the laity in the Church:

> The Church's mission of salvation in the world is realised not only by the ministers in virtue of the sacrament of Orders but also by the lay faithful ...

> The pastors, therefore, ought to acknowledge and foster the ministers, the offices and roles of the lay faithful that find their foundation in the sacraments of Baptism and Confirmation, indeed for a good many of them in the sacrament of Matrimony *(The Vocation and Mission of the Laity, Christifideles Laici, n 23)*

ii) The Priest as Teacher of his People:

Experience shows that lay people turn to the priest for knowledge about the Christian way of life. Because of his years of formation and training they expect of him a certain level of knowledge, wisdom and insight which will shed spiritual light on their personal struggles and dilemmas. In particular, people look to their priests for guidance in new moral issues thrown up by contemporary culture and technological progress. If the priest is to satisfy their hunger and give them the enlightenment and guidance they are seeking he must be intellectually alive. He must be widely read, taking an interest in new ideas and intent on expanding the horizons of his mind through argument and discussion, as well as through reflection and prayer. People today are asking questions of the priest about what faith and ministry means to him personally. If the priest is not to spurn genuine questions or take refuge in worn-out cliches he must be able to articulate his own personal faith. Questions are a point of contact between faith and life. They provide a valuable opening into people's lives and where they stand *vis-à-vis* their own faith. They are opportunities for evangelisation. Questions are often a sign of the Spirit of God at work in people. They come in all forms and guises – out of anger, cynicism or mere curiosity. The priest should welcome questions rather than shun them. After all did not Jesus provoke a storm of questions in his day? Did he not leave us with many unanswered questions?

The priest who relies totally on his own personal experience is unlikely to be able to understand or help those with genuinely searching questions. Ongoing study, reading widely and wisely must be an integral part of the life of every priest. 'In particular, continuing theological study is necessary if the priest is to faithfully carry out the ministry of the word, proclaiming it clearly and without ambiguity, distinguishing it from mere human opinions, no matter how renowned and widespread these might be' (John Paul II, 'Post Synodal Apostolic Exhortation on the Formation of Priests in the Circumstances of the Present Day', *Pastores Dabo Vobis*, n 72). There is no other way of bringing the wisdom of generations of lived faith to bear on contemporary issues and problems; there is no other way of preserving a freshness and originality in one's preaching.

In guiding his people in the ways of faith the priest is obliged to put before them the integral faith and tradition of the Church. 'The priest will wisely avoid falsifying, reducing, distorting or diluting the content of the divine message' (Congregation for the Clergy, *Directory on the Ministry and Life of Priests*, n 45). He speaks in the name of the Church as a whole; he is its spokesperson. Hence, it is his duty to teach and preach the Church's mind on all issues, not his own personal views. Pope Paul VI impresses upon priests their duty and responsibility in this regard when he writes:

> The effectiveness of evangelisation will be gravely diminished if the preachers of the gospel are divided among themselves in various ways. Is not this one of the great obstacles to evangelisation at the present time? If the gospel which we preach appears to be rent by doctrinal disputes, by opposing opinions or even by mutual recriminations between Christians – according to each individual's views about Christ and the Church and according to differing opinions about society and human institutions – is it not inevitable that those to whom our preaching is directed will be troubled, led into error, and, indeed, scandalised .... Since we are preachers of the gospel we must appear before the faithful, not as

men disputing and disagreeing about controversies that can give no edification, but rather as men strong in the faith who are able to come together, in spite of differences, which may now and then arise, united in a sincere, disinterested search for the truth (*Evangelisation in the Modern World, Evangelii Nuntiandi*, 8/12/1975, n 77, Flannery, vol II, pp 752-753).

Thus the priest must not place obstacles in the way of the Christ's saving power by equating his own views with those of the Gospel or by projecting his own prejudices. 'The obligation to follow the Magisterium in matters of faith and morals is intrinsically united to all the functions which the priest must perform in the Church. Dissent in this area is to be considered grave, in that it produces scandal and confusion among the faithful' (Congregation for the Clergy, *Directory on the Ministry* ... n 62).

He exercises his teaching role through a variety of ways and in constantly changing circumstances. He is to instruct the faithful through the homily, through pre-sacramental preparation and through adult religious education. A ten-minute weekly homily for the adult majority of the Church is hardly adequate to nourish faith and sustain hope. The priest's responsibility as teacher of his people does not begin and end with the Sunday homily. Rather he constantly seeks out new ways and means for imparting the truths of faith in an increasingly secular and, even sometimes, a hostile environment (cf *Evangelisation in the Modern World*, n 54, Flannery, vol II, pp 735). Priests might consider collaborating with neighbouring parishes and enlisting the help of religious and other competent lay people in discharging more effectively this task of evangelisation. In the words of Pope John Paul II, it is the duty of 'priests and religious to assist the lay faithful in their mission' (*The Vocation and Mission of the Laity* ... n 61).

In addition to adult and pre-sacramental preparation of both children and parents, the priest is to have a special care for the Catholic education of children and young people. With the collaboration of the faithful, he is to make every effort to bring the gospel message to those who have given up religious practice or who do not profess the true faith' (c 528 #1).

Local Radio – an instrument of evangelisation: A valuable instrument in the whole area of teaching and evangelisation is the phenomenon of local radio. It is truly amazing the number of people who tune into local radio and particularly those programmes dealing with religious topics. Good religious broadcasting does not consist so much in giving people answers to their problems but rather in reminding them of the important questions in their lives and helping them to find their own answers. Local radio is in many respects a kind of modern-day pulpit. As the number of people attending church regularly on Sunday begins to decline it is imperative that the priest and the believing community make maximum use of the airwaves. Local radio reaches into the homes and work-places of people who may have long since severed all formal contact with the institutional Church. Local radio personnel are welcoming and cooperative and are anxious to have 'religious' as part of their team. The priest should avail of this goodwill.

iii) The Priest as Leader of his People in Prayer and Worship:

The priest is the official proclaimer of the Christian message and at one and the same time the president of the eucharistic celebration. In order to lead his people in prayer and worship he must himself be seen to be a man of prayer, a man of God. The priest exercises his priestly role primarily through his celebration of the Eucharist. 'For this reason the daily celebration of it is earnestly recommended. This celebration is an act of Christ and the Church even if it is impossible for the faithful to be present' (*Vatican II, Decree on Ministry* ... n 13, Flannery, vol 1, p 888). In addition he continues the priesthood of Jesus Christ through his celebration of the sacraments and the Divine Office. 'By their fulfilment of the Divine Office priests themselves should extend to the different hours of the day the praise and thanksgiving they offer in the celebration of the Eucharist. By the Office they pray to God in the name of the Church for the whole people entrusted to them and in fact for the whole world' (*ibid* n 5, p 872).

In addition to official and formal prayer the priest needs to spend some time each day in private, personal prayer or meditation. He needs courage to face God, in the nakedness and emptiness of of his own heart (cf Ray Brady, 'Priesthood at Risk: Courage to Be', in: *The Furrow*, January 1989, p 11). Insofar as possible the priest should try to set aside a definite period each day for prayer and eucharistic adoration (cf *Congregation for the Clergy,*

Directory on the Ministry ... n 50). The words of Pope John Paul II to priests and seminarians at Maynooth are particularly apt here:

> Your first duty is to be with Christ. You are called to be 'a witness to his Resurrection' (Acts 1:22). A constant danger with priests, even zealous priests, is that they become so immersed in the work of the Lord that they neglect the Lord of the work' (*The Visit, John Paul II in Ireland*, Veritas/A.C.W., 1979, p 75).

In all liturgical celebrations he exercises a ministry of leadership among the many ministries which facilitate the building up of God's Kingdom on earth. It pertains to the Bishop 'to ensure that abuses do not creep into ecclesiastical discipline, especially concerning ministry of the word, the celebration of the sacraments and sacramentals, the worship of God and the cult of the saints, and the administration of goods' (cs 392 #2 & 835 #1). Hence, with regard to the liturgy the priest 'must not add, remove or change anything by his own initiative' (Congregation for the Clergy, *Directory on the Ministry* ..., n 64).

The quality of the priest's presence in worship is crucial if people are to be drawn into the mystery being celebrated. By his very words and gestures he communicates a sense of the holy. He can no longer rely on the automatic or *opus operatum* effect of his ministry. He is required to do his best to create in his people that level of personal faith that will make the sacraments which he celebrates truly 'sacraments of faith'. He should remember that to sacramentalise people without first evangelising them is to do them a serious disservice and ultimately to undermine the very truthfulness and integrity of the sacraments. The revised liturgy frequently calls for adaptation in style and and approach. A real concern for authenticity over and above the requirements of validity and lawfulness must inspire every liturgical celebration. The *1994 Directory on the Ministry and Life of Priests* lays particular emphasis on this aspect of priestly ministry:

> ... a lack of attention to the symbolic aspects of the liturgy, and even more, carelessness and coldness, superficiality and disorder empty the meaning and weaken the process of strengthening the faith. Those who improperly celebrate the Mass reveal a weakness in their faith and fail to educate others in the faith (n 49).

Finally, in his role as leader the priest is not just a liturgical functionary. He is above all a pastoral leader. While one can be an effective pastoral minister without being a sacramental minister,
one cannot be an effective sacramental minister without also
being a pastoral minister in that community. He sees to the spiritual and even at times to the material needs which enhance the
human dignity of the people who live within the parish.

iv) The Priest as Servant/King:

The priest's sharing in the Kingship of Christ takes effect in and
through his service to his people. Jesus set the pattern for this
service at the Last Supper when he washed his disciples' feet.
Like all the People of God, the priest is called to serve others or
as Pope John Paul II reminds us: 'You priests, however, are expected to have a concern and a commitment greater than and
different from that of the lay person. And this is because you
share in the priesthood of Jesus Christ in a way that differs 'essentially and not only in degree' (L.G. n 10) from the manner in
which they share' (Holy Thursday Letter to Priests, 1979, n 5,
Flannery, vol II, p 351). When it comes to serving people priests,
therefore, are expected to be 'artists' of pastoral care, to be models and paradigms of ministry in a community hosting a multitude of ministries.

> Our vocation demands that we be close to people in their
> problems, whether personal, family or social. But it also de-
> mands that we be close to them in a priestly way. Only thus
> do we remain ourselves in the midst of these problems. If we
> are to be of assistance to people in their problems, and they
> can be very difficult, we must keep our identity and remain
> really faithful to our vocation (*ibid*, n 7, p 353).

v) The Priest as Herald of Hope:

In his day-to-day ministry the priest encounters many people
weighed down by a profound sense of helplessness and despair.
Of those who claim to be unbelievers some do so because they
see no point in believing. Pointlessness and aimlessness are
often more of a problem than actual unbelief. In reaching out to
such people the priest must himself be a man of hope. He must
breathe new hope into them, not just talk about it or bemoan its
absence. What people today need above all is hope – a real sense
of God-with-them in the ups-and-downs of life; a sense of God

being on their side and at hand to assist them in their struggles. The priest mediates hope through his preaching and by the witness of his life. The fact that he professes hope does not immunise him from weakness and failure in his own personal life. Nor does the fact of failure take from the good he has already done (cf *Catechism*, n 1550).

2. Ongoing Formation

Both Pope John Paul II in his Post Synodal Apostolic Exhortation on the *Formation of Priests in the Circumstances of the Present Day, Pastores Dabo Vobis* and the 1994 *Directory on the Ministry and Life of Priests*, devote entire final chapters respectively to the matter of 'Ongoing Formation'. Pope John Paul speaks of it as

> an intrinsic requirement of the gift and sacramental ministry received; ... it proves necessary in every age. It is particularly urgent today, not only because of rapid changes in the social and cultural conditions of individuals and peoples among whom priestly ministry is exercised, but also because of that 'new evangelisation' which constitutes the essential and pressing task of the Church at the end of the second millennium (n 70).

It helps the priest to overcome the temptation to reduce his ministry to the provision of impersonal services, even if these are spiritual or sacred, or to a business-like function which he carries out for the Church. The very nature of priestly vocation presupposes it. One is called not merely to priesthood but also 'within' the priesthood to reaffirm anew that original 'yes' given at ordination. Vocation is not just a once-off response but a continuing 'yes' to the grace of the Holy Spirit. For this reason it is not something confined to a particular age group.

> Ongoing formation is a duty, in the first instance for young priests. They should have frequent and systematic meetings ... to help one another by exchanging experiences and reflecting on how to put into practice the ideals of the priesthood and of ministry which they have imbibed during their seminary years (*ibid* n 76).

> Ongoing formation is a duty also for priests of middle age. They can face a number of risks precisely because of their age ... Often enough, the older priest has a sort of interior fatigue which is dangerous. It can be the sign of resigned disillusion-

ment in the face of difficulties and failures. Such situations find an answer in ongoing formation ...

Ongoing formation should also involve those priests who by their advanced years can be called elderly ... for these priests (it) will not be a matter so much of study, updating and educational renewal, but rather a calm and reassuring confirmation of the part which they are still called upon to play in the presbyterate ...(*ibid* n 77).

Inner Conversion: the Root of all Ongoing Formation:

In order that the priest be effective in carrying out his threefold ministry, he must himself be open to that same conversion which he preaches to others. 'We shall never be in a position to correct the lives of others as long as we neglect our own' (St Gregory the Great). This conversion means experiencing God's graciousness and love and responding accordingly in the changing circumstances of life. Though conversion takes place within the inner life of each person, it entails every facet of one's life - intellectual, affective, social, spiritual, moral and ecclesial. Conversion is by its very nature a life-long endeavour. Hence priestly formation is not something that can be accomplished and completed in one's seminary days but rather an ongoing call to conversion.

> Personal growth, continuing formation, theological education and human development, all of which lead to greater service to the People of God, are woven throughout the priest's entire life and ministry. A priest who takes advantage of these opportunities enhances his personal life and, more importantly, ministers to others with renewed vision and imagination' (National Conference of Catholic Bishops (NCCB) of the United States of America, *The Continuing Formation of Priests, Growing in Wisdom, Age and Grace*, 1984, p 6).

Ongoing formation and in-service training must be an integral part of priestly ministry today. It is long since an accepted part of the business world and professional life. For the priest it is all the more imperative given the nature of his ministry and that he is today addressing an increasingly educated people living in the midst of the contradictions and pluralisms of a secularised world. How is he to interpret and proclaim Christ's message to people with any hope of success if he has no contact with modern theology, a theology that is attempting to consider and cope with all these critical enquiries addressed to Christianity by the world today? How can he interpret and preach on the scriptures if he is not seeking to apply the methods of modern scriptural exegesis? To be effective in proclaiming God's word, 'the preacher must', in the words of Karl Barth, 'have the Bible in one hand and the daily newspaper in the other'.

The Church in which many priests were ordained is very different to its post-conciliar counterpart. The Second Vatican Council enunciated a new ecclesiology, giving birth to new structures and ministries within the Church such as the Council of Priests, Pastoral Councils and Finance Committees, etc.. The Apostolic Exhortation of John Paul II, *The Vocation and Mission of the Laity*, 1988, calls for a new style of ministry and new skills if the priest is to work collaboratively with his people. He must work towards becoming an effective leader who encourages the full and active participation of the laity. To do this he will need to develop certain skills and qualities such as sincerity of heart, a constant concern for justice, fidelity to one's word, courtesy of manner, restraint, and kindliness of speech. As a significant part of the priest's ministry is spent in dealing with people's problems, courses in counselling and personal development are strongly recommended (cf Congregation for the Clergy, *Directory on the Ministry* ... n 75).

The priest has an obligation to himself and his people to update himself theologically, pastorally and spirituality. Otherwise he runs the risk of being unable to distinguish the substance of the faith from its time-conditioned expression, and perhaps imposing on people faith-burdens which they are not bound to bear and perhaps cannot bear anyway. Making pastoral decisions as to who should be admitted to the sacraments is a case in point.

Given the demands of parish life, it is possible for the priest to maintain only a very limited contact with modern academic theology. He must, however, do his best to keep in touch with modern-day scholarship and pastoral issues by subscribing to and reading some theological reviews or journals (e.g. *The Furrow; Doctrine and Life; The Way, Scripture in Church, Review for Religious* etc.) and books (a list of up-to-date books on various topics appear at the end of each section of this *Directory*). If he is to carry out his work responsibly he ought to seek opportunities for further study and renewal courses. Diocesan Conferences should provide the opportunity to become acquainted with topical issues of immediate pastoral concern. *The 1994 Directory on the Ministry and Life of Priests* recommends that the Bishop in consultation with the Council of Priests set up a committee to advise him with regards to such topics, sessions, courses, (cf ns 89-90).

The priest then must have a positive attitude to theology. A good grasp of theology helps him to express more clearly and succinctly what he proclaims. He must always read discriminately and set a certain time aside for this if he is not to fall back to an immature grasp of the faith. Where possible the clergy should have the courage to do some biblical theology, working together in preparing homilies, etc..

It is the duty of the Bishop to ensure 'that they (the priests) have the means and the institutions needed for the development of their spiritual and intellectual life.' (c 384). 'Sabbatical periods' for study and updating are recommended (cf *Directory on the Ministry and Life of Priests* n 83).

3. Spiritual Growth

A primary consideration for every priest must be his own spiritual growth and holiness. He is called and challenged to that same perfection and holiness to which he calls his people. This is no easy task, given the varying circumstances in which priests must work and live. Yet it is probably the most urgent need facing today's priest. The words of advice given by St Charles Borromeo to his clergy seem particularly apt and relevant today:

> Do not neglect yourself. Do not give yourself to others to such an extent that nothing is left of yourself for yourself. You should certainly keep in mind the souls whose pastor you are, but without forgetting yourself. My brothers, do not forget that there is nothing so necessary to all churchmen than the meditation which precedes, accompanies and follows all our actions: I will sing, says the prophet, and I will meditate (cf Ps 100:1). If you administer the sacraments, my brother, mediate upon what your are doing. If you celebrate Mass, meditate upon what you are offering. If you recite the psalms in choir, meditate to whom and of what you are speaking. If you are guiding souls, meditate in whose blood they have been cleansed. And let all be done among you in

charity (1 Cor 16:14). Thus we will be able to overcome the difficulties we meet, countless as they are, each day. In any event, this is what is demanded of us by the task entrusted to us. If we act thus, we will find the strength to give birth to Christ in ourselves and in others (*Acta Ecclesiae Mediolanensis*, Milan 1599, 1178, cited in: *Pastores Dabo Vobis*, 1992, n 72).

How does the priest nourish his inner spiritual life? Each day prime time must be given to prayer and reflection. 'Prayer is essential for maintaining pastoral sensitivity to everything that comes from the Spirit, for correctly discerning and properly employing those charisms that lead to union and are linked to priestly service in the Church' (John Paul II, *Holy Thursday Letter to Priests*, 1987, n 12). One cannot live off past gains. Days of recollection and afternoons of prayer are organised for this purpose. In addition priests are required to do an annual retreat (cf *Directory on the Ministry* ... n 85). A Directed Retreat regularly is something that should be considered. The many renewal programs advertised in *Intercom* and elsewhere should be availed of.

4. The Priest and his own health

To be effective in his ministry the priest is challenged to be a mature, human person who has a healthy relationship with God, with himself and with others. There is today in the human sciences a growing awareness of the interdependence of the physical, emotional and spiritual dimensions of our being. Hence, problems in one area can often produce effects in another. The priest therefore must take care of his physical and emotional health.

Taking care of one's physical health constitutes an authentic expression of Christian self-love. It is difficult for a priest genuinely to love others and to invite them to love themselves when he consistently exempts himself from this caring. Care for himself exhibits itself in the simplest of ways: eating properly, getting enough sleep, taking regular exercise, seeing a doctor regularly, taking time off, and observing moderation in the use of alcohol and other drugs. Simple physical fitness, achieved and maintained in this way, will significantly enhance a priest's ministry. He will be less prone to fatigue, better able to tolerate stress, and generally be more alert, less tense and less subject to depression (National Conference of Catholic Bishops of the United States, *The Priest and Stress*, 1982, p 17).

The priest's health is frequently not unrelated to his living conditions. The presbytery should primarily be a home where he
lives, rather than a base from which he works. It should be comfortable and well-kept. It should be a place into which he feels
free to invite people, especially his brother priests and members
of his family. Hospitality towards one's fellow priests is a value
that should not be forgotten or sacrificed in the name of
progress. Poorly kept presbyteries can only lead to low morale
among priests and ultimately constitute a disincentive to at-
tracting vocations. People expect their priests to live in as comfortable surroundings as they themselves do. A lackadaisical
approach to one's living conditions can only do a disservice to
the priesthood that he represents and constitute a deterrent
when it comes to promoting vocations to the priesthood.

Equally important is the priest's emotional health. Frustration,
loneliness, depression and irritability can result from the priest
neglecting his genuine emotional needs. The priest is called
upon to live a celibate way of life in a society where many do not
understand or appreciate celibacy as a value. Celibacy is a gift of
the Spirit, an eschatological sign and a symbol of availability
for service.

> Through his celibacy, the priest becomes the 'man for others'
> differently from the way that a married man becomes, as a
> husband and father, a 'man for others' ... The priest in re-
> nouncing the fatherhood proper to married men seeks an-
> other fatherhood and even another motherhood ..., (John
> Paul II, *Holy Thursday Letter to Priests*, 1979, n 8, Flannery, vol
> II, p 355).

In living out his vocation to celibacy the priest needs above all
the support and encouragement of his brother priests. He needs
their companionship and that of his family and friends, both
male and female. There is an ordinariness, an everydayness,
about family life that a celibate priest needs. But despite all of
these supports there are times when that commitment that he
knowingly and freely made to life-long celibacy will be put to
the test.

> At such times he must look for support in more fervent
> prayer. Through prayer he must foster humility and sinceri-
> ty before God and his own conscience. Prayer imparts
> strength to faltering resolution and induces a confidence

PRIESTHOOD

akin to that of which St Paul speaks: 'I can do all things in him who strengthens me' (Phil 4:13). Many priests can confirm this from their own experience. It is a proven fact of life (*ibid* n 9, p 356).

It is well to recall that the life-long commitment expected of married people involves similar obligations. It sometimes exposes husbands and wives to similar trials and experiences, affording them the opportunity of proving the worth of their love. In being faithful to his own vocation, the priest extols the value of fidelity that the Church expects of married couples.

At critical times in his life he may find professional counselling to be valuable. Counselling should not be considered extraordinary; nor should it be confused with spiritual direction nor indeed with psychiatric care. In short a priest owes it to himself and his people to obtain whatever help may be necessary in order to grow in holiness and be more effective in his ministry.

Holidays and recreation help to build up the priest and enable him to be happy in himself so that he can have the energy and enthusiasm to do his work well. Every priest is entitled to four weeks vacation each year (cf c 533 #2), excluding spiritual retreats and renewal courses. Priests are strongly encouraged to take vacations and regular time off.

5. Morale of Priests

In the life of a priest there are many areas of concern. Today there are symptoms of low morale. Some priests feel weighed down by the burdens of ministry. Others feel that they are not doing important things with their lives. Some priests are hesitant to encourage actively vocations to priesthood. The causes of low morale can be identified and remedied. With a deepening sense of vocation through ongoing spiritual formation the priest realises the value of his ministry. An adequate system of accountability, feedback and evaluation offers the affirmation and supports that are necessary for a certain satisfaction and encouragement from the priest's work. The setting of measurable goals allows the priest to take responsibility for his work and not feel guilty because he cannot achieve everything all at once. There are many areas that bring unease, not least being the number of child sexual abuses cases and scandals within the Church.

Thirty years ago, 'the priesthood' was able to carry or give credibility to individual priests. Today, because of the scandals, the
opposite is rapidly becoming the case. It is now a matter of the
individual priest, through his ministry and example, 'carrying'
or giving credibility to 'the priesthood'. There are increasing
signs that the faithful too are beginning to realise this.

6. The Priest and the Presbyterate

The priest with the bishop and his fellow-priests shares in the
ministry of Christ. It is as a member of the Diocesan Presbyterate
that each priest has responsibility for the mission of the Church.
The priest can never be a 'solo runner'. Rather, he is part of a
diocesan team exercising a ministry of leadership in the pastoral
care of people. He must, therefore, be concerned for the welfare
and health of his brother priests by visiting them when they are
ill and by being ready to help them out when indisposed or on
vacation. It pertains to the Vicars Forane in particular to be concerned for their brother priests 'who are in difficult circumstances or are troubled by problems' (c 555 #2, 2).

> When he has come to know that parish priests (or other
> priests) of his district are seriously ill, the Vicar Forane is to
> ensure that they do not lack spiritual and material help.
> When they die, he is to ensure that their funerals are worthily
> celebrated. Moreover, should any of them fall ill or die, he is
> to see to it that books, documents, sacred furnishings and
> other items belonging to the Church are not lost or removed
> (c 555 #3).

In this diocese it is customary for the Vicar Forane, in the absence of a curate or an assistant priest in the parish, to receive
the funeral remains of a brother priest and to concelebrate at the
funeral Mass. It is his task also to install or assist at the installa-
tion of new parish priests in his deanery.

Pastoral effectiveness is enhanced and the bond of priestly
brotherhood strengthened by the readiness of priests to work as
a team both at local and deanery level. Priests of neighbouring
parishes might very usefully collaborate in areas of Adult
Religious Education, Pre-Sacramental Preparation, Parish and
School Retreats, etc..

At a very practical level priests express their unity within the
presbyterate by supplying for one another when away or on va-

cation. In days when housekeepers are more the exception than the norm, priests who live in close proximity to each other might consider sharing a common table for their main meal each day. After all it was in the context of a meal that Christ ordained the first priests and prayed for unity among them.

This unity finds liturgical expression in concelebration, especially in the Chrism Mass of Holy Thursday. It is also realised in the various groups that express fraternity among priests, e.g. the Charles De Focauld Priests' Fraternity, Emmaus Spirituality, Ministry to Priests Programme, etc.. Other gatherings of priests whether for pastoral, recreational or educational purposes are strongly encouraged. All of them help to cement a sense of brotherhood among priests and strengthen the bonds that unite them in the presbyterate. Offering hospitality to one's fellow priests when they visit the parish on the occasions of weddings, funerals, etc. is one of the key ways of promoting this sense of unity and brotherhood for which Christ prayed at the Last Supper.

7. The Priest and the Missions

The Second Vatican Council reminds us that the Church by its very nature is missionary (cf *Decree on the Church's Missionary Activity, Ad Gentes Divinitus*, n 2, Flannery, vol 1, p 814). Recent years has witnessed a growing desire on the part of diocesan priests to help the missions by volunteering for missionary work. Some dioceses have adopted parishes in Latin America or Africa while others have opted for working in close collaboration with existing missionary organisations and societies, e.g., St Columban's Missionary Society, Navan; St Patrick's Missionary Society, Kiltegan. Hence, it is diocesan policy to facilitate any priest wishing to work on the missions. Priests intending to do so should consult with the Bishop in good time so that the necessary arrangements both at home and abroad can be made.

Priests who spend some time working on the missions 'enjoy all the rights in their diocese of origin, in which they have been incardinated, as if they had been involved in the sacred ministry there without interruption' (Congregation for the Clergy, *Norms for Co-operation Among Local Churches and for a Better Distribution of the Clergy, Postquam Apostoli*, 25/3/1980, n 30, Flannery, vol II, p 378.

Recommended Reading:

Vatican II, Decree on the Life and Ministry of Priests, Presbyterorum ordinis, Flannery, vol 1, 863-902.

John Paul II, *Holy Thursday Letter to Priests,* 1979, Flannery vol II, 346-360.

Post-Synodal Apostolic Exhortation, *The Formation of Priests in the Circumstances of the Present Day, Pastores Dabo Vobis,* 7/4/1992.

Congregation for the Clergy, *Norms for Co-operation Among Local Churches and for a Better Distribution of the Clergy, Postquam Apostoli* 25/3/1980.

Directory on the Ministry and Life of Priests, Veritas, Dublin, 1994.

Being a Priest in Ireland Today, (Papers of the 1988 Annual Conference of the NCPI), Dominican Publications, Dublin, 1988.

National Conference of Catholic Bishops of the USA,

   The Priest and Stress, 1982.

   The Health of American Catholic Priests, a Report and a Study, 1985.

   A Shepherd's Care, Reflections on the Changing Role of Pastor, 1987.

Connolly, F.B., *Growth in Priesthood,* Asian Trading Corporation, Bangalore, 1986.

Bausch, W.J., *Ministry, Traditions, Tensions, Transitions,* Twenty-Third Publications, Mystic, Connecticut, 1982.

Bausch, W.J., *Take Heart Father,* Twenty-Third Publications, Mystic, Connecticut, 1986.

Lane, Tom, *A Priesthood in Tune,* The Columba Press, Dublin, 1993.

Power, D.N., *Gifts That Differ: Lay Ministries, Established and Unestablished,* Pueblo, New York, 1980.

O'Meara, T.F., *Theology of Ministry,* Paulist, New York, 1983.

Mitchell, N, *Mission and Ministry, History and Theology of the Sacrament of Order,* Glazier, Wilmington, Delaware, 1982.

CHAPTER 7

Marriage and the Family

1. Introduction

Married Christians, in virtue of the sacrament of matrimony, signify and share in the mystery of that unity and
fruitful love which exists between Christ and his Church;
they help each other to attain to holiness in their married life
and in the rearing and education of their children (Sacred
Congregation for Rites, *Introduction to Rite of Marriage*,
19/3/1969).

Marital love is rooted in the conjugal covenant of irrevocable
personal consent. Through this act of consent spouses mutually
bestow and accept each other in their strengths and weaknesses.
In the words of the Second Vatican Council they bring into being
an 'intimate partnership', a 'conjugal covenant' of life and love
(*Pastoral Constitution of the Church in the Modern World, Gaudium
et Spes*, n 48, hereinafter *G.S.*, Flannery, vol I, pp 950-952). It is
the duty of the priest and indeed of the whole Christian community to assist those preparing for marriage, and those already
married to achieve these high ideals in their own particular circumstances.

Speaking to his brother Bishops, Pope Paul VI urged them to assume a 'concerted pastoral role' in preserving and improving
the quality of Christian marriage:

We invite you all, we implore you, to give a lead to your
priests who assist you in the sacred ministry, and to the faithful of your diocese and to devote yourselves with all zeal and
without delay to safeguarding the holiness of marriage …
Look upon this mission as the most important work and responsibility committed to you at the present time (*Encyclical
Letter on the Regulation of Births, Humanae Vitae*, 25/7/1968, n
30, cf Flannery, vol II, pp 413-414).

2. Preparation

Preparation for marriage, which is always required, takes place in stages and at different levels. Responsibility for providing it devolves upon the Bishop, priests and the whole ecclesial community (cf c 1063). The 1983 *Code of Canon Law* makes it clear that such preparation may no longer be equated with merely determining the absence of canonical impediments and completing the necessary pre-marriage documentation, etc.. Indeed, a complete new section has been added to the Code dealing specifically with pre-marriage preparation (cf cs 1063-1072).

In his Apostolic Exhortation, *The Christian Family in the Modern World, Familiaris Consortio,* 22/11/1981, n 65 – hereinafter *Familiaris Consortio,* (cf Flannery, vol II, pp 868-871) Pope John Paul II identifies the different stages in this work of preparation: remote, proximate and immediate preparation.

i) Remote Preparation:

The most fundamental and effective preparation for marriage begins in the home. It is in the family setting that a person acquires his/her basic attitudes to love, sexuality, caring forgiveness and living with others. In the words of Pope John Paul II:

> It is the period when esteem for authentic human values is instilled, both in interpersonal and social relationships, with all that it signifies for the formation of character, and for the control and right use of one's inclinations, for the manner of regarding and meeting people of the opposite sex and so on (*ibid*, n 66, p 869).

What is begun in the home is built upon and continued in the school. The latter plays an important part in shaping and forming attitudes and values. A formative programme in human relationships based on the values of Christ ought to be an integral part of the school's curriculum. Accord, at the invitation of the school authorities, will be happy to give whatever assistance it can in this area.

ii) Proximate and Immediate Preparation:

Courtship and engagement are times for personal growth and maturation for the couple. It is a time when they experience love freely given and received and at a progressively deeper level.

They begin to understand the wholeness of love – its emotional, intellectual and spiritual dimensions. Engagement is a time when the couple's attitude to life and love are in the process of final formation, and they are open to being influenced for good in a special way.

Immediate preparation for marriage extends to several different areas – pastoral, spiritual, liturgical and canonical.

a) Pastoral and Spiritual:

Every marriage is the wedding of two unique persons and never to-be-repeated personalities. Each marriage is a unique creation in the eyes of God. Husband and wife in their love for each other share in God's love, making it visible and tangible in their life together. Indeed, it is the presence of this very love that makes marriage sacramental. Marriage then is a sacrament not because it is celebrated in a church but rather by virtue of what it is in itself. Sacramentality is not something superimposed or added to the natural reality of marriage but rather marriage in its concrete reality viewed from the standpoint of Christian faith. Hence, the Church has always spoken of Christ 'elevating' natural marriage to the dignity of sacrament rather than trans-forming it into a sacrament. Neither is sacramentality something which is over and finished with on the wedding day. It is the subsequent living out of total and unconditional love for each other amid the ups-and-downs of life that gives vitality and meaning to the sacrament of Marriage. Since married-love mir-rors the love which Christ has for his Church it too has to be sac-rificial, forgiving and enduring (cf Eph 5: 25-30). Just as the love between Christ and his Church is never a fifty-fifty relationship, neither can it be expected that the reciprocal love between hus-band and wife will be a fifty-fifty relationship. The self-giving of one partner will seldom be matched by an equal level of self-giving on the part of the other.

Of all the sacraments Christian Marriage in its concrete living out is the one that most reflects the Paschal Mystery – suffering, death and resurrection. The partners must continually die to self before they can be born into that oneness of mind and heart and soul which marriage is.

To help them realise these high ideals of their calling every couple needs the help of a priest. He should be somebody who has time

MARRIAGE

for them and is concerned for the quality of their marriage. For many young couples it may be their first personal contact with a priest as adults. The environment should be comfortable and hospitable and the meeting itself should not be rushed. The priest of the bride (or of the Catholic party in a mixed marriage) must satisfy himself that the couple are adequately prepared for marriage. In encouraging the couple to attend the Pre-Marriage Course the priest should inform the couple that it is not a series of lectures telling people what to do, but rather a means of helping the couple to learn about each other, their expectations, their values and their attitudes. It is an introduction to living out the vocation of Christian marriage in today's world. The times and venues for these pre-marriage courses are published annually in the *Ossory Diocesan Directory*.

The spiritual preparation of the couple and the liturgical preparation of the wedding ceremony will normally go hand-in-hand. This pertains to the priest of the bride or jointly to the priest of the bride and the priest or deacon officiating at the wedding ceremony. Like all of the other sacraments Marriage too is a sacrament of faith but in its own proper and unique way. 'Priests should first of all strengthen and nourish the faith of those about to be married, for the sacrament of matrimony presupposes and demands faith' (*Sacred Congregation for Rites, Introduction to Rite of Marriage*, n 7). The priest should encourage the couple to prepare spiritually for their marriage by prayerful reflection on the actual texts of the rite and by reception of the sacrament of Reconciliation. The priest is encouraged to pray with the couple for the success of their marriage.

b) Liturgical:

Christian marriage will normally take place within the context of a liturgical celebration. A carefully planned and well-celebrated wedding can be a moving and memorable experience not only for the couple themselves but also for all present. It can in fact be a special moment or occasion of evangelisation for those who only infrequently attend Church. Priests should remind couples that the liturgy is a sacred and public action of the whole Church, and not merely a private celebration for this particular couple. Pope John Paul II draws particular attention to this aspect of marriage:

Inasmuch as it is a sacramental action of the Church, the liturgical celebration of marriage should involve the Christian community, with the full, active and responsible participation of all those present, according to the place and task of each individual: the bride and bridegroom, the priest, the witnesses, the relatives, the friends, the other members of the faithful ...' (Op cit, n 67, Flannery, vol II, p 871).

Selecting the Readings, Prayers and Marriage Texts:

Couples should be encouraged to take an active part in preparing their wedding liturgy. The priest introduces them to the different options available for the particular parts of the wedding ceremony and invites them to select those prayers and formularies which they prefer. In this way they can enter into the spirit of the liturgy and truly make it their own. *The Celebration of Marriage*, Veritas 1980, should be used. In choosing the form of consent couples should be encouraged to select the strength and richness of the longer formularies rather than the shorter one, requiring the simple answer 'I do' ...

A full selection of the readings for marriage from vol III of the *Lectionary*, pp 263-289 should be made available to them. This does not, of course, eliminate other suitable, biblical readings. Non-biblical readings may never be used instead of the word of God. They may, however, be incorporated as commentaries, meditations or communion refections. The priest and couple together prepare the intentions for the Prayer of the Faithful, taking into account the liturgical character of these prayers and the liturgy being celebrated. Being a friend or relative of the bride or groom does not necessarily qualify a person to be a reader at a wedding. What is essential is that the reader be competent and be well prepared, spiritually and technically. Insofar as possible they should be present for the rehearsal in order to familiarise themselves with the sanctuary area and amplification system. Normally the bride and groom do not act as readers. Indeed, it might be preferable to involve people other than the witnesses at the marriage. They are already fulfilling an important ministry in their own right as official witnesses.

Selecting music and singers:

Music is the servant of the liturgy. In helping the congregation to worship more effectively, it gives glory to God and adds beauty and splendour to the celebration. It helps create an atmosphere of festivity and joy. Hence, it is especially appropriate for weddings.

All music and hymns should be chosen in consultation with the priest, the organist or other instrumentalists and soloist (cantor or psalmist). Ultimately it is the responsibility of the priest of the church in which the marriage takes place to ensure that the celebration be conducted in an appropriate liturgical manner, musically as well as otherwise. This may entail providing the couple with a selection of suitable hymns and music in good time from which they can then choose. Such a list has been made available on a special leaflet by the Irish Episcopal Conference, i.e. *Christian Marriage, preparation and celebration, For the Musician,* 1990. A copy of this available from the Irish Institute of Pastoral Liturgy, College Street, Carlow. The purpose of this document is to assist the couple to select suitable music for their wedding.

The music chosen should serve the liturgy and be in keeping with its sacred character. Music and songs which express a purely superficial understanding of marriage and love, or which because of their association with the cinema, television or music hall may prove distracting, are not permitted.

Soloists should be discretely weaned away from the singing of certain items customarily requested at weddings in the past, e.g. *Panis Angelicus* and Gounod's or Schubert's *Ave Maria* which are little suited to the occasion. The renewed liturgy offers the soloist opportunities of contributing in a valuable way to the celebration. He/she may for instance sing the responsorial psalm, lead the people in the acclamations, sing the Alleluia, encourage the congregation in their own singing. (*The Celebration of Marriage,* 1980, *Pastoral Notes,* p 7).

Finally, each piece of music should be appropriate to the particular part of the liturgy at which it is being used.

Organ music at weddings is normally the responsibility of the parish organist. If an outside organist is to be engaged this should be done in consultation with the parish organist. Since the wedding is not a private or family affair, but a celebration of the whole congregation, the choice of music should be such that all can join in at the appropriate moments.

MARRIAGE

c) Canonical:

When a person intimates to his/her priest the intention to marry, the priest completes Part A of the 'Pre-Nuptial Enquiry Form'. The priest will then be in a position to indicate to the person what further documentation will be required, e.g. a baptismal certificate not more than six months old, a confirmation certificate, letters of freedom from parishes where the person lived for six months or more after the age of sixteen; in the case of non-Catholics and non-baptised, letters from parents, relatives or employers or a civil affidavit testifying to the person's freedom to marry, etc.. If a record of Baptism cannot be located, the testimony of one reliable witness to the Baptism suffices to prove it took place (cf c 876). It often transpires that a person's freedom to marry is established not so much on the basis of any single document but rather through a combination of documents and circumstances taken together.

In addition, the priest will discuss with the couple the form of pastoral and spiritual preparation best suited to their circumstances. He will encourage them in the strongest possible way to participate in a Pre-Marriage Course without making it a *sine qua non* condition for getting married. Effective participation at a pre-marriage course is best achieved by voluntary attendance. In the event of this not being possible he will either arrange with an Accord counsellor for a private course for the couple or undertake to prepare them himself. (cf Appendix I for suggested topics and guidelines for three meetings with a couple.) Preparation for marriage must never be omitted and responsibility for this devolves upon the priest, not Accord. The latter's function is simply to assist the priest in this very important task.

Finally, it should be remembered that in accordance with a *Decree of the Irish Episcopal Conference*, effective from Easter Sunday 1981, all couples planning to get married are required to give three months notice to the priest. Ideally this notice should be given to the priests of both parties, assuming that the place of marriage is the bride's parish. The Bishop alone may dispense from this three months notice requirement. As the decree itself does not indicate to which priest the notice should be given, it suffices that it be given to one of the priests of either the bride or groom.

It should be noted that according to the 1983 *Code* the parish of both the bride and groom now enjoy equal standing as the possible place of marriage. The preference given by the Irish Bishops after the publication of the 1983 *Code of Canon Law* to the parish of the bride no longer applies (cf *Pre-Nuptial Enquiry, Pastoral Guidelines*, Veritas, 1991, p 22).

If the marriage is to be celebrated outside of Ireland, all marriage documentation is to be sent to the Diocesan Office for issue of the *Litterae Testimoniales* and onward transmission to the appropriate Diocesan Office for issue of the *Nihil Obstat* and subsequent forwarding to the parish where the marriage is to take place (cf *ibid* p 15).

3. Couples Needing Special Care

The priest must keep in mind that 'every man and every woman, having reached marriage age and having the necessary capacity, has the right to marry and establish a family without any discrimination whatsoever … ' (Holy See, *Charter of the Rights of the Family, Art. 1a*, Veritas, l983). If, however, a priest has serious reservations about the suitability of one or both parties for marriage he must refer the matter to the Bishop and inform the couple of the right of the Bishop to postpone the marriage (c 1077 #1). This referral should take place before the couple have been given a date for the wedding. It may be necessary in a variety of situations. Its principal aim is not to stop the wedding from taking place but to ensure that those needing special care and preparation receive it.

i) The Very Young Couple:

The marriage of the very young must be a cause of serious concern for all. Statistics show the highest failure rate among people in this category. When the priest is approached by a couple, one or both of whom are very young, he should see them at least once separately and once together, and, if possible interview their parents also. Before making a judgement he should consider:
  - their home background and culture;
  - the nature and duration of their relationship;
  - the seriousness of their intention to marry;
  - their practical preparedness in terms of money, employment and accommodation, etc..

Like every other couple they should be advised to do a pre-marriage course. Marriage counsellors can be of invaluable help to the priest in helping prepare such a couple for marriage. Priests require the permission of the local Ordinary to assist at the marriage of a minor (i.e. under 21) who wishes to marry against the reasonable wishes of his/her parents (c 1071 #1.6).

ii) Pre-Marital Pregnancy:

There is much evidence to suggest that a marriage which takes place when the girl is already pregnant is at risk. Pregnancy is not a reason for getting married; nor is it grounds for obtaining a decree of nullity subsequently. When confronted with this kind of case the priest should make the following enquiries:
- whether the pregnancy has been confirmed;
- the duration of the couple's relationship;
- when the couple actually decided to marry;
- when the baby is due;
- what was their immediate reaction to the discovery of the pregnancy;
- seek the views of both sets of parents, wherever possible.

Should the priest conclude that the pregnancy is the sole reason for the marriage and that the couple are not yet adequately prepared to take this step, he should advise a substantial postponement. 'When the bride-to-be is pregnant, it is often advisable to try to persuade the couple to have the marriage postponed at least until after the baby is born. This is because of the real danger that the existence of pregnancy may cause pressure to be put on the couple, either by their families or by one another; so that the decision to marry may not be entirely free and mature' (Irish Bishops' Pastoral, *Love is for Life*, Veritas, 1985, n 83, p 24). If the priest's advice is not accepted he may refer the matter to the Bishop, informing him of the full circumstances of the case in question. The Bishop alone has the right to defer a marriage for a grave reason and only for as long as this grave reason persists (cf c 1077 #1).

iii) Older Couples

Special consideration should be given during the process of marriage preparation for older couples. While pre-marriage preparation may never be omitted, some modifications might be necessary in order to address the particular needs of the couple, e.g.

MARRIAGE

a few meetings with the priest or marriage counsellor rather than a formal pre-marriage course.

By virtue of their longer and richer life-experiences they have particular needs that younger couples would not have. The fact that each person brings to the marriage a lifestyle formed by habit over an extended period of time may in itself be a hindrance to that total self-giving of persons which Christian marriage is. It cannot be assumed that a couple is ready for marriage in the church simply because they are older. Statistics indicate that such marriages are also subject to failure mainly because of the inability to compromise individual independence for the mutual interdependence of the marriage relationship.

iv) The Apparently Unsuitable Couple:

From time to time the priest will have a distinct unease about the suitability of a couple to marry each other. This unease may arise from any of the following:
   - one or both parties has suffered from severe mental illness;
   - one or both parties show signs of serious immaturity, inadequacy or instability;
   - a history of promiscuity, fleeting and superficial relationships, alcoholism and compulsive gambling;
   - great discrepancy in age or cultural outlooks between the parties.

Great tact and sensitivity is required on the priest's part when dealing with this type of situation. The priest should point out to the couple the reasons for his reservations, and should they still persist, discuss the matter with the Director of Accord and the Bishop.

v) The Disabled:

The priest must show particular care and sensitivity when a disabled person requests marriage in the church. The disability may be either of a physical or mental nature, or a combination of both. Each situation must be assessed individually and a determination made only after consultation with family and professionals who are in a position to assess the person's level of independence and ability to make and sustain a permanent commitment.

vi) The Paraplegic:

Occasionally the priest will be approached by a couple where one or both are paraplegic. Serious doubts may arise about the individual's capacity to consummate the marriage. It should be noted that for as long as such doubt persists the canonical impediment of impotence does not arise (c 1084 #2). Competent advice, particularly medical, should be sought before making any assessment of the situation.

vii) Chemical Dependency/Alcoholism:

Special care and concern should be taken to assess the effects of alcohol and/or chemical abuse on the capacity of a person to enter into and sustain the essential duties and obligations of Christian marriage (cf c 1095 #3). Such dependency is often the symptom of a more deep-seated problem. In assessing particular situations the priest may need the help of Accord personnel or some other professional evaluation.

viii) The Uncommitted Catholic:

Marriage, like all other sacraments, is a sacrament of faith. Not infrequently, however, priests come across people requesting marriage whose faith and affiliation to the Church are minimal or even non-existent. In these circumstances the priest finds himself in somewhat of a dilemma. On the one hand, it is his duty to safeguard the sacredness and dignity of the sacrament and on the other, he must remember that the only form of marriage open to this baptised though non-practising Catholic which would be valid in the eyes of the Church, is in fact a church marriage (c 1055 #2). The priest should invite non-practising Catholics to articulate their reasons for requesting a church marriage. Social convention, parental expectations or the church setting do not provide sufficient justification for marriage in the Catholic Church. The ensuing dialogue provides the priest with a valuable 'catechetical moment' for encouraging a return to an active practice of the faith.

What is of vital importance is the manner in which the priest meets and receives the couple. They often come with a heightened sense of anxiety and feelings of awkwardness caused by unfamiliarity, not really knowing what form of marriage they want. Their motives for requesting a church marriage are at best mixed, i.e. often of a social and family nature rather than religious as such.

MARRIAGE

In these and other similar situations (e.g. the admission of children of non-practising parents to baptism, etc.) the priest must always be motivated by genuine pastoral concern for the people in question. He must not allow his own personal prejudices and feelings to interfere in this process. Such feelings and prejudices can easily override pastoral principles. When dealing with such people the priest, therefore, might usefully pose to himself the following questions:

1) Do I need to be in control of all situations? Does my latent hostility towards non-practising Catholics arise more from a sense of helplessness and loss of control over them rather than from a genuine pastoral concern for their spiritual good ?

2) When I am dealing with people who do not share my religious values and expectations, do I feel threatened? Do I immediately create an adversarial situation: me-against-them, and as a result become aggressive and overpowering?

3) Do I feel used and manipulated by couples who do not practise their faith but want a church wedding? Is it my own self-esteem that is hurt or am I genuinely concerned for their spiritual welfare?

4) Do I feel overly responsible for the manner in which this couple live out their life? Do I interpret it as my having failed them as a pastor?

5) Do I mistrust people who are not practising even before I get to know them?

Some of the above issues very often constitute a hidden motive for the priest in these and similar circumstances. He should remember, however, that his primary task is to be a shepherd to his people. He must make every effort to rekindle and nourish that spark of faith which they may have. In particular he should be prepared to enter into an honest dialogue with the couple, meeting them where they are at in the hope of accompanying them along the road of conversion. He might indeed take the Emmaus Story (Lk 24:13-35) as a model and guide for making real contact with the couple, i.e. be-friending them along their road of life, listening to their story, opening up the Scriptures to them in a new way, accompanying them to the crossroads of decision but allowing them to choose the road they wish to take. In this way it is hoped that they will approach the sacrament(s) they wish to celebrate more honestly and less awkwardly. It may indeed transpire that they are ripe for marriage but almost like the catechumens of old not yet ready for the Eucharist. Thus, it may be a celebration of the sacrament of Marriage outside of the eucharistic context that is most suited and acceptable to the couple at this stage in their conversion journey. The one thing that the priest must guard against at all costs is rushing people into sacraments that they neither want nor understand. Father Michael Paul Gallagher S.J. in his very useful booklet on this whole topic warns against sacramentalising people before they are ready. He writes:

> To put it negatively, there is a temptation when confronted with the typical unbeliever or half-believer, to opt for shortcuts of sacramentalising at all costs. From my own experience, as well as from the wider wisdom of the RCIA, that if the preparatory efforts of slow listening and suitable evangelising are skimped, the outcome could be a token and short lived conformism rather than any genuine step to conversion (*Walking with Unbelievers*, Veritas, 1985).

In dealing with this kind of case the priest is advised to take into account the principle of gradualness as enunciated by John Paul II in *Familiaris consortio*: 'permanent conversion ... is brought about concretely in steps that lead us ever forward' (Flannery, vol II, p 821). Thus he must be guided by the teaching of the Pope on this issue and not by any personal prejudices of his own. A church marriage may be refused only when the couple 'reject explicitly and formally what the Church intends to do when marriage of baptised persons is celebrated' (Op cit, n 67, Flannery, vol II, p 873). One must be careful not to equate marriage with the other sacraments when it comes to determining who should receive it.

> The sacrament of Matrimony has this specific element that distinguishes it from all the other sacraments: it is the sacrament of something that was part of the very economy of salvation; it is the very conjugal covenant instituted by the Creator 'in the beginning'. Therefore the decision of a man and a woman to marry in accordance with this divine plan, that is to say, the decision to commit by their irrevocable conjugal consent their whole lives in indissoluble love and unconditional fidelity, really involves if not in a fully conscious way, an attitude of profound obedience to the will of God, an attitude which cannot exist without God's grace (*ibid* p 872).

Hence, the Church does admit to a church marriage people who might not be considered properly disposed for receiving other sacraments. Because of the uniqueness of Christian marriage, the criteria which might be applied to other sacraments do not necessarily apply to it. In fact, only those who 'reject explicitly and formally what the Church intends to do when the marriage of baptised persons is celebrated' (*ibid*, p 873) may be refused a church marriage.

Those who formally leave the Church i.e. renounce their allegiance to it by joining some other church or sect are not bound to observe canonical form (c 1117). If such a person, however, wishes to marry a Catholic, that marriage is to be treated as a mixed marriage (c 1071 #2).

ix) The Cohabiting Couple:

Closely linked to the question of faith and religious commitment is the situation of the cohabiting couple. The Irish Bishops in their Pastoral Letter, *Love is for Life*, speak of these so-called 'stable sexual relationships' or 'trial marriages' as recipes for future marital instability and infidelity.

> 'Trial marriages', instead of being a preparation for successful marriage, are instead a psychological and moral preparation for instability in a future marriage. Having each experienced the other's readiness for one tentative 'affair', a couple will find it more difficult to trust each other totally in a true marriage. They may even find it harder themselves to resist temptation to marital infidelity. There is no better foundation for trusting and trustworthy married love than for each partner to know that the other has had sexual relationships only with him or with her. Pre-marital chastity means being determined to keep the gift of oneself for the person one loves alone. It is the manifestation of true love (n 80, p 23).

The priest must always put before people the Church's moral teaching on this issue. She does expect chastity of her single members even though this might appear today to be old fashioned. She does so because she is convinced that there is no true love without discipline and that chastity allows one to see the other from the purest perspective.

Having put before them the Church's teaching the priest then invites the couple to reflect on their particular situation. A question or two put in the right spirit might help in this process, e.g. when you visit your parents' home for an over-night stay, do you live as man and wife?

The whole purpose of both the questions and the discussion is to help the couple appreciate the Church's position on this matter. Normally parents and other family members are happy that the couple are being challenged in this way and are ready to be supportive in whatever way they can. Challenging a couple to reverse their decision of cohabiting is in fact a call to conversion. It requires time, patience and community support. Hence, the vital role of the family and friends.

If the couple refuse to reflect seriously on their situation, the priest might explain to them that perhaps the more honest form of marriage ceremony best suited to their circumstances would appear to be a celebration of marriage outside of Mass.

x) Mixed Marriages:

The preparation, celebration and pastoral care of couples in mixed or interchurch marriages present the priest with a unique pastoral challenge. It requires great sensitivity, tact and skill and presents a special opportunity for ecumenical dialogue and co-operation.

The relevant norms and guidelines concerning mixed marriages are to be found in the *Directory on Mixed Marriages* of the Irish Episcopal Conference (Veritas, 1983) and in the *1993 Directory for the Application of Principles and Norms on Ecumenism* of the Pontifical Council for the Promotion of Christian Unity. It suffices here to draw attention to the following sections in these Directories:

- the pre-marriage promises to be made by the Catholic party (pp 17-18). The text of the promises reads as follows:

   I declare that I am resolved, as God's law demands, to preserve my Catholic faith, and to avoid all dangers of falling away from it. Moreover I sincerely undertake and I will, as God's law also requires, do everything possible, so far as in me lies, to have all the children of our marriage baptised and brought up in the Catholic Church (p 17).
- the permission of the local Ordinary of the Catholic party (pp 21-23).

- dispensation from canonical form (pp 25-26);
- liturgical celebration and participation by the clergy of the respective churches (pp 25-28);
- registration of mixed marriages and those contracted with dispensation from canonical form. The latter are registered in the Diocesan Offices of the diocese that granted the dispensation and in the parish of the Catholic party (c 1123 #3). The 1983 edition of the *Directory* relates the law existing prior to the promulgation of the l983 *Code of Canon Law*.
- pastoral care after marriage (pp 30-31).

Should there be difficulties with regard to the pre-marriage promises required from the Catholic party, the matter should be referred to the Bishop.

The 1993 Directory for the Application of Principles and Norms on Ecumenism, introduced a few notable changes in existing discipline. It lists for the first time the particular reasons which might constitute a 'just cause' for the granting of a dispensation from canonical form. 'Among these reason for the dispensation may be considered the maintaining of family harmony, obtaining parental consent to the marriage, the recognition of the particular religious commitment of the non-Catholic partner or his/her blood relationship with the minister of another Church or ecclesial community' (n 154). While the reading of Scripture during the course of a eucharistic celebration is normally reserved to Catholics, 'on exceptional occasions and for a just cause, the Bishop of the diocese may permit a member of another Church or ecclesial Community to take on the task of the reader' (n 133).

4. Celebration

Time: In the Diocese of Ossory marriages are not celebrated on Sundays or holy days of obligation or after 4 p.m. on Saturdays. If marriage is celebrated on a solemnity the Mass of the day is used with the nuptial blessing and, where appropriate, the special final blessing. The readings are usually a combination of those proper to the solemnity being celebrated and those given in the Lectionary for marriage.

The Church: Marriages are celebrated only in parish churches. The church should be inviting, well lighted, heated and hospitable for all marriages. No special honour or favouritism should be shown to any particular couple.

Place of Ceremony: Normally the couple are located in the sanctuary and the guests in the nave. Whatever arrangement is opted for it should be conducive to fruitful and active participation in the liturgy. In an unusually large church it might be necessary to re-arrange the seating or use another chapel or area within the church. The conventional division of the congregation into the bride's people and the groom's people is scarcely desirable. There is no such division at the reception later.

The Homily: The gospel is always followed by a homily which deals with the mystery of Christian marriage, the dignity of married love and the responsibilities of married people, keeping in mind the circumstances of the particular marriage. The homilist should be especially sensitive to the make-up of the particular congregation. It will include members of both families, other married couples, young people preparing for their marriage and people who may have given up the practice of their faith, as well as members of other Churches perhaps. The homily and indeed the whole wedding ceremony should be an occasion of grace and spiritual nourishment for all who are present at it.

Location of Couple: The traditional arrangement whereby the couple have their backs to the congregation scarcely does justice to the role of the congregation as witness. An alternative possibility is for the couple to face each other at least during that part of the ceremony where they are addressing each other. Such an arrangement makes for better visibility and greater audibility and participation.

Communion Under Both Kinds: For several years now it has been standard practice for the bride and groom on their wedding day to receive Holy Communion under both kinds. That privilege has now been extended to others present provided that in the judgement of the celebrant they have been sufficiently instructed about this matter. In the case of Mixed Marriages, celebrated within the context of Mass, the Catholic party might opt to forgo receiving Holy Communion.

Signing the Register: This is required by civil law. It takes place either before the final blessing at a table in the sanctuary (not on the altar) or in the sacristy afterwards. The altar is neither a writing desk nor a table of convenience.

In a letter to the editor of *Intercom*, 17 December 1989, the

Registrar General's Office, draws attention to the difficulties that can ensue if this form is not completed correctly. 'The procedure for amending a marriage certificate after it has been registered involves filling out Deposition forms before a District Justice sitting in the district in which the marriage took place and providing satisfactory evidence. The papers then have to be sent to this Office and the appropriate local Office for noting. This can be a time consuming process and can cause delays for the couple in the transaction of legal business in the future'. To avoid unnecessary difficulties the Registrar General suggests that the parties to the marriage be asked to check the Form at the wedding rehearsal, so that any errors can be detected and corrected at this stage.

Photographs and Video-taping: The Church's discipline on this matter is that 'great care should be taken to ensure that liturgical celebrations, especially the Mass, are not disturbed or interrupted by the taking of photographs. When there is good reason for taking them, the greatest discretion should be used and the norms laid down by the local Ordinary should be observed' (*Sacred Congregation for Rites, Instruction on the Worship of the Eucharistic Mystery, Eucharisticum Mysterium*, 25/5/1967, Flannery, vol I, p 116).

Photographers, to avoid any confusion or misunderstanding, should consult with the presiding priest before the wedding begins. Nowadays, there should hardly be any need for auxiliary lighting.

Concelebration: Any semblance of discrimination in favour of any family on the occasion of weddings is strictly forbidden. In some cases concelebration may be appropriate. Parish priests and administrators of parishes may permit concelebration on the occasion of weddings provided the following conditions are adhered to:

1) that not more than one priest of the parish where the wedding is taking place joins in the concelebration;
2) in the case of the four Kilkenny city parishes that not more than one priest from each of the city parishes joins in the concelebration;
3) that no extra stipend or offering be made merely for concelebrating;

Flowers: The use of flowers and plants, if arranged tastefully, can enhance the liturgical environment and the marriage ceremony. However, over-decoration and the placing of flowers in unsuitable locations can take from it. Artificial flowers or such decorations are better avoided.

Rehearsal: For an orderly and dignified celebration of marriage, a rehearsal is almost indispensable. In addition to the bride, groom and witnesses, all those having a special ministry at the wedding - readers, musicians, etc. – should be present for the rehearsal.

5. Particular problems and related issues

i) Validations:

A couple who have failed to comply with the requirements of canonical form (c 1108) may have their marriage validated in the Church provided no other obstacles stand in the way of its lawful and valid celebration (cf cs 1156-1160). The usual pre-marriage documentation is required and the marriage is registered in the normal way in the Church Register and civilly also if the couple are free to marry according to civil law. If the marriage has already been registered civilly (e.g. Register Office Marriage) a note to this effect is made in the church register and it is not re-registered civilly.

The couple should be prepared pastorally and spiritually for the sacrament of Marriage. At an opportune time they receive the sacrament of Reconciliation. In such circumstances the couple may opt for a marriage liturgy within Mass or a simple, semi-private celebration consisting of a liturgy of the word and the rite of marriage.

ii) Marriage in Church after a previous non-Canonical Union:

If a Catholic marries civilly or before a non-Catholic minister without the appropriate permission and dispensation from canonical form (c 1127 #2), he/she marries invalidly. Though strictly speaking canon law does not require a Declaration of Nullity by reason of Defective Form in respect of the former marriage (cf *Pontifical Commission for the Authentic Interpretation of the Code of Canon Law,* June 24, 1984) in practice such a Declaration is normally the best way of establishing with moral certainty that the previous non-canonical marriage was never in fact validated in the Church. This is achieved by having a search

MARRIAGE

done of Catholic Church records of marriage in the various parishes where the person lived for the duration of the previous marriage and the issuing in due course of the Declaration of Nullity by the Bishop.

Before assisting at such marriages priests should take special care to enquire about any natural obligations that the previous union may have created towards a third party and children (cf c 1071 #1, 3). The Church must not be seen as interested only in the second marriage while ignoring the welfare of the former spouse and children, if any.

With regard to the civil registration of the said marriage consult the guidelines given hereunder in Section iii, and seek competent legal advice.

iii) Marriage after a Church Annulment:

In addition to the standard pre-nuptial documentation the priest needs the relevant Decree of Nullity from the Court of Second Instance. This is filed away with the other marriage papers. In some instances the said Decree of Nullity may include a bar or prohibition against re-marriage. The Bishop alone may remove this prohibition or *Vetitum* and hence no plans or arrangements for a marriage should be made until this matter has been satisfactorily resolved. Priests should advise the person that this could take a considerable time and should refrain from taking a booking for the proposed marriage. Even if there is no such obstacle, the priest is required nevertheless to consult the Bishop before proceeding with such a marriage. The Church must be seen to be concerned for the natural obligations towards a former spouse or possible children of a previous union (cf c 1071 #1, 3).

Registration: These marriages are entered in the normal way in the Church Register but cannot be registered civilly unless the individual is free to marry in the eyes of the State, i.e. has obtained a civil divorce which is recognised by the State. In the event of the person not being civilly free to marry, the marriage is registered in the Church Register only. It is futile completing a civil registration surreptitiously or based on false declarations. Since such marriages cannot be recognised by the State the couple will not be entitled to avail of the various legal protections reserved to married couples, e.g. concerning inheritance entitlements for spouses (rights which will be retained by the first spouse), a marriage certificate and the benefits accruing from it. It has been suggested in the Dáil, for instance, that a wife's right to a barring order against a husband would not be available to a woman in such a situation. This matter would now seem to have been addressed by recent legislation. In any event, the couple should always be advised to seek competent, legal advice concerning the registration of children and property rights, etc.. Ultimately, it is the joint responsibility of the couple themselves (as stated on the reverse-side of the registration form), and not that of the priest, to see to the civil registration of their marriage.

The criminal law is another important consideration for those who involve themselves in a marriage in such circumstances. Any person who enters into a marriage ceremony while already married can be prosecuted for the crime of bigamy and if convicted can be sentenced to a maximum sentence of 7 years imprisonment. This applies also to the priest who officiates at such a marriage (cf M. O'Flaherty, 'The Priest, Marriage and the Law', in: *Intercom*, September 1990, p 5).

If the person who has been granted an Annulment has also obtained a civil divorce, it is assumed that it is the name by which the person is now known that will appear in both the civil and ecclesiastical registration of the new marriage. If the marriage cannot be registered civilly, the woman in question may opt for either her married or maiden name.

iv) Marriage after Church Annulment and Foreign Divorce:

Closely allied to the latter case is the situation of the party who has already obtained an ecclesiastical Decree of Nullity/Dissolution of a former marriage and a Foreign Divorce. In addition to the regular preparation – canonical, pastoral and spiritual – which is always required, the priest must be concerned that the said person is honouring his/her natural obligations towards the former spouse and possible children resulting from that union (cf c 1071 #1, 3).

A copy of the divorce decree should be filed with the pre-marriage documentation.

Registration: In order that the new marriage be registered civilly, prior recourse must be made by the party in question to the Registrar General's Office, Civil Marriage Section, Floor 2, Joyce

House, 8/11 Lombard Street, Dublin 2, requesting recognition of the divorce duly granted. A special form, available from the local Registrar's Office, must be completed and forwarded in good time to the Registrar General's Office, together with the Divorce Decrees, Nisi and Absolute, (and certified translation(s) into English, if necessary, and any other relevant details and documentation. The Registrar General will in due course inform the party as to whether or not the divorce in question can be recognised in Irish Civil Law. This procedure normally takes about three weeks and so it is preferable to have the papers submitted in good time. It is advisable to seek competent legal advice in this whole area.

v) Civil Law Requirements for Marriage in the Irish Republic: Minimum Age for Marriage in the Irish Republic:
The Marriage Act, 1972 determined that a boy or girl under the age of sixteen years may not marry validly, unless prior permission has been obtained from the President of the High Court or some other High Court Judge, designated by him. Application may be made by or on behalf of either party to the marriage, through the Registrar of Wards of Court, Four Courts, Dublin 7. Even if such permission is granted, there is no legal obligation placed upon any religious body to marry the parties concerned. The Judge will normally interview both parties and their parents or guardians, if possible. This service is provided free of charge.

Consent of Parents/Guardians of Minors: Section 7 of the same Marriage Act, 1972 provides that if either party to a proposed marriage is under twenty-one years (and not a widower, widow, or Ward of Court), he/she must have the prior consent of his or her parents/guardians (or of the sole parent/ guardian, if there is only one). This will normally mean that the consent of both parents is required. If there is no parent or guardian or if the said person cannot be contacted or traced without unreasonable difficulty, the requisite consent can be secured from the President of the High Court or his designate.

Where parental consent (or that of guardian) is refused or withheld, an application may be made – through the Registrar of Wards of Court – to the President of the High Court (or other designated Judge), who may, if he thinks fit, grant the permission necessary for the marriage. The Judge will normally interview the couple and their parents/guardians with a view to establishing whether their refusal or withholding of consent is reasonable or otherwise. This service is provided free of charge.

vi) Marriages of Irish Couples in Rome:

In recent years a number of Irish couples have travelled to Rome to get married. While this arrangement may suit particular circumstances, there is often little necessity for couples going to Rome for their wedding. Priests should gently discourage couples from making such arrangements by pointing out that their wishes can probably be accommodated by marrying elsewhere in Ireland. Should a couple wish to be married in Rome the following documents are required:

Church Documents: All the usual documentation is required for both parties. When assembled these documents are forwarded to the Bishop of the bride for his *Litterae Testimoniales*, and forwarding to Rome to the priest looking after the arrangements there. This documentation should reach him at least one month prior to the proposed date of the marriage.

Civil Document: This is known as the *Nulla Osta* document. Application for it must be made to the Department of Foreign Affairs in Dublin. The Department will forward it through the Irish Embassy in Rome to the priest nominated by the couple to make their wedding arrangements there. Hence, before requesting this document the couple should have the name of a priest in Rome who will make the necessary arrangements as well as the name of the church where they intend getting married. Most Irish weddings in Rome take place either in the Irish College Chapel, St John Lateran Basilica (near the Irish College), the Church of San Silvestro (Irish Pallottine Fathers) or St Patrick's Church (Irish Augustinian Fathers). Couples intending marrying in Rome should allow at least three months for obtaining and transmitting the necessary documentation to Rome. They should be told that there can be no wedding without the *Nulla Osta* document. Non-Irish citizens (i.e. holders of other than an Irish passport) can expect additional complications when applying for the *Nulla Osta*.

For further information contact:
    The Rector, Pontificio Collegio Irlandese,
    Via dei SS. Quattro 1, 00184 Roma, Italy.
    Tel 7315766 - 737295 - 736649. Fax 738453

MARRIAGE

vii) Marriages of Travelling People:

These marriages should always be referred to the parish priest for travelling people or to the person in the diocese responsible.

6. Ministry to the Family

The priest's ministry to couples does not cease on their wedding day. He should be concerned for the overall quality of marriage among his people. In particular priests should encourage and assist 'the various groups and numerous movements engaged in various ways … in the pastoral care of the family' (John Paul II, *Familiaris Consortio*, n 72, Flannery, vol II, p 876).

i) The Newly Married:

Newly Married couples in the early years of marriage often feel lonely and isolated. It is important that they be made feel welcome by the parish community and integrated into its various activities. The current Pre-Nuptial Enquiry form makes provision for informing the priest of the parish of the imminent arrival of a newly married couple.

ii) Parents and Children:

Parents need help in coping with issues that arise at different stages in their children's growth and development. Courses in the skills of parenting are encouraged. Apart from being of great help and benefit to parents, they provide an excellent means for lay people to exercise their prophetic role within the Church. It pertains to the priest in collaboration with parents and teachers to encourage and facilitate such courses in whatever way he can. He will already be involved in the pre-sacramental preparation of parents and children for First Confession, First Communion and Confirmation. The promotion of courses in parenting is the logical continuation of his involvement in the Christian education of parents and their children (cf D. Connolly, 'The Role of Parenting Today', in: *Intercom*, April 1984, pp 10-11). Finally, he will try to impress upon parents that they are the first teachers of their children in the ways of faith. In the school they learn about their faith, in the Church they celebrate it and in the home they live it.

iii) The Elderly; the Widowed; Single Parent Families:

Couples whose families have grown up and departed are often

subject to loneliness and feelings of no longer being useful to the community. They should be encouraged to get involved in areas of the apostolate formerly out of their reach because of work and family ties. Pope John Paul II when speaking of the specific mission of the older person in the Church and in the world refers to him/her as 'the symbol of someone rich in wisdom and the fear of the Lord (Sir 25:4-6)' and as a 'witness to tradition in the faith both in the Church and in society (cf Ps 44:2; Ex 12:26-27), the teacher of the lessons of life (Sir 6:34; 8:11-12), and the worker of charity (*The Vocation and Mission of the Laity, Christifideles Laici*, n 48).

Priests should show special concern for the widowed through their encouragement and support for them in their time of personal loss. This support should not be confined to the time of the funeral of their loved one. Bereavement is a long process. The priest through his pastoral care and concern can help in this healing process.

Unmarried mothers and single parent families need a pastoral care that is imbued with tact and sensitivity. They should be encouraged in every possible way to bring up their children in the practice of the faith and accompany them to the sacraments. Unmarried parent status does not in any way constitute a barrier to that person's full participation, sacramental or otherwise, in the life of the Church.

iv) The Irregular Union:

Not infrequently the priest will come across unions which in the eyes of the Church are irregular. It is important that the priest should visit such families. Great tact and sensitivity is called for because such people often feel hurt and rejected by the Church. Some have great difficulty in accepting why the Church can grant laicisations to priests and permit them to marry while denying the right of a second chance to a person who has made a terrible mistake with regard to his or her first partner. The fact that one is a matter of divine law and the other a matter of ecclesiastical law rings hollow to them. The priest's visit will provide an opportunity for both priest and couple to clarify the Church's position with regard to their particular circumstances and their own personal views and feelings on the issue. It is the duty of the priest to encourage the couple to seek an external forum solution by approaching the representative of the Regional Marriage Tribunal. It often transpires that some couples living together in irregular unions are in fact canonically free to marry but do not realise it.

The Irish Bishops' Pastoral, *Love is for Life*, adverts to the growing number of such unions:

> Many pressures in modern society lead to an increase in civil unions and unions without any form of marriage. When Catholics unfortunately enter such irregular unions, they still remain in the Church's care and must not be allowed to feel rejected from her love (n 257, p 84).

Pastoral care of such couples is both difficult and delicate. They may reject the priest's initiative and concern. Authentic pastoral concern challenges the priest to emulate Jesus in his encounter with the woman at the well (Jn 4:5-30). He entered into dialogue with the woman and brought her to faith despite her many attempts to evade the deeper issues concerning her life. He didn't postpone his approaching her until after she had straightened out her marital affairs. She was the object of his love and concern precisely as she was.

Sometimes, however, the particular problems are such as cannot be resolved through the external forum and the couple, because of their commitment to each other and their children, are not in a position to separate. In these circumstance the priest must 'make sure that they (the divorced and remarried) do not consider themselves separated from the Church, for as baptised Christians they can, and indeed must, share in her life' (*Familiaris Consortio*, n 84, Flannery, vol II, p 888). The Pope goes on to specify exactly how such people can share in the life of the Church:

> They should be encouraged to listen to the word of God, to attend the sacrifice of the Mass, to persevere in prayer, to contribute to the works of charity and to community efforts in favour of justice, to bring up their children in the Christian faith, to cultivate the spirit and practice of penance and thus implore, day by day, God's grace. Let the Church pray for them, encourage them and show herself a merciful mother, and thus sustain them in faith and hope.

> However, the Church reaffirms her practice, which is based upon Sacred Scripture, of not admitting to eucharistic communion divorced persons who have remarried. They are unable to be admitted thereto from the fact that their state and

MARRIAGE

condition of life objectively contradict the union of love between Christ and the Church which is signified and effected by the Eucharist. (*ibid*, pp 888-889).

Neither can they be admitted to the sacrament of Reconciliation until they 'are sincerely ready to undertake a way of life that is no longer in contradiction to the indissolubility of marriage' (*ibid*, p 889).

Some couples have great difficulty in accepting this teaching, especially those who have sincerely tried to save their first marriage and are subjectively certain in conscience that their previous and now irreparably destroyed marriage had never been valid. Indeed the Pope explicitly calls on priests to exercise careful pastoral discernment of such situations because 'there is in fact a difference between those who have sincerely tried to save their first marriage and have been unjustly abandoned, and those who through their own grave fault have destroyed a canonically valid marriage' (*ibid*, p 888). The Pope stops short of specifying the concrete consequences of this pastoral discernment, leaving it instead to the wise pastoral judgement of the individual adviser. Some pastors have already taken up this challenge.

Joint Pastoral Letter of Three German Bishops
of the Upper Rhine Province (1993):

In a joint pastoral letter (10 July 1993) three German Bishops (Karl Lehmann of Mainz, Oskar Saier of Freiburg and Walter Kasper of Ruttenburg-Stuttgart), in searching out this pastoral discernment, have noted 'that there cannot be a simple, smooth solution to the complex situations of divorced-and-remarried people' (*Origins*, March 10, 1994, vol 23, p 673). They acknowledge the limitations of canon law and procedural law in particular. 'It cannot', they say, 'regulate all of the often very complex individual cases' (*ibid*). With regard to discerning who should receive Holy Communion the Bishops call for the establishment of a 'pastoral dialogue' to determine 'whether that which is generally valid applies also in a given situation. This cannot be generally presumed, especially when those involved have, based on good grounds, satisfied their consciences of the nullity of their first marriage but no legal proofs exist to obtain a declaration of nullity from an ecclesiastical tribunal. In these and similar cases a pastoral dialogue can help those involved to reach a personal and responsible decision according to the judgement of their own consciences that must be respected by the Church and the congregation' (ibid). The role of the priest in this situation is one of accompaniment, helping the people in question 'to clarify and evaluate these various situations and circumstances' in which they find themselves. The priest is not in any sense to be seen as an alternative to the marriage tribunal. 'The priest does not pronounce any official admission in a formal sense' but in an unbiased way helps individuals sharpen their consciences in acknowledging their responsibilities (ibid, p 675). Ultimately the decision to receive Holy Communion 'can only be made by the individual in a personal review of his or her conscience and by no one else' (ibid, p 674) .

The above pastoral proposal clearly goes beyond what might be called the common doctrine and discipline of the Church in this matter. While the bishops in question would seem to be acting on their own initiative, it is nevertheless the collective teaching of the episcopate of an ecclesiastical province. Besides, two of the bishops in question are president and vice-president respectively of the German Episcopal Conference, and two of them are theologians of international repute (cf Ladislaus Orsy, 'Divorce and Re-marriage: a German Initiative', in: The Tablet 18 June 1994, p 787).

Rome's Reponse:

In September, 1994 the Congregation for the Doctrine of the Faith issued a Letter to the Bishops of the Catholic Church concerning the Reception of Holy Communion by Divorced and Remarried Members of the Faithful. The Congregation, while clearly having in mind the pastoral letter of the three German Bishops, reaffirms Church teaching as contained in Familiaris Consortio, n 84 and the Catechism of the Catholic Church, n 1650. It rules out what it calls 'a tolerant and benevolent pastoral solution in order to do justice to the different situations of the divorced and remarried' (n 3) indicating that the teaching of Familiaris Consortio on this matter 'cannot be modified because of different situations' (n 5). What is perhaps most significant about this Letter is that it now appears to preclude that invitation extended to priests 'to exercise careful discernment of situations' of 'those who have sincerely tried to save their first marriage and have been unjustly abandoned, and those who through their own grave fault have destroyed a canonically valid marriage' (*Familiaris Consortio*, n 84). The German Bishops identified this opening or invitation and proceeded to explore what they saw to be its implications. The Congregation for the Doctrine of the Faith now seems to equate this 'discernment' with the external forum of the Church, that which establishes objectively the nullity or otherwise of a particular marriage (cf n 9). It explicitly states that personal conscience cannot be considered the final arbitrator when it comes to deciding the existence or otherwise of a previous marriage and the value of the new union (cf n 7) because one cannot be in communion with Christ without being at the same time in communion with his Church (cf n 8).

Subsequent Clarification by the Three German Bishops

Shortly after the Congregation for the Doctrine of the Faith issuing its letter, 'Concerning the Reception of Holy Communion by Divorced and Remarried Members of the Faithful', the three German Bishops directed a letter of clarification to their respective flocks of the Upper Rhine Region.

They insist that the (the three Bishops) do not find themselves in doctrinal disagreement with the Congregation for Doctrine of the Faith. Rather 'the difference has to do with the question of pastoral practice in individual cases' (*Origins* 24 (1994) p 343). In defending their right to differ at this level they appeal to the traditional teaching of the Church which invokes both the concept of *epikeia* and canonical equity (*aequitas canonica*) when it is a matter of applying the general norm to concrete persons in their individual situations. 'It is not a question here,' they state, 'of doing away with the law that is in force or the valid norm. Rather it is a matter of applying them in difficult and complex situations according to justice and equality in such a way that the uniqueness of the individual person is taken into account. This has nothing to do with the so-called 'situational pastoral practice' (*ibid*).

The Bishops go out of their way to point out that they are not enunciating a new discipline on admitting the divorced-and-remarried to the Eucharist but merely facilitating them to approach the eucharistic table after appropriate guidance by a priest. 'The distinction between admission and approach is fundamental to us' (*ibid*). What they seem to be advocating is the toleration of an alternative pastoral practice rather than any change in existing Church discipline. They argue for a 'pastoral flexibility' which does not in any way threaten the indissolubility of marriage. On the contrary, they see it as their duty to uphold the generally valid doctrine of the Church as well as the unity of the Church while at the same time taking into account the spiritual well-being of people in existentially difficult situations.

What is significant about this letter is that the Bishops in question do not modify their earlier position despite the issuing of the Congregation's letter in the meantime and their 'thorough-going discussion' with the same Congregation.

By way of conclusion it must be said that the question of admitting divorced and re-married to Holy Communion remains a vexed and complicated issue. The recent advice given by the French Bishops on this subject is perhaps as much as one can hope for:

> Do what can be done in full communion with the Church rather than dream about the impossible. Peace of heart can be rediscovered, the path lived in union with the suffering of Christ. In their longing to return to the eucharistic table, some even rediscover the meaning of the much forgotten 'communion of desire' (*Pastoral Statement of the French Bishops*, 29 March 1992).

Finally, priests should remember that their stewardship does not involve taking responsibility for how people actually choose to live out their lives. Above all they must not be burdened with feelings of guilt in relation to those who reject their teaching or fail to respond to appeals to change their ways. To show compassion is not to condone the way of life a particular couple have chosen to adopt.

Blessing Irregular Unions:

With increasing frequency priests are asked to bless irregular unions or at least to acknowledge their existence in some formal way, e.g. by the celebration of a special Mass. Pope John Paul II rules out ritual and formal prayers that approach an official liturgical act. Priests are forbidden 'for whatever reason or pretext even of a pastoral nature, to perform ceremonies of any kind for divorced people who remarry. Such ceremonies would give the impression of the celebration of a new sacramentally valid marriage, and would thus lead people into error concerning the indissolubility of a validly contracted marriage' (*Familiaris Consortio*, n 84, Flannery vol II, p 889). The Bishops of the Upper Rhine concur with this policy in every detail and go on to warn that:

> Misrepresentations in such situations are almost unavoidable. This is especially true of special Masses celebrated at specific times, namely in conjunction with the civil marriage. In the interests of a specific pastoral care, the pastor can and must avoid public appearances of this kind. Divorced-and-remarried people must not ask this of him. One can express support in other ways such as through visits, discussions, letters and the like (*Op cit* p 75).

Recommended Reading:

The Rite of Marriage, Introduction and Pastoral Notes, Veritas, Dublin, 1980 (The introduction and pastoral notes are new and should be studied by every celebrant.)
John Paul II, *Apostolic Exhortation, the Christian Family in the Modern World, Familiaris Consortio*, 22/11/1981, Flannery, vol II, pp 815-898.
Letter to Families for the International Year of the Family, 2/2/1994.
Irish Bishops' Conference, Pastoral Letter, *Love is For Life*, Veritas, Dublin, 1985.
Archdiocese of Dublin, *The Pastoral Care of Marriage and the Family*, The Chancellery, Archbishop's House, Dublin, 1982.
Schillebeeckx, E., *Marriage: Human Reality and Saving Mystery*, Sheed and Ward, London, 1976.
Dominian, J., *Christian Marriage*, DLT, London, 1967.
— *Marital Breakdown*, Penguin, Middlesex, 1968.
— *Marriage, Faith and Love*, DLT, London, 1981.
— *Marital Pathology*, DLT, London, 1980.
— *An Introduction to Marital Problems*, Collins, London, 1968.
Gallagher, M.P., 'Walking with Unbelievers' in *Struggles of Faith*, The Columba Press, Dublin, 1990, 61-71).
Kasper, W., *Theology of Christian Marriage*, Seabury Press, N.Y., 1980.
Macken, T., *What is Marriage?*, Paulist Press, New York, 1982.
Reidy, M., *Freedom to be Friends: Morals and Sexual Affection*, The Columba Press, Dublin (Useful background reading for priests preparing people for marriage.)
O'Flaherty, M., 'The Priest, Marriage and the Law', *Intercom*, September, 1990, 4-5.
Magee, Brian (ed), *Readings for your Wedding*, Veritas, Dublin, 1995.

MARRIAGE

CHAPTER 8

The Celebration of Sunday

1. Introduction: The Centrality of Sunday

'Whenever the community gathers to celebrate the Eucharist, it announces the death and resurrection of the Lord, in the hope of his glorious return. The supreme manifestation of this is the Sunday assembly' (*Congregation for Rites, Instruction on the Worship of the Eucharistic Mystery, Eucharisticum Mysterium*, 25/5/1967, ch II, 2a, Flannery, vol I, p 117). Gathering on Sunday for the celebration of the Eucharist has been an enduring characteristic and hallmark of the life of the Church. From the very beginning of christendom Sunday and the eucharistic celebration have been inseparable. Participation in the Sunday Eucharist was regarded as the hallmark and authentication of being Christian. The Lord's Day and the Lord's Supper went hand-in-hand. Christians assembled for Sunday Eucharist not out of a sense of obligation but rather out of an inner conviction and a deeply felt spiritual need to share in the life of the risen Christ. This became real when they met together to relive what he had said and done. Sunday was primarily the commemoration and memorial of the resurrection. It was the 'original feast day', a kind of weekly Easter. By absenting themselves Christians felt they were cutting themselves off from the very source of life itself, i.e. the risen Christ. But even more importantly, they were conscious of diminishing and weakening the very fabric of the Christian community. Their overriding conviction was 'lest any man diminish the Church by not assembling, and cause the Body of Christ to be short a member' (*Didascalia Apostolorum*). We must try to recover these ancient insights in order to celebrate Sunday more fittingly.

i) The Sunday Liturgy: a barometer of faith

The Sunday liturgy is the celebration of the faith-life and charity of the parish community and for this reason the Catholic Church has always placed a high premium on participating in Sunday worship. In the mind of the Church, the liturgy acts as a kind of barometer of faith and holiness. Traditionally the sacraments were often used as a gauge of faith. Today the parish liturgy provides a coherent sign of its spiritual well-being. 'The Sunday Eucharist is the foundation and confirmation of all Christian practice. For this reason, the faithful are obliged to participate in the Eucharist on days of obligation, unless excused for a serious reason (for example, illness, the care of infants) or dispensed by their own pastor. Those who deliberately fail in this obligation commit a grave sin' (*Catechism of the Catholic Church*, n 2181).

Recent years have witnessed a decline in the number of people going to Church regularly. 'A common reason given for dropping the practice of Sunday Mass is boredom with the service. In an age when entertainment is much sought after and professionally packaged, boring the congregation must be avoided.' (T. Prior, 'A Living Liturgy ... Every Sunday?', in *Intercom*, September 1990, p 10.) If a person's experience of Sunday Eucharist is cold and uninspiring, the sense of community is weakened and the bonds of faith and love are diminished as a result. Consequently, no effort should be spared when it comes to preparing for and celebrating the Sunday Eucharist. It takes precedence over everything else a priest has to do in his parish during the week. It must never be displaced by other celebrations, e.g. weddings, etc.. Funerals which occur on Sunday should be handled with sensitivity. The Presider must do his best to integrate both the Sunday and funeral liturgy, especially in his homily.

ii) The Eucharistic Assembly: a sign of faith

The assembly of the faithful is one of the chief ways in which Christ is present in the Eucharist (*Vatican II, The Constitution on the Sacred Liturgy, Sacrosanctum Concilium*, n 7, cf Flannery, vol I, pp 4-5). Among the symbols that make up the liturgy, none is more important than the assembly of believers. We frequently underestimate it or we take it for granted. It is not merely in the eucharistic species that the risen Christ is given and received but also in and through the mutual presence of Christians to one another. Each person comes to the eucharistic celebration not just to be nourished himself/herself but to nourish others as well. We do this in and through our presence at the eucharistic celebration and above all by our active participation in it. If we are

not prepared to put something into the celebration, it is highly
unlikely that we will receive anything from it. If we come to our
Sunday Eucharist empty-handed, we will go away from it in the
same frame of mind.

The Sunday Eucharist, then, is the principal *locus* where Christians
share their life of faith with people proclaiming that same vision.
It is here that they are surrounded by the signs of faith. By
absenting themselves from the Sunday Eucharist they are separ-
ating themselves from these signs of faith and weakening the
faith fabric of the whole community. Not infrequently priests
meet people who claim to be believers but not church-goers. It is
difficult to fathom this apparent contradiction. How does one
respond to such people?

The Church is not just a spiritual reality and Christianity is not
simply a private and individual matter. In the Judeo-Christian
tradition salvation is essentially communitarian, i.e. we are
saved not as individuals but as members of his chosen people.
This is because God '... willed to make men holy and save them
not as individuals without any bond or link between them, but
rather to make them into a people who might acknowledge him
and serve him in holiness' (*Vatican II, The Dogmatic Constitution
on the Church, Lumen Gentium*, n 9, Flannery, vol I, p 359). The
liturgy is the primary locus which gives expression to this fact.
Indeed, it is worth recalling that the root-meaning of *Anamnesis*
(the ancient Greek word for what happens in the liturgy and in
the Eucharist in particular) is not 'remembering' but 'not forget-
ting'. We all forget, we all falter, we all need to be reminded regularly of who we are and what we are called to be. This takes
place in and through our Sunday Eucharist. If we are to grow in
our understanding and appreciation of the Christian life, we
need direction for that growth from the ecclesial community.
How are we to receive any direction if we deliberately cut ourselves off from it?

2. Preparation

Good liturgy doesn't just happen – it requires preparation, time,
commitment and pastoral concern. This preparation cannot be
confined simply to the liturgy. The liturgy is primarily a celebration of what we are and what we are called to be. If there is no
sense of unity or community among the people in the parish

before they come to Sunday worship, it is difficult to see how this can be created through the liturgy. If there is no sense of commitment to common values and ideals, this will be reflected in the liturgy. Ritual or liturgy merely gives public expression to what is already happening in our life. Liturgy does not create experience. Instead it brings experience to expression and endeavours to move it on to a new level. The trouble very often with eucharistic celebrations is not with the ritual as such – it can be clinically perfect – but with the failure of those participating to get in touch with their experience. The experience in question is invariably a series of dyings and risings. It may be a line of Scripture, a phrase from the homily, a piece of music or even a single word that makes that vital contact with one's experience. Hence, the importance of knowing one's people – their struggles, their cares, their joys, their hopes – in order to be able to touch their lives by what we say and do.

At the level of celebration, symbols and actions are the language of the liturgy and consequently the language of faith. Great care and attention should be given to these symbols, i.e. whether they be objects (light, incense, cross, book, water, bread, wine), spaces (arrangement of furnishings, location of people, processions, etc.), times (feasts, seasons, etc.), posture (standing, kneeling, bowing, genuflecting, processing, uplifted arms, joined hands etc.), gestures or actions (sign of the cross, laying on of hands, washing, blessing, receiving, elevating, sprinkling, offering, breaking, welcoming, gathering, inviting, greeting, proclaiming, praying, singing, keeping silence). Symbols well used and gestures properly executed nourish and deepen faith; symbols of poor quality and gestures carelessly executed destroy faith. Hence, a procession from the front pew to the altar is not a procession in the liturgical sense. Likewise, a miniature crucifix placed on a coffin and seen by nobody contradicts what a sign should be. It is of the essence of a sign to be seen. A stub of a Paschal Candle may emit the same amount of light as a proper candle but it lacks the splendour and beauty demanded by the very nature of the liturgy. Objects, gestures, movement and volume of one's voice should be according 'to scale', i.e. the size of the liturgical space and the number of people present. Liturgy will be according 'to scale' when the physical, psychological and spiritual needs of the particular community are taken into account. There is really no such thing as a 'generic' celebration.

SUNDAY

Liturgy must always be tailored to fit the particular circumstances.

i) Remote Preparation: the Liturgical Environment
The eucharistic celebration, as such, focuses on the altar, ambo and president's chair. These liturgical furnishings, like all other symbols used in the liturgy 'should be distinguished by a noble simplicity' (SC 34, cf Flannery, vol I, p 12). They should be the best the community can provide, exhibiting honesty and authenticity with regard to materials and craftsmanship. They should above all harmonise with one another and the whole liturgical environment. 'Marbleised' wood and other artificial materials should be assiduously avoided. They are unbecoming of the mystery being celebrated.

The liturgical books (Altar Missal; Lectionary; Rite of Baptism; Order of Christian Funerals; Book of Blessings, etc.) should be current and in good trim. Vessels, vestments and altar linen should be of a quality and condition befitting the celebration that is taking place. Priests are reminded that books (especially those in constant use) and vestments need to be replaced periodically. Shabbiness is to be avoided at all costs. These criteria should be observed not merely with regard to parish churches but also with regard to other churches and oratories where the liturgy is celebrated on a regular basis.

Indeed, the entire space and atmosphere for the liturgical celebration deserve special attention. A well-prepared space coupled with appropriate furnishings, vestments and books which are in good condition make for a more dignified and ultimately a more prayerful celebration of the liturgy. They invite contemplation and participation.

Attention to the physical environment in the form of appropriate lighting, good heating and sound system is indispensable. Like all other items, they should be the best that the community can afford.

The appropriate arrangement of furnishings is essential if one is to promote 'that full, conscious and active participation in liturgical celebrations which is demanded by the very nature of the liturgy' (SC 14).

Finally, the skills of artists and artisans in the parish might be utilised to bring out the diversity of liturgical themes being celebrated throughout the liturgical year. Flowers, plants and other decorative items, tastefully arranged, create an appealing and prayerful atmosphere. Flowers remind us that it is not our toiling or our spinning or our gathering into barns that are important in God's eyes but rather what we are. Banners and hangings of various sorts are appropriate, provided that the nature of these forms is respected. They are creations of form, colour and texture rather than signboards to which words must be attached.

Attention is drawn to the 1994 *Pastoral Directory on the Building and Reordering of Churches, The Place of Worship* of the Irish Episcopal Commission for Liturgy. It contains current thinking with regard to the reordering of churches as well as some very useful hints concerning the correct ordering of existing liturgical space.

ii) Proximate Preparation: the Parish Liturgy Group

The liturgy is the celebration of the parish as a believing community and not just of the priest alone. 'In the community which assembles to celebrate Mass everyone has the right and duty to take an active part, though the ways in which individuals do so will differ according to the status and function of each. Each one, whether cleric or layman, should do all of, but only, those parts pertaining to his/her office, so that from the very way in which the celebration is organised, the Church may be seen to consist of different orders and ministries' (*General Instruction on Roman Missal*, 26/3/1970, n 58, hereinafter *G.I.R.M.*, cf Flannery, vol I, pp 179-180). The smooth and dignified celebration of the liturgy requires that those exercising different ministries should be properly prepared. The celebrant must be part of this preparation. He can delegate this task only to an alternative presider. 'Presidency of the assembly begins long before the scheduled hour of preparation. It is the responsibility of the leader of prayer to take a leading role in planning the celebration with the other ministers and with all who have a special responsibility for the community's prayer. As one who will normally participate in the planning meeting, the leader of prayer must be equipped for this ministry by prayerful reflection on the Word of God, a solid mastery of the revised rites, and an intimate knowledge of the celebrating community'. (K. Hughes, *Lay*

Presiding, the Art of Leading Prayer, The Pastoral Press, Washington D.C., 1988, pp 41-42). A liturgy group trying to plan a liturgy in the absence of the presider is like a Cabinet trying to make a decision in the absence of its Leader. It does not work. Presiders are called upon to inspire and guide the planning process by the transparency of their own faith, their knowledge and understanding of the Church's prayer traditions and the liturgical year. A vibrant and active parish liturgy group can be of invaluable assistance to the priest in preparing ministers and planning the Sunday liturgy and indeed other liturgies also.

a) Readers:
Among the ministries requiring constant and ongoing attention and motivation is that of reader. What the ancient Christian writer Tertullian said of Christians many centuries ago, might be equally applied to readers: 'Good readers are made, not born'. They may acquire the basic skills through a short course of preparation but each time they read the Scriptures in church is a new experience and a new challenge. They must be helped to deepen their knowledge and appreciation of the Scriptures so that they may be able to proclaim them with ever greater competence and authority. It is strongly recommended that one of the readers be responsible for co-ordinating them and that they meet on a weekly or fortnightly basis to prepare and pray about the readings. It is only through praying over the Scriptures and taking them to heart that the reader will be able to proclaim them with faith and conviction. One of the priests should try to be present at their meetings to encourage and help them in this most important and demanding task. Besides, it can be an excellent sounding board for the priest in the preparation of his Sunday homily. The U.S. Bishops' Committee on Priestly Life and Ministry suggest such a format for homily preparation in their 1982 document on preparing the Sunday homily *Fulfilled in Your Hearing*, cf pp 36-38).

Readers should be encouraged to read the word of God from the Lectionary rather than from a missalette. Light and amplification should be adequate. A voice that shouts in a small church is as annoying as a weak and mumbling voice in a big church. Equally important is the pace and rhythm the reader uses. Reading too quickly expects too much of the listener; reading too slowly leads to apathy and somnolence. Posture and dress are also important because the reader is never there in a private capacity but as spokesperson for the word of God. Dress and deportment betrays the person's attitude to the word. Finally the reader should be taught to make use of silence. 'To speak or read without silence is to kill the word, converting the reading into a boring monotony. The pause helps assimilate the reading, it interiorises the word' (Spanish Bishops' Conference, 'The Ministry of Reader', in: *Intercom* December/January 1991, p 9).

Parishes are encouraged to avail of courses for readers organised by the *Diocesan Liturgy Committee* or indeed to take the initiative themselves to provide suitable training in the scriptures on an ongoing basis. Right now there is an intense hunger for the word of God among our people. Co-ordinators for readers should avail of scripture courses and workshops organised by the *Diocesan Adult Education Committee – Creidim.*

All scripture readings, with the exception of the gospel, are to be proclaimed by lay people. They may also announce the intentions of the Prayer of the Faithful. These norms still hold even though ministers of higher rank may be present (cf *General Instruction on the Roman Missal*, n 66, Flannery, vol I, p 182).

b) Music:

> Liturgical worship is given a more noble form when it is celebrated in song …. Indeed, through this form, prayer is expressed in a more attractive way; the mystery of the liturgy, with its hierarchical and community nature, is more openly shown, the unity of hearts is more profoundly achieved by the union of voices, minds are more easily raised to heavenly things by the beauty of the sacred rites … Pastors of souls will therefore do all they can to achieve this form of celebration' (Congregation for Rites, *Instruction on Music in the Liturgy, Musicam Sacram*, 5/3/1967, n 5, cf Flannery, vol 1, p 81).

In the liturgy and particularly in the area of sacred music the Church recognises the principle of progressive solemnity, i.e. from small and humble beginnings one can build up a more complete repertoire. 'A repertoire of well known, easy-to-sing hymns is within the scope of every parish. Gradually this can be enlarged and hymns suitable to the different feasts and seasons can be learnt. In this way confidence is built up and the problem of monotony overcome' (Vincent Ryan, *Welcome to Sunday*, p 69).

Congregational singing is clearly the ideal and goal. However, this is not something which is either easily or readily realisable. Hence, as the 1967 Instruction on Music in the Liturgy urges:

> Provision should be made for at least one or two properly trained singers, especially where there is no possibility of setting up even a small choir. The singer will present some simpler musical settings, with the people taking part, and can lead and support the faithful as far as is needed (Sacred Congregation for Rites, n 21, cf Flannery, vol I, p 86).

In parishes where there are choirs 'the directors of these choirs and the rectors of the churches should take care that the people always associate themselves with the singing by performing at least the easier sections of those parts which belong to them' (*ibid*, n 20, p 86).

When it comes to singing, preference should be given to the more significant parts of the Mass, especially the eucharistic acclamations (Sanctus, Eucharistic Acclamation, Great Amen) and Alleluia verse. To facilitate this each parish should have a number of cantors. The *Diocesan Liturgy Committee* and *Creidim* arranges courses and workshops for those involved in the music ministry.

With regard to musical instruments, the pipe organ or other instruments, provided they are suitable for sacred use or can be adapted to it, may be used. 'The use of musical instruments to accompany the singing can act as a support to the voices and render participation easier, and achieve a deeper union in the assembly' (*ibid*, n 64, p 96). Care must be taken to ensure that the presidential prayers of the Eucharist, the scripture readings and homily, etc. are never overlaid with music or song. When choosing hymns and music, care should be taken to ensure that they are of a sacred-nature and that they are in keeping with the liturgical season and the theme of the particular celebration. The theme will normally be taken from the scripture readings of the Sunday.

c) Special Ministers of the Eucharist:
Parishes should ensure that there is a sufficient number of duly authorised special ministers of the Eucharist who will help with the distribution of Holy Communion. When they were introduced in 1973, one of their primary tasks was to assist priests in

distributing Holy Communion so that it might not be unduly pro-
longed (cf *Congregation for Divine Worship, Instruction on Facilitating
Sacramental Eucharistic Communion in Particular Circumstances,
Immensae Caritatis*, 25/1/1973, n 1, Flannery, vol I, p 227).

Special ministers of the Eucharist are commissioned for a period
of three years, renewable for two further periods of three years
each. Training courses for new eucharistic ministers are held
each year during Lent in each of the deaneries so that the new
eucharistic ministers are ready for commissioning in their own
parishes and communities at the Mass of the Lord's Supper on
Holy Thursday.

Following the Eucharist on Sundays and holy days of obligation, it is strongly recommended that these special ministers
bring Holy Communion to the sick and elderly members of the
community who cannot be present. The parish should make a
sufficient number of pyxes available for this purpose. One of the
ministers might be designated to act as co-ordinator.

d) Commentator:
The *General Instruction on the Roman Missal* of 1970 makes provision for a commentator in the celebration of the Eucharist but
current thinking seems to be moving away from the idea. While
a commentator is hardly necessary at the regular Sunday liturgy, he/she can play a worthwhile role at a liturgy with which
people are less familiar, e.g. Easter Vigil. In particular a commentator can provide that unifying thread to a liturgy that
might otherwise appear disjointed. All commentaries, whether
by a commentator or presider, should be brief and succinct.

Ordinarily no one person should exercise more than one
liturgical ministry at a given Mass. Ministers should be present
for and participate in the entire celebration. This also applies to
the ministry of preaching. With regard to their placement in the
church, ministers should take their places among the people and
come to the altar as their ministry requires.

e) Altar Servers:
Altar servers are an integral part of the Sunday liturgy. Their
presence enhances the overall quality of the celebration. They
should be properly trained and attired for the role they play in
the liturgy. Since March 1994 Rome recognises the legitimacy of

SUNDAY

altar girls while still encouraging 'the noble tradition of having altar boys serve at the altar' (Congregation for Divine Worship and the Discipline of the Sacraments, *Circular Letter to Presidents of Episcopal Conferences*, 15/3/1994).

iii) Immediate Preparation:

To reduce the rush and 'busyness' that often precede the liturgy and detract from the needed recollection and preparation by the priest and ministers, it is suggested that each church have a trained sacristan. The sacristan will see to it that the liturgical environment (lighting, heating, sound system, liturgical books, vessels, etc.) is ready for the celebration and release the priest to concentrate on the liturgy about to begin.

3. Celebration

i) The Liturgy of the Word – telling our story:

When we come together at our tables for feasting and celebrations, we tell the story of who we are as a family and of our life together. We tell our tales of joy and sorrow, of good times and of bad, of promises made and promises broken. They help us remember who we are and who have gone before us. So, too when the Christian family gathers it tells its stories of faith, of hope and of God's presence to his people. These stories have been handed down to us. In their retelling we are strengthened and inspired to continue our faith-journey.

a) Proclaiming the Word:

Christ is truly present in the proclamation of the word. Hence, the Lectionary demands the same level of respect and dignity as the chalice and paten do. The Lectionary is the 'chalice' of God's word and should be treated as such. To read the word of God from a disposable missalette is like putting the Blood of the Lord into a paper cup. Missalettes are suitable for preparing the readings and for private meditation but not for proclaiming the Lord's word from them in the assembly. They should be kept out of the sanctuary. The Lectionary alone should be used for the proclamation of God's word. Proclaiming it from anything less devalues the word and enfeebles its effectiveness.

As a sign of the dignity of God's word, the ambo is especially reserved for the proclamation of the word. It is a primary symbol within the liturgical space. It should be fixed, somewhat elevated and of suitable design and nobility for proclaiming the word. Only the liturgy of the word should take place at the ambo (*G.I.R.M.*, n 272, Flannery vol I, p 192) – the presider takes his place at the president's chair for the entrance and concluding rites. A smaller, mobile lectern or stand may be used by the cantor and commentator (cf *Place of Worship*, p 28).

The presider does not read the gospel if he is accompanied by a concelebrant or deacon (*G.I.R.M.*, n 34, p 171). When present, a deacon seeks and receives a blessing from the presider, but another priest does not, unless the presider is a bishop (*Ceremonial of Bishops*, 1989, nn 74 & 173).

b) Gospel Procession:
The Church has always venerated sacred Scripture as it venerates the Body of the Lord. Hence, we speak of the two tables - the table of the word and the table of the Eucharist. 'This love of Scripture can only be made manifest by the honour given to the Lectionary, carried in procession between two lighted candles with incense, reverently kissed and placed on the ambo , saluted with song and with acclamation. The book of the Gospels should therefore be a distinct book, well printed and decorated to impress upon all the esteem we need to have for this book' (Spanish Bishops' Conference, *art cit*, p 9). Hence, a dignified gospel proclamation with candles and incense should be an integral part of the principal Mass on Sunday and on other special occasions. It serves to highlight the importance of the gospel message. Attention to sacramental symbols applies not only to things or objects but to ritual actions as well. Liturgical minimalism and an unyielding concern for practicality are the enemies of ritual.

c) The Homily:
The purpose of the homily is to nourish the faithful with the bread of the word. It should apply the Scriptures to contemporary experience and to everyday life. It is not an academic lecture on the truths of faith but a humble sharing of God's graces and insights. It should give hope and courage to people. 'At all Masses on Sundays and holydays of obligation, celebrated with a congregation, there is to be a homily and, except for a grave reason, this may not be omitted' (c 767 #2). One does not begin or end the homily with the sign of the cross as the homily is an integral part of the liturgy as such.

A recent survey (1989) sponsored by the Irish Episcopal Conference on preaching and the liturgy of the word makes the following observations: 'Homilies, should be brief, clear and audible. Many agree that the homily should interpret the word of God by applying it to life. Lay people prefer that preachers draw on their own experience to do this. Otherwise they like to hear experiences of fellow Christians. Storytelling is rated highly in this approach. Good homilies are brief (five to seven minutes), have one clear message, and interpret the word of God by applying it to daily life. Such homilies make use of concrete language, as well as illustrations, stories and images drawn from the experience of the preacher himself and of the congregation' (cf *The Furrow*, August 1989, pp 502-504). 'Apart from a prophetic jolt, what the people want from a preacher are enthusiasm, joy, encouragement .... People know too that the holiness of a celebrant gives a special meaning to a service; at the same time holy men preach long tedious homilies' (T. Prior, 'A Living Liturgy ... Every Sunday?', in: *Intercom*, September 1990, p 11).

Effective preaching presupposes that the preacher knows his people and the matters that are crowding through their minds right now - the fear of losing one's job, bad news from the hospital, etc.. The task of the preacher is to uplift people with a word of hope and consolation crafted from the word of God.

The liturgy of the word concludes with the Prayer of the Faithful. Care should be taken to preserve the integrity and structure of these prayers. They are prayers of intercession rather than prayers of thanksgiving and an exercise of the priesthood of the laity. In the Roman rite the classical model for this prayer is that of prayers of intercession on Good Friday. When introducing the Prayer of the Faithful the celebrant does not begin with 'The Lord be with you'. His words should echo the theme of the Scripture readings or the feast. The intentions themselves should not be mini-homilies, nor occasions for a particular message, and not divisive of the community. Excessive wordiness should be avoided. Books containing prayers of intercession should be used as aids and models for creating one's own prayers and petitions. While the prayers should be tailored to suit the particular occasion and circumstances, the temptation to over-localise them should likewise be resisted. The Congregation for Divine Worship in 1973 stated that it is inappropriate to conclude them with a Marian prayer such as the 'Hail Mary' (cf B. Magee, 'Prayer of the Faithful', in *Intercom* April, 1991, p 29).

ii) The Liturgy of the Eucharist – doing what Jesus did:

The liturgy of the Eucharist recalls the actions of Jesus at the last Supper: the priest takes the eucharistic elements at the preparation of the gifts, he blesses them during the eucharistic prayer, he breaks the host before distributing it and gives it during communion. However, it should be remembered that the Eucharist is not a dramatic re-enactment of the last Supper but a liturgical remembrance of it. Hence, the priest does not break the bread at the words of institution.

The eucharistic prayer is to be prayed with power and expression. The presider, with warm and generous gestures, leads the assembly in this great prayer of thanksgiving. He must create an atmosphere of reverence for the sacramentality of word, gesture and object. The people's response through the acclamations - Holy, Holy, Holy; Memorial Acclamation and Great Amen are of the greatest importance. They must not be allowed to become the sole property of the choir or cantor.

Insofar as possible the Holy Communion which is distributed at Mass is to be consecrated at that particular Mass. The unnecessary accumulation of consecrated hosts in the tabernacle is to be avoided.

a) Reception of Holy Communion – the different options:
On the tongue or in the hand: The reception of Holy Communion in the hand became possible in the early 1970s. In 1969 the Congregation for Divine Worship stopped short of giving blanket and universal approval for communion in the hand. Having consulted with Bishops throughout the world, the Holy Father decided not to change the existing practice. Instead he left it up to the particular Episcopal Conferences to seek such permission and to the individual Bishop within his diocese to implement it as he saw fit.

As the change in question did not pertain to the area of doctrine but merely to the domain of ecclesiastical discipline such permissions were readily given. Furthermore, the change being introduced was not something totally new but merely the restoration of an earlier practice already alluded to by Cyril of Jerusalem in the fourth century when he wrote:

When you approach, do not go stretching out your open hands or having your fingers spread out, but make the left hand into a throne for the right which will receive the King, and then cup your open hand and take the Body of Christ, reciting the Amen (*Mystagogic Catechesis*).

Reception of Holy Communion in the hand remained the standard and universal practice in the Church until the ninth century. Its disappearance was not unassociated with a new understanding of the Eucharist which saw it more in terms of an object to be adored rather than an action to be celebrated. Eucharistic piety of the period placed much emphasis on personal unworthiness on the part of the recipient when approaching the Lord in Holy Communion.

Today Communion in the hand is normal practice throughout the Church. It recognises the dignity of all believers. They too have been consecrated by Baptism and hence touching the host is no longer seen to be reserved to the 'anointed hands of the priest'. Besides, receiving Holy Communion in the hand is a more adult and hygienic way of doing so.

It should be remembered that the option of receiving Holy Communion in the hand belongs to the individual communicant and not the minister distributing it. Care should taken to ensure that the host is always distributed with due respect and reverence. The communicant receives the host on uncovered hands as the Eucharist is and must be seen to be real food. One does not eat with covered hands.

Of special concern is the case of young children. Care should be taken to ensure that the host is placed on the tongue before they leave the communion area. Parents of first communicants should be encouraged to discuss and decide with their child the manner in which they wish him/her to receive the host and in addition to take responsibility for the child in order to instil a sense of reverence and respect for the Eucharist. The communicant should place the host in his/her mouth before leaving the place of receiving. Priests in their teaching and preaching should from time to time remind people of how to receive Holy Communion with reverence and of the necessity of proper disposition (Congregation for Divine Worship, *On Holy Communion and the Worship of the Eucharistic Mystery outside of Mass, Eucharistiae Sacramentum*, 21/6/1973, n 23, Flannery, vol I, p 248).

Under both species: Although 'Christ whole and entire and true' (Trent, DS 1729) is received under one species alone, the Second Vatican Council permitted that, in certain cases, the faithful should be able to receive Holy Communion under both species 'in order that the fullness of sign in the eucharistic banquet may be seen more clearly by the faithful' (Congregation for Divine Worship, *Instruction on the Extension of the Faculty to Administer Holy Communion under Both Kinds*, 29/6/1970, Introduction). The occasions on which Communion Under Both Kinds were permitted were listed in the *G.I.R.M.*, n 242, (cf Flannery, vol I, pp 187-188).

In 1991 the Irish Catholic Bishops requested and obtained permission from the Holy See to make Holy Communion under both kinds more readily available to the faithful. The Rescript of the Holy See granting this favour specified certain conditions under which Holy Communion under both kinds may be given. It may be given on Sundays and Holy Days of Obligation and on weekdays if in the judgement of the Ordinary, Communion can be given in an orderly and reverent way. It may not be given:

1. At Masses celebrated in the open with a great number of communicants.

2. At other Masses where the number of communicants is so great as to make it difficult for Communion under both kinds to be given in an orderly and reverent way.

3. At Masses where the assembled congregation is of such diverse nature that it is difficult to ascertain whether those present have been sufficiently instructed about receiving Communion under both kinds.

4. When circumstances do not permit the assurance that due reverence can be maintained towards the consecrated wine both during and after the celebration (cf *Inaestimabile Donum*, nn 19-14).

In the final analysis that method of distribution should be chosen which ensures that Communion can be received with dignity, devotion and reverence.

When distributing Communion from the chalice care should be taken to ensure that the symbolism of giving and receiving is preserved. Thus, a eucharistic minister or somebody else designated by the priest should minister the chalice to the faithful. With regard to introducing Holy Communion under both kinds priests might find the following observations helpful:

SUNDAY

a) The practice should be introduced gradually, initially on weekdays and then at the less-crowded Masses on Sundays and Holy Days. In addition, special celebrations during the liturgical year might be marked by Communion under both kinds e.g. the Mass of the Lord's Supper on Holy Thursday and the Feast of Corpus Christi, the Easter Vigil, the feast of the patron of the parish and diocese, special parish celebrations, etc.. It is felt that by having Communion under both kinds at every Mass, even if it were feasible, would devalue the symbolism involved. The practice of Communion under both kinds should first be explained and introduced at the main Mass in the parish on weekdays. One could then progress to introducing it at the smaller Masses on Sundays, etc.. Experience tells us that this is the preferable approach.

b) The practice should be positively encouraged and promoted at small-group Masses, e.g. groups on retreat, prayer groups, house Masses, etc.. This could be invaluable in preparing people little by little for its introduction at parish level.

c) It would appear inadvisable for Masses celebrated in the context of First Communion and Confirmation. On such occasions one is likely to encounter a congregation of such diverse nature that it would be difficult to ascertain if they have been sufficiently instructed about receiving Communion under both kinds (cf art 3 of *Rescript of Congregation for Divine Worship and Sacraments*). The same would probably apply also to weddings and funerals. In these instances the matter is best left to the discretion and judgement of the priest.

Practicalities of distributing Holy Communion under both kinds:

a) The wine to be consecrated should be placed in a large chalice or pitcher or flagon of such design and quality as befits the celebration of the Eucharist. Like a chalice the pitcher or flagon used would be reserved for this purpose only. At the Communion of the Mass it is subdivided into a number of smaller chalices for distribution. (A number of small glass or ceramic chalices, polished on the inside to ensure they are non-absorbent would seem ideal for this purpose. There is a definite aesthetic merit in having all chalices of similar size and material. Besides, there is the advantage of both eucharistic ministers and communicants growing accustomed to a particular style of chalice more readily. Indeed, there might even be a value in recommending a particular type of chalice for general use throughout the diocese.

Because of its sign value and the need to preserve ritual honesty and authenticity, Communion from the chalice is always preferred to any other form of ministering the precious blood. 'Drinking from a shared cup is the full symbolic action: dipping the consecrated bread in the cup is not symbolic because it is not drinking. It also deprives communicants of the right to receive directly from the chalice' (E. Matthews, 'The Chalice and Hygiene', in *Intercom*, July/August 1987, p 14).

b) The chalice is always offered to the communicant with the words: 'The Blood of Christ' to which the communicant responds 'Amen'. That part of the chalice that has come into contact with the communicant's lips is always wiped with a purificator both inside and outside before being offered to the next person. This presupposes a good supply of purificators. Ministers should be reminded that there is little point in wiping the rim of the chalice with the same part of the purificator after each communicant. Finally, it is also customary for the minister to rotate the chalice slightly after each communicant has received. The chalice may never be left on the altar for the communicant to help himself/herself to it, nor must it be passed from one to the other. The Lord's gesture of giving us his body and blood must be preserved in symbol.

c) The right to receive or not to receive Communion from the chalice belongs to the individual communicant. The only exception might be that of children whom the minister might deem of insufficient age or maturity to have been instructed about receiving from the chalice.

d) A greater number of Ministers of Communion will obviously be needed. When Communion is to be given from the cup, generally there should be two ministers of the consecrated wine for each minister of the consecrated bread. In some churches the practice exists of ministers distributing Communion at different points around the church. This would not appear to be a realistic option with regard to the chalice. In a confined space the risk of spillage increases. The same must be said of Masses celebrated in the open with a large number of communicants. In fact the Rescript of the Congregation explicitly prohibits Communion under both kinds on such occasions.

e) Ministers of the Eucharist will need to familiarise themselves with distributing the consecrated wine. As a rule communicants and ministers alike tend to be more nervous when handling the chalice. Some chalices because of their shape and size may be unsuitable for this purpose.

f) Should there be a mishap, for example if the consecrated wine is spilled from the chalice, the area should be washed and the water poured into the *sacrarium*.

g) The amount of wine to be consecrated should be carefully measured so that none remains afterwards. It is forbidden to store consecrated wine in the tabernacle except for those who being ill are unable to receive Communion under the form of bread. Wine may not be consecrated at one Mass and used at another. Any consecrated wine remaining must always be consumed as soon as the distribution of Communion has finished.

h) All vessels used for the distribution of consecrated wine must be properly purified at the end of Mass in the same way as the chalice is purified. 'After Mass, all chalices should have their rims dipped in hot, soapy water, just as we would wash any vessel after a meal. Ceramic chalices can more easily be washed. It goes without saying that courtesy will suggest that those temporarily suffering from severe colds or cold sores, should refrain from the chalice while the conditions persist' (*ibid*).

Communion from the Chalice and the health factor:
People today are more conscious of hygiene than ever before and of the risks of catching communicable diseases by receiving from a common chalice. The U.S. Bishops' Committee on the Liturgy, on the occasion of introducing Communion under both kinds in 1985 consulted the then available medical opinion to be told:

> Since laboratory studies have shown that bacteria and viruses can contaminate a silver chalice and survive despite the alcohol content of the wine and wiping or rotating the cup, the potential exists for an ill parishioner or asymptomatic carrier to expose other members of the congregation by contaminating a common cup. If any diseases are transmitted by this practice, they most likely would be common viral illnesses such as the common cold, but transmission of other illnesses cannot be entirely excluded. During the past four years since AIDS has been studied, there has been no suggestion of transmission of the virus that causes AIDS by sharing utensils, including the common cup, or through any other means involving saliva.

We are not aware of any specific episodes or outbreaks of any illness that have been associated with use of common communion cup. However, it is important to understand that health officials would only become aware of health risk from such a practice if it resulted in the transmission of unusual diseases or large clusters of common illnesses and subsequent investigation were successful in determining the vehicle of transmission. Viral respiratory disease might be transmitted frequently by a common cup, but the association may not be recognised or the disease may be attributed to respiratory or other forms of person-to-person contact. We are not aware of any epidemiological studies that have attempted to study the importance of a common communion cup in disease transmission. The lack of documented occurrence of disease is reassuring that the practice is not gravely hazardous, but it should not imply that there are no risks.

In summary, we cannot quantify a risk for disease transmission by use of a common communion cup nor can we provide an absolute endorsement that the practice is safe (*Canon Law Digest*, vol XI, p 235).

From the chalice only: The present discipline concerning communion for coeliacs is that they receive from the chalice only. This should be done discreetly and with sensitivity.

The use of gluten-free hosts for coeliacs has long been the subject of uncertainty. On June l9th 1995 the Congregation for Doctrine of the Faith issued norms concerning their use. They area as follows:

1. Special hosts from which the gluten has been removed (*quibus glutinum ablatum est*) are invalid matter for the celebration of the Eucharist.

2. Low-gluten hosts are valid matter, provided that they contain the amount of gluten sufficient to obtain the confection of bread, that there is no addition of foreign materials and that the procedure for making such hosts is not such as to alter the nature of the substance of the bread (cf *Origins* 25(1995) p 192)

Communion Plates: Given the fact that many people today receive Communion in the hand, and the greater number of people distributing Holy Communion, communion plates would seem obsolete. Their use is often more a hindrance than a help. The 1970

SUNDAY

General Instruction on the Roman Missal omits all reference to them.

Mitigation of Eucharistic Fast: The current discipline concerning eucharistic fast is to be found in the 1983 *Code of Canon Law, Immensae Caritatis* (1973) and *Eucharistiae sacramentum* (1973). The faithful are required to abstain from all food and drink, with the exception of water or medicine, for one hour prior to receiving Holy Communion (cf c 919 #1).

Eucharistic Fast for the sick and housebound: The sick and housebound have always merited special consideration with regard to eucharistic fast. The current norms are to be found in the Instruction *Immensae caritatis*, 1973 and are as follows:

The period of time of the eucharistic fast or abstinence from food and alcoholic drink is reduced to approximately one quarter of an hour for the following:
a) the sick in hospital or in their homes even if not confined to bed.
b) The faithful advanced in age who must remain at home because of age or are living in a home for the aged.
c) Sick priests, even if not confined to bed, and elderly priests who wish to celebrate Mass or receive Holy Communion.
d) Persons looking after the sick and aged, as well as those relatives of the sick and aged wishing to receive Holy Communion with them, whenever they are unable to observe the fast of one hour without inconvenience (cf Flannery, vol I, p 231).

The spirit of the above regulations is such that the time factor is of lesser significance. What matters most is that the sick and housebound be permitted to receive Holy Communion without inconveniencing themselves and those who care for them or the minister of Holy Communion. Hence, if the minister of Holy Communion should arrive unexpectedly one does not have to wait until fifteen minutes have elapsed since the consumption of food or drink other than water. Such would obviously be contrary to the biblical notion of fasting from which the idea of eucharistic fast emanates. In the New Testament feasting is a sign of the Lord's presence while fasting is sign of his absence. Fasting creates in us a longing to be with the Lord.

A priest who has to celebrate more than one Mass on the same day is not obliged by the eucharistic fast (c 919 #2).

SUNDAY

Holy Communion twice on same day: It is now permissible to receive Holy Communion twice on the same day but only within the context of a full Mass (cf *Reply of the Pontifical Commission for the Authentic Interpretation of the Code of Canon Law*, 26 June 1984).

b) Lighting Candles around the Tabernacle:
The practice of lighting candles around the tabernacle during the eucharistic celebration at the distribution of Holy Communion is non-liturgical. During the celebration of the Eucharist lighted candles are placed on or near the altar which is central to the celebration. Lighted candles elsewhere only serve to detract from the central action taking place.

4. Particular Problems and Related Issues

i) Concelebration – Pastoral and Liturgical Guidelines:
Concelebration, which has been restored to the Western Liturgy since 1965 (cf Congregation for Rites, *Decree on Concelebration and Holy Communion Under Both Species, Ecclesiae Sempre*, 7/3/1965, Flannery, vol I, pp 57-60) manifests in an exceptional way the unity of the priesthood. It should be remembered that concelebration is a liturgical option, the use of which or otherwise depends both on pastoral and practical considerations. Insofar as possible it is something that should be planned and organised, and not haphazard. The following guidelines should be kept in mind when arranging a concelebration:

1) It is for the diocesan Bishop to determine concelebration policy for his diocese especially with regard to weddings, funerals, etc.. Any semblance of favouritism or 'renting' priests for the occasion must be avoided. That which is primarily an expression of unity must not be allowed to become a source of disunity, division and liturgical disorder (cf *G.I.R.M.*, n 155).

2) It is for the priest of the church in consultation with the chief celebrant, and in accordance with diocesan policy, to determine what is practicable. The overall dignity and decorum of the celebration must never be sacrificed in order to 'pack-in' more concelebrants. However, celebrants should be sensitive to the wishes of those who have come from a distance intending to concelebrate. Like any other form of ritual, concelebration too should be according 'to scale', i.e. the number of concelebrants should not numerically overwhelm the number of people in the assembly, nor should it ever be seen as a form of domination over people.

3) All concelebrants must be vested in at least an alb and stole. The chief celebrant always wears a chasuble.

4) In the entrance procession concelebrants are preceded by altar servers, (at an ordination by a deacon carrying the book of the gospels, followed by the *ordinandus*) and make the usual bow/genuflection as well as kissing the altar at the beginning of Mass. At the final procession the main body of concelebrants omit kissing the altar (cf *G.I.R.M.*, nn 163 & 208). This is to avoid confusion and liturgical disorder.

5) Nobody should join a concelebration after it has already begun (*G.I.R.M.*, n 156).

6) Ordinarily a deacon or concelebrant reads the gospel as this is a ministerial rather than a presidential function. The deacon asks for the blessing from the chief celebrant but a concelebrant only if the former is a bishop (cf *Ceremonial of Bishops*, nn 74 & 173).

7) The number of concelebrants that can be comfortably accommodated in the sanctuary area are located in this space while the remainder take up their positions in the front pews. They remain there for the entire celebration so as not to block the view of the other participants (*G.I.R.M.*, n 165)

8) Except when proclaiming that part of the eucharistic prayer assigned to him, a concelebrant is not heard. He recites that part of the eucharistic prayer said in common, in a low voice so as not to drown out that of the chief celebrant.

9) At a concelebration concelebrants should try to harmonise their gestures. It makes for a more dignified and aesthetic celebration. At the *epiclesis* all concelebrants extend hands towards the gifts with palms facing downwards. This is the only gesture required of concelebrants; the other gesture, that of pointing to the eucharistic elements during the words of institution is optional (cf *G.I.R.M.*, n 174 a & c).

All bow profoundly when the celebrant genuflects at the words of institution. During the *anamnesis* and post-consecratory *epiclesis* all concelebrants extend hands.

10) During the doxology, which concelebrants say in a low voice with the celebrant, only one chalice and paten are elevated. This is to bring out the symbolism of one bread, one cup.

11) The sign of peace should not be over-extended to the extent that it creates disorder.

12) The 'Lamb of God' is intended to accompany the breaking of the bread. This should be repeated as often as is necessary.

ii) Keeping Sunday Holy:

The celebration of Sunday must not be confined to attendance at the Eucharist. Sunday is the Lord's Day and should be kept sacred. It is the day in the week when we take leave of our daily routine in order to rest awhile. It is above all a day to be spent with one's family, a day for visiting relatives and friends or some elderly or sick person at home or in hospital.

In their 1988 Pastoral Letter the Bishops of the Tuam Province focus attention on the disturbing tendency to secularise Sunday. Sunday is a unique day - the Lord's Day; it is the day of Assembly for Christians for nearly 2,000 years and a day set aside for rest and relaxation (cf Sunday Celebration, in; *Intercom*, June 1988, p 7). While acknowledging that some people must work on Sundays, either because of economic necessity or because their particular job requires it, Christians should, nevertheless, when given the choice, opt not to work or shop on Sundays. Abstaining from unnecessary servile work is not something that has gone out of date. As a general rule, however, we must aim at preserving the sacred character of Sunday. 'We are strongly convinced that if Sunday were to become a full trading day it would have devastating effects on the day of the Lord .... The time that should be given to the Lord, to others, and to rest would be given to trading .... Sunday itself should not be traded at any price (*ibid*).

The new *Catechism* re-affirms the sacred nature of Sunday:

> Sanctifying Sundays and holy days requires a common effort. Every Christian should avoid making unnecessary demands on others that would hinder them from observing the Lord's Day. Traditional activities (sport, restaurants, etc.), and social necessities (public services, etc.). require some people to work on Sundays ... public authorities should ensure citizens a time intended for rest and divine worship. Employers have a similar obligation towards their employees (n 2187).

iii) Rationalising the number of Sunday Masses:

Recent years have seen the introduction of the vigil Mass on Saturday evenings. In many instances this means an additional Mass and an extra burden for all concerned with authentic liturgical celebration. With the population falling in many of our parishes and a decreasing number of priests, the time has come

SUNDAY

for reviewing the number of Masses needed in a parish at weekends. Sunday Masses should not be needlessly duplicated simply for convenience. With fewer Masses priests are more likely to approach the Sunday Eucharist with greater prayerfulness and enthusiasm. The reduction in the number of Sunday Masses allows a better utilisation of eucharistic ministers, readers, choir-members and musicians, etc.. Besides, too many Masses fragment the worshipping community and render full, active and conscious participation in the liturgy next to impossible (cf Congregation for Rites, *Eucharisticum Mysterium*, 25/5/1967, ch II, 2b, Flannery, vol I, p 118). It is difficult to preach with either conviction or enthusiasm to half-empty pews. On a very practical level, when it comes to holiday time, one is more likely to find a supply for a lesser rather than a larger number of Masses.

In reviewing the number of Masses needed, and arranging Mass schedules, neighbouring parishes should work in close collaboration with one another.

iv) Lay Preaching:

Liturgical preaching (i.e. in the context of the liturgy) is reserved to a priest or deacon (c 767 #1). As this matter pertains to liturgical rather than disciplinary law, the local Bishop may not dispense from it (cf *Pontifical Commission for the Authentic Interpretation of the Code of Canon Law, Private Reply*, 3/12/1987). However, in addition to the homily of the priest or deacon a lay person may on occasions preach at Mass, e.g. special appeals such as a mission collection , famine relief, vocations to religious life, etc.. In this instance the homily is not omitted. Rather another form of preaching is added for that special occasion. In some instances it might be more appropriate that the appeal be made after the post-communion prayer of the Mass.

During Church Unity Week ministers of the other churches may extend their greetings to the congregation or preach after the post-communion prayer.

The 1973 *Directory on Children's Masses*, permits lay persons to preach a homily to the children after the gospel, especially if the priest has difficulty in adapting himself to the mentality of the children' (n 24, Flannery, vol I, p 262). The 1988 *Directory for Sunday Celebrations in the Absence of a Priest*, permits the lay presider to give 'an explanation of the readings' or read a homily prepared by the pastor (n 43).

v) Place of Silence:

The place of silence in the liturgy is often overlooked. In order to hear and to listen, silence is necessary. Attention needs to be given to the importance of silence at the times designated within the celebration, such as the penitential rite, after the invitation to prayer, throughout the liturgy of the word and after Communion. The unnecessary proliferation of words, even if intended as commentary or instruction, as well as superfluous actions, detracts from the liturgy.

vi) Missa pro Populo:

Parish priests and administrators are bound on each Sunday and holy day of obligation to apply the Mass for the people entrusted to them (cf cs 534 #1 & 540 #1). Should a priest obliged by the *missa pro populo* obligation celebrate more than one Mass on a Sunday or holy day of obligation, he is, according to more probable canonical opinion, entitled to retain one offering for himself (cf c 951 #1). This interpretation is based on the norm that a priest is bound to offer Mass only for those intentions for which an offering has been made and accepted (cf c 948) and no offering as such has been made for the *missa pro populo* (cf R. A. Hill, 'Missa pro populo', in: *The Jurist* 44 (1984) pp 243-244 .

vii) Concerts in Churches:

On November 5, 1987 the Congregation for Divine Worship issued a letter to the world's bishops on the use of churches for concerts of vocal or instrumental music. The letter sets about working out a suitable balance between preserving the sacred character of the church building and opening its doors for concerts and musical recitals.

When particular churches are requested for concerts or organ recitals the priest of the church must first consult the Bishop before giving permission.

In the event of permission being granted the following norms should be observed:
- entrance to the church must be free and open to all;
- the performers and audience must be dressed in a manner which is fitting to the sacred character of the place;
- the musicians and singers should not be located in the sanctuary. The greatest respect is to be shown to the altar, the president's chair and the ambo.

SUNDAY

- the Blessed Sacrament should be removed and reserved in another suitable place.

viii) Notices:

The proper place for the reading of notices and making announcements is after the post-communion prayer and before the final blessing. They should be brief but sensitive to the needs of the community. Additional notices and information can be incorporated into the parish bulletin.

ix) Collections:

Particular groups who have the prior approval and permit of the *Gardaí* are entitled to take up collections outside the church gate but never inside it. They cannot be prevented from doing so. Nevertheless, such groups are not entitled to position themselves in such as way as to hinder or impede access to the church grounds. As a general rule collections are not to be taken up within a distance of twenty metres of all entrances to church property.

Only church-related collections may be taken up indoors. If there are two collections the first should be taken up at the preparation of the gifts and the second after Communion. The proceeds of special collections should be sent to the Diocesan Offices as soon as possible.

Recommended Reading:

The General Instruction on the Roman Missal, 26/3/1970, (G.I.R.M.), at beginning of Altar Missal or Flannery, vol I, pp 154-205.
Cong. for Sacs. and Divine Worship, *Introduction to the Lectionary for Mass* (2nd Ed.), 21/1/1981, cf Flannery, vol II, pp 119-152.
Cong. for Divine Worship *On Holy Communion and the Worship of the Eucharistic Mystery outside of Mass*, 21/6/1973, Flannery, vol I, pp 100-136.
Catechism of the Catholic Church, Veritas, Dublin, 1994.
Spanish Bishops' Conference 'The Ministry of Reader', in: *Intercom*, December 1990/January 1991, pp 8-9.
Smolarski, D.C., *How not to Say Mass*, Paulist Press, New York/Mahwah, 1986.
Kavanagh, A., *Elements of Rite*, Pueblo, New York, 1982.
Emminghaus, J.H., *The Eucharist, Essence, Form, Celebration*, Liturgical Press, Collegeville, 1978.

SUNDAY

Ryan, V., *Welcome to Sunday*, Veritas, Dublin, 1980.

Swayne, S., *Communion, The Rite of Mass*, Veritas, Dublin, 1980.

Matthews, E., 'The Chalice and Hygiene', in *Intercom*, July/August 1987, pp 13-14.

Prior, T., 'A Living Liturgy ... Every Sunday?', in *Intercom*, September 1990, pp 10-11.

Bredin, E., *Praxis and Praise*, The Columba Press, Dublin, 1994.

CHAPTER 9

Diocesan and Parochial Administration

1. Ownership of Church Property

The Diocese as a whole and each individual parish within it are owners of certain temporal goods and properties. These goods and properties belong to the juridical person which has lawfully acquired them. Physical persons are never the subjects of ownership of Church property, but only its administrators or stewards. The Bishop in the diocese (c 393) and parish priests in their respective parishes (c 532) are entrusted with the task of administering these temporal goods and safeguarding them on behalf of God's People. Together with other artifacts these constitute the Church's patrimony.

2. Administration of Church Property

Administrators of Church property are charged with managing it in a way that is consistent with the teachings of the Church, the needs of God's People and the norms of Canon Law (cs 1276-1289). In discharging this task administrators of property are assisted by various structures and committees.

i) Ossory Diocesan Trust:

This is a Body Corporate, which by virtue of a licence issued under and having effect by virtue of the Companies Act 1963, is registered under that Act without the addition of the word 'limited' or 'Teoranta' and is a qualified person within the meaning of Section 45 #1 (v) of the Land Act 1965. Its Registration No is 66457.

All properties acquired by parishes in the diocese must be registered in the name of this Trust. In the event of there being any transactions concerning parish buildings or lands currently not registered in the name of the Trust, the property should be transferred into it. In this way it is hoped that all parish and diocesan property will eventually be registered in the name of the Trust.

ii) Diocesan Finance Committee:

This Committee was established in the diocese in 1965. It is a mandatory body (c 492) whose function it is to monitor diocesan finances and investments. It assists the Bishop in drawing up an annual budget of income and expenditure for the diocese and advises him in all areas pertaining to finances, etc.. Presently it consists of seven priests and seven lay people. The Bishop needs its consent together with that of the College of Consultors to alienate property (cf c 1292 #2), the market value of which lies between £100,000 and £1m pounds sterling (cf 'The Decrees of the Irish Episcopal Conference' , No 17, in: *Intercom*, December 1987/January 1988, pp 12-13). In addition the Bishop must consult it before carrying out acts of administration of property which, in the light of the financial situation of the diocese, are of major significance (cf c 1277).

iii) Diocesan Deposit and Loans Scheme:

This scheme was established in the diocese in 1982. It acts as a kind of agency through which parishes with surplus finances at a given time can be of practical assistance to parishes needing to loan money for building and renovation purposes. The parish investing the money receives only slightly less than the going bank rate while the borrower pays considerably less than the commercial lending rate. It is monitored by the Diocesan Finance Committee and its success obviously depends upon the extent to which parishes with surplus funds at their disposal are prepared to use it. Ultimately it works for the good of the diocese as a whole. In a very real way it gives tangible expression to the notion of the diocese as a 'communio' of God's people.

Any parish wishing to invest in this Scheme or obtain a loan from it, should contact the Diocesan Offices.

iv) Parish Finance Committee:

In each parish there is to be a finance committee to help the parish priest in the administration of the goods of the parish, ...' (c 537). This Committee is required by Canon Law. Its purpose is to advise the Parish Priest/Team Leader in all areas pertaining to the financial management and administration of parochial property and goods. This entails advising and helping the Parish Priest/Team Leader in matters such as:

  - compiling an accurate and up-to-date inventory of all

parochial property and equipment;
- drawing up an annual budget of income and expenditure for the parish;
- preparing the Parish Account Book;
- safeguarding the ownership of parish goods and property; - the acquisition and alienation of parish goods and property;
- adequate security, insurance and fire-safety precautions for all buildings and properties for which the parish has responsibility;
- operating a parish fund-raising policy. Care should be taken to ensure that whatever form of fundraising undertaken is within the parameters of the law (cf M. O'Flaherty, 'Fundraising and the Law', in: *Intercom* December 1991/January 1992, p 20).

Each parish is to have one Parish Finance Committee for the whole parish. The Parish Priest and the Curate(s) of the parish are members of it *ex officio* as well as at least four lay people, two of whom should be women. The Committee meets at least three times a year and matters discussed at meetings are to be kept confidential, unless otherwise advised by the Committee.

The Parish Priest or his delegate is chairman of the Committee. Other relevant norms and guidelines governing these Committees are to be found in Appendix II at the end of this *Directory*.

3. Church Property

The Church's property consists of buildings, lands, monuments, cemeteries, registers, books, manuscripts, and other artifacts of religious, cultural or historical value such as chalices, monstrances, vestments, works of art, etc..

i) Acquisition and Alienation of Parish Property:

Before acquiring or disposing of any land or property, the parish must obtain the prior permission of the Bishop. No agreements, verbal or otherwise, should be entered into without this permission. It pertains to the Bishop in consultation with the Diocesan Buildings and Properties Committee to sanction the acquisition or alienation of all parochial lands or properties. It likewise pertains to him to convey this information to the parish concerned. All lands or property acquired must be registered in the name of the *Ossory Diocesan Trust*, Reg No 66457. It is the policy of the diocese to divest itself of lands and properties surplus to parish needs in the present and in the future insofar as these can be reasonably forseen.

ii) Building or Renovating:

Before architects are asked to draw up detailed plans for the construction or renovation of parochial buildings, the advice of the *Diocesan Buildings and Properties Committee* and the permission of the Bishop must be sought. Requests of this nature should be submitted in writing to the Diocesan Office in good time together with sketch plans for the proposed project. This will enable members of the Committee to visit the location in question prior to the meeting. The dates on which the Buildings and Properties Committee meet are published annually in the *Ossory Diocesan Directory*. Priests' attention is drawn to the fact that all projects costing £10,000 or more, irrespective of the origin of the funds, require prior episcopal approval, as indeed does all internal restructuring of parochial houses.

When building or renovating priests should be conscious that they are not merely carrying out this work for themselves but also for their successors. Work should be carried out to a taste and standard acceptable to other priests and people. Hence, personal likes and idiosyncrasies should not find expression in parochial buildings.

Churches and Sanctuaries: Of particular concern is the building and renovation of churches and sanctuaries. Providing a proper, aesthetic and worthy environment for worship ranks among the primary tasks of every priest. When contemplating structural changes and renovations of the worshipping environment, the priest's attention is drawn to the 1994 *Pastoral Directory on the Building and Reordering of Churches, The Place of Worship*, published by the Irish Episcopal Commission for the Liturgy. Both priests and people engaged in church building or renovation should consult and study the relevant sections of that *Directory*.

Priests and Religious Superiors who intend changing sanctuaries must submit architects plans for specific episcopal approval before proceeding with the work. All materials used in both construction, alteration and furnishing of the liturgical environment should be characterised by their nobility and simplicity. Shoddiness and shortcuts with regard to materials or craftsmanship must be avoided at all costs.

ADMINISTRATION

Sacred places frequently contain items of Christian heritage which deserve special respect and care. Such items may be altars, tabernacles, ambos, communion rails, baptismal fonts, Stations of the Cross, altar plates, stained glass, mural paintings and monuments to the dead. When refurbishing and renovating churches great tact and sensitivity is called for so as not to offend the sensibilities of donor's or their relatives. This holds true also for other monuments of the Christian heritage.

With regard to the proper preservation of stained-glass windows, storm-glazing may be necessary, especially if the windows are the work of well-known artists.

When disposing of surplus church furnishings (e.g. pews, altars, stations of the cross) every effort should be made to ensure that their future use be in a sacred rather than a secular environment.

iii) Planning Permission:

Planning permission is required for the construction of all new buildings and for structural alterations of existing ones. This must be obtained from the local statutory Planning Authority of the area where the building is to be located. The requisite planning guidelines and applications can be obtained from the the the Secretary, Planning Section, of the appropriate local authority.

Planning permission can be sought in different ways:
a) Full Planning Permission so that the project may commence as soon as the permission is given;
b) Outline Planning Permission means that the Planning Authority is asked to make known its attitude to the proposed development. It does not authorise the commencement of the development. In this instance the applicant needs the approval of the Planning Authority before commencing the project.

In the event of planning permission being refused, or what the applicant considers inhibiting conditions or restrictions being attached, appeal may be made to *An Bord Pleanála*.

The obtaining of outline planning permission is probably the most effective approach to any development. This is done by forwarding in triplicate an Ordnance Survey map of the location in question together with the request to build or extend the facility in question (i.e. church, school, house, etc.). Notice must also

14

be put in the local paper or national paper or displayed in position on the site for a month. At the stage when approval is sought, an architect or at least a draughtsman's service is required. Great care should be taken to ensure that he (the architect or draughtsman) clearly understands his terms of reference. The advice and expertise of a competent member of the Parish Finance Committee can be of invaluable assistance in this regard. The Diocesan Clerk of Works is also available to act on any construction project to ensure that the work is carried out according to specification and standards submitted in the tender.

iv) Maintenance of Church Property:

The proper maintenance of Church and parish buildings is the concern of the entire parish community. It is in the interest of the whole community at both parish and diocesan level to ensure that buildings do not fall into serious disrepair necessitating large capital expenditure. To ensure that all parochial buildings are kept up to standard and in a sound state of preservation, and in order to offset extensive renovations at a future date, a detailed report on same must be submitted to the Diocesan Offices every seven years. This report is presented to the members of the Buildings and Properties Committee for their consideration. The appropriate forms are available from the Diocesan Offices. The particular parishes required to submit reports are published in the *Ossory Diocesan Directory* at the beginning of each year.

Parish lands not being used by the parish should be rented out at a competitive rate through a proper legal agreement drawn up by a solicitor. This is to ensure that the parish receives a realistic income from its assets and that the tenant does not acquire any rights over and above those guaranteed in the agreement. If it is foreseen that such lands are unlikely to be of use to the parish in the future, it is diocesan policy to dispose of same.

Fire Safety and Security: People today are more conscious of the hazards of fire than ever before. Parish halls in particular should meet current fire safety standards and regulations for public buildings. Lightning conductors where deemed necessary should be attached to church buildings and spires. Security of church buildings and priests' houses is a matter of urgency. Burglar alarms are to be installed in every house with some form of 'panic' button to summon help quickly in the event of attack. Different types of alarm systems are available.

ADMINISTRATION

Proper safes should be installed in all priests' houses. It is strongly recommended that these be either bolted to the floor or embedded in the wall. Excess cash, especially that accruing from collections should not be kept in the house for any longer than necessary. It must be deposited in the bank as soon as possible after collection.

Insurance: All church buildings, properties and any other items of considerable value must be adequately insured against fire and theft.

Cemeteries: 'Where possible, the Church is to have its own cemeteries ...' (c 1240 #1). The manner in which cemeteries are kept is an indication of the community's respect for its dead. Priests might motivate people to maintain their family graves and ask them not to place on or around graves structures which make cemetery maintenance difficult and awkward. Public Mass for the deceased might be celebrated in the cemetery once a year.

4. Safeguarding the Christian Heritage

In addition to buildings and lands, the Church has inherited several other items pertaining to the Christian heritage. These include Registers, Documents, Books and other Artifacts such as chalices, monstrances, ciboria, vestments, etc..

i) Registers:

The status of people within the Church is recorded in Church Registers. Apart from supplying important data to the priest, registers constitute part of our cultural and religious heritage. It is the duty of every priest to safeguard this valuable heritage by taking good care of old registers and making the appropriate entries in current ones.

In each parish there are to be registers of Baptism, Confirmation and Marriage. It is the responsibility of the parish priest to ensure that entries are accurately made and that the registers are properly cared for and preserved (cf c 535 #1). To ensure this the following guidelines are to be observed:

a) Entries should be made as soon as possible after the religious ceremony. In particular the priest's attention is directed to the canonical requirement of sending notification of marriage to the place of baptism of the spouses (cf c 1122 #2) and of ensuring that marriages contracted with a dispensation from canonical form are registered in the parish of the Catholic party (cf c 1121 #3).

Such registrations are of vital importance when it comes to determining the freedom or otherwise of people to marry.

In addition to the above, the following matters are to be recorded in their appropriate registers:
- Baptism (cs 877 & 878) ;
- Confirmation (cs 895 - 896) ;
- Marriage and marriage dispensations (cs 1121-1123; 1081);
- decree of nullity and dissolution; non-consummation; prohibition against re-marriage (cs 1123; 1685 & 1706);
- sacred Orders (cs 1053 & 1054).

(For further information concerning registration in particular circumstances consult the relevant sacrament in this Directory). On the occasion of Confirmation in the parish the Bishop will inspect all current parochial registers (cf c 535 #4).

b) Registers should be kept in a fire-proof and damp-proof place. Being confidential documents, they should be locked away in a secure place. The Parish Priest is to take care that they do not fall into unauthorised hands (cf c 535 #5). Generally speaking, access to current church records is restricted to the person in question or his/her immediate relative, e.g. parent.
c) Surnames and first names (of the baptised, confirmed, married, ordained and professed) should be written in capital letters. All other information should be written in legible handwriting.
d) Good quality, non-fading ink should be used.
e) No alterations may be made in an existing document without the expressed permission of the Bishop and then only by way of adding to what is already there for the sake of clarification.

Old Registers: Old registers constitute an invaluable part of our Christian and cultural heritage. Every effort should be made to ensure that they do not become damaged through overexposure to light, etc.. Faded writing cannot be restored except by means of a specialised process used on valuable manuscripts. The practice of indexing and computerising old registers is to be commended. However, before embarking on any such project the Bishop should be consulted.

ii) Documents:
a) Property Documents: All deeds, and important evidence relating to ownership of churches, presbyteries, parish halls and lands should be forwarded to the Diocesan Office for safe keeping.

ADMINISTRATION

b) Parish Inventory: In accordance with the Norms for Parish Finance Committees of the diocese, the parish shall have in its files an up-to-date and comprehensive inventory of all parochial property and equipment. A copy of this is to be sent to the Diocesan Office to be lodged in the diocesan archives (cf c 1283 #2 & 3).

iii) Books:

a) To preserve the dwindling number of *The History and Antiquities of the Diocese of Ossory* (William Carrigan) in the ownership of priests of the diocese, priests should not sell them or give them to anybody other than diocesan priests or to St Kieran's College. Executors of wills should take particular note of this.

b) Insofar as possible other books of local and historical interest should be bought by and retained by the parish in question.

iv) Artefacts:

Chalices, monstrances, etc. distinguished by reason of age, artistic beauty or financial value should, when not in use, be kept in a locked safe. Particular attention should be given to those of great cultural and historical value. It may indeed be necessary to withdraw them from regular use.

5. Collections

Almsgiving: Almsgiving is an integral part of being Christian (cf Paul VI, *Apostolic Constitution on Penance, Paenitemini* 17/2/1966, Flannery vol II, pp 1-12). Since Apostolic times it has been customary to take up a Sunday collection on behalf of the poor and needy (cf 1 Cor 16:2). Many parishes have branches of the St Vincent de Paul Society. This Society depends entirely on the voluntary contributions of the faithful, taken up through parish collections. In parishes where the St Vincent de Paul Society does not exist, alternative structures should be provided to help the poor and needy. Every parish has its own share of poor and needy people.

Support of the Clergy: Priests should periodically remind the faithful of their 'obligation to provide for the needs of the Church, so that the Church has available to it those things which are necessary for divine worship, for apostolic and charitable work and for the worthy support of its ministers' (c 222 #1). A

ADMINISTRATION

number of collections each year enable the faithful to fulfil this obligation.

6. Wills

Priests' Wills: The attention of priests is directed to n 325 of the Maynooth Statutes.

a) Priests must place a valid Will in the Diocesan Archives. It must be renewed every 10 years. At least one executor must be a priest of the diocese.

b) Wills should be drawn up by a solicitor whose name and address must be shown on the envelope containing the Will with the date of execution and names of executors.

c) The priest executor is responsible for ensuring that the death of the priest is registered. One copy of the Death Certificate must be sent to the Diocesan Office.

Lay People's Wills: Except in case of necessity priests should not involve themselves in the making of lay people's wills (Maynooth Statues, 1956, no 36).

7. Foundation Masses

Pious Foundations exist in some parishes. The Mass obligations arising from them are celebrated at double the diocesan stipend or offering (Maynooth Statutes, n 328). Nobody may accept or establish a Pious Foundation without the prior written permission of the Bishop (cf c 1304 #1). In future such Foundations are established for a period not exceeding 20 years.

8. Parish Computer

Some priests are making increasing use of computers for the keeping of parish records, accounts and other data. The practice is highly commended. In order to reap maximum benefit and use out of such data priests might consult with one another before embarking on this task. They are encouraged to seek competent advice as to the type of computer that will best serve their needs and that of their successors in the parish. Finally, attention is drawn to the terms of the Data Protection Act 1988. Anybody keeping on computer personal data relating to racial origin, political opinions or religious beliefs and physical or mental health are required by law to register with the Data Protection Commissioner. Registration forms and a Guide to the Act are available on request from:

Office of the Data Protection Commissioner,
Earl Court,
Adelaide Road,
Dublin 2.

Recommended Reading:

Irish Episcopal Commission for Liturgy, *The Place of Worship*,
Veritas, Dublin, 1994.

ADMINISTRATION

CHAPTER 10

Religious in the Parish and in the Diocese

Many parishes are blessed by the presence of Religious Priests, Brothers, and Sisters. Some assist in running parishes, others work in the field of education and still others in a wide range of caring ministries. The spiritual and material well-being of our people is greatly enriched and enhanced by their presence and their work. We are, all of us, Diocesan and Religious, partners in carrying out the Lord's work. Co-operation and collaboration, therefore, should be the hallmarks of the relationship between diocesan priests and Religious in the diocese or as St Paul would have it: 'there must be no competition among you, no conceit; but everybody is to be self-effacing. Always consider the other person to be better than yourself, so that nobody thinks of his own interests first but everybody thinks of other people's interest instead. In your minds you must be the same as Christ Jesus' (Phil 2:3-5).

All of us together are working in the same vineyard for the good of the Lord's people.

> Between diocesan clergy and religious communities, efforts should be made to create new bonds of fraternity and co-ordination (CD 35 #5). Great importance should therefore be attached to such ways and means, including simple and informal ones, as may serve to increase mutual trust, apostolic solidarity and 'fraternal harmony' (ES I, 28) (Congregation for Religious and Secular Institutes, *Directives for Mutual Relations between Bishops and Religious in the Church, Mutuae Relationes*, 23/4/1978, n 37, Flannery, vol II, p 232).

1. Areas of Co-Responsibility and Collaboration

i) Apostolic Work:

Changing pastoral circumstances coupled with a decline in the number of people entering religious life has necessitated the un-

RELIGIOUS

dertaking of new forms of apostolate for some religious institutes. While regretting the fact that many institutes are finding it increasingly difficult if not impossible to continue in their traditional apostolates such as teaching, health-care and social services, etc. the Church welcomes the new apostolic initiatives being undertaken by these institutes. Some are in the process of adopting new forms of apostolic presence such as parish ministry, caring for the elderly, etc.. These initiatives are warmly welcomed and encouraged. It pertains to the Bishop in consultation with the religious Superiors, taking into account the most urgent needs of the Church, the directives of the Magisterium and the distinctive character of the Institute, to evaluate all apostolic innovations and experimentation.

ii) Parochial Ministry:

In a number of parishes throughout the diocese members of religious institutes are directly involved in parochial ministry either as parish priests or associates. Their duties and obligations *vis-á-vis* the people of God are identical with those of the secular clergy. Their terms of appointment are determined in accordance with the provisions of c 682 of the *Code of Canon Law*.

Serious consideration must be given to the involvement of female religious in different areas of pastoral ministry in the parish. Because of their innate qualities of womanhood and their wealth of experience in the field of education, administration or in the caring professions, they have much to contribute to the enrichment of parish life, e.g.
- in preparing the Sunday liturgy – co-ordinating and training readers, choirs, etc.;
- visiting the sick and elderly in their homes and in hospital, etc.;
- bereavement counselling, etc.;
- pre-sacramental preparation of parents of First Confession, First Communion and Confirmation children (cf c 776);
- Adult Religious Education in the parish;
- leading people in prayer.

iii) Promotion of Vocations:

Experience testifies to a diversity of vocations within the local Church. Hence, the collaboration between secular and religious in the work of promoting vocations can only be for the enrich-

RELIGIOUS

ment of the local Church itself. *Response* (the national body for co-ordinating the promotion of Religious vocations) arranges for the visitation of post-primary schools by representatives of three different Religious institutes each year in connection with vocations promotion.

iv) Missionary Awareness:

In addition to vocations promotion Religious are also engaged in promoting missionary awareness among the People of God. This entails visiting parishes and schools and preaching at weekend Masses on behalf of the Missions. The response of our people to Mission Appeals has always been most generous.

2. Relationship between Bishops and Religious

This matter is clearly spelt out in different Church documents. Nowhere is it more clearly dealt with than in the document *Mutuae Relationes*. The pastoral meaning of exemption is under-scored in a particular way:

> Of its nature exemption, is no obstacle either to pastoral co-ordination or to mutual happy relations among the People of God. In fact, 'it relates to the internal organisation of these Institutes. Its purpose is to ensure that everything is suitably and harmoniously arranged within them and the perfection of the religious life is promoted …

> Therefore exempt religious Institutes, faithful to 'their own proper character and function' (PC 2, 6), should cultivate above all special docility to the Roman Pontiff and to the Bishops, placing their liberty and apostolic eagerness at their disposal with good will and in accordance with religious obedience. Similarly, they should with full awareness and zeal, apply themselves to the task of creating and manifesting in the diocesan family the specific witness and the genuine mission of their Institute (22, *ibid* pp 224-225).

In concrete terms this means that:

> All religious, whether exempt or non-exempt, are subject to the authority of the local Ordinary in the following matters: public worship - without prejudice however, to the diversity of rites - the care of souls, preaching to the people, the religious and moral education, catechetical instruction and liturgical

formation of the faithful, especially of children. They are subject to diocesan rules regarding the comportment proper to the clerical state and also the various activities relating to the exercise of their sacred apostolate. Catholic schools conducted by Religious are also subject to the local Ordinaries as regards their general policy and supervision, without prejudice, however, to the right of Religious to manage them. Likewise, Religious are obliged to observe all those prescriptions which episcopal councils or conferences legitimately decree as binding on all' CD 35 #4 & 5; ES I, 39 (n 44 *ibid* pp 234-235)

This same discipline is re-affirmed in c 678.

Members of Religious Institutes working in the Diocese:
In order to minimise misunderstandings in this area the law stipulates that there be a written agreement entered into between the diocesan Bishop and the competent Religious Superior setting down expressly and accurately the work to be done, the members to be assigned to it and the financial arrangements (cf c 681 #2).

With regard to members of Religious Institutes holding ecclesiastical office in the diocese, he/she is appointed by the Bishop on presentation by, or at least the consent of the competent Superior. Likewise he/she is removed from office at the discretion of the Bishop, with prior notice being given to the Religious Superior; or by the Religious Superior with prior notice being given to the Bishop. Neither requires the other's consent (cf c 682).

For a very grave reason a diocesan Bishop can forbid a member of a Religious Institute to remain in his diocese, provided the person's major Superior has been informed and failed to act (cf c 679).

Recommended Reading:
Congregation for Religious and Secular Institutes *Directives for Mutual Relations between Bishops and Religious in the Church, Mutuae Relationes*, 23/4/1979, Flannery, vol II, 209-243.

CHAPTER 11

Vocations to the Priesthood and Religious Life

1. Fostering Vocations to the Priesthood and Religious Life

'God our Saviour, desires all men to be saved and come to the knowledge of the truth' (1 Tim 2:3). But 'how are they to hear without a preacher? And how can men preach unless they are sent'? (Rom 10:14 ff.). Conscious of both the urgency and enormity of the task of providing workers for the Lord's vineyard the Congregations for Oriental Churches, for Religious and Secular Institutes, for the Evangelisation of Peoples, and for Catholic Education convened an International Congress of Bishops and Others with Responsibilities for Ecclesiastical Vocations, in Rome in May 1981. The objective of the Congress was to analyse the whole issue of religious vocation in the Church today and to propose a plan of action which would help particular churches in the promotion of vocations to the priesthood and religious life. The deliberations of that Congress were subsequently made available in what is called *The Conclusive Document*, 2 May 1982. This document is presented as the framework and blueprint for the promotion of religious vocations.

On Vocations Sunday, 1989 the Irish Bishops' Conference, published a pastoral letter on vocations, entitled: *Come, Follow Me*. It is against the background of these two documents that the following observations and recommendations are made.

The Second Vatican Council in its *Decree on the Training of Priests*, *Optatum Totius*, 23/11/1965, reminds us that 'The duty of fostering vocations falls on the whole Christian community, and they should discharge it principally by living full Christian lives (n 2, cf Flannery, vol I, p 708).

The Difficulties:
In his article in *The Furrow* (August, 1984) Father Donal Neary

articulates some of the difficulties militating against pursuing a religious vocation. The faith-culture and religious milieu for young people has changed greatly in the past twenty years.

> The young person has grown up in a world of moral ambiguity and global uncertainty, of marital conflict and infidelity. He has been educated in a religious atmosphere of questioning and tolerance. He has grown up in a world where inequality and injustice are deeply felt in the people and structures of his Church. In Ireland he has grown up through fifteen years of religious intolerance and killings. He has grown up also in a 'culture of experience' where immediate gratification is desired and almost sanctified by consumerism, thus placing a high value on experience and the place of feelings in the making of a decision. He has come to sexual awareness and maturity through many doubts and the ambiguities of differing adult advice, having received his sexual education within a Church that is publicly divided on many issues. He has probably experienced some sexual relationships, a fact that will make celibacy more difficult for him than if he hadn't. An affluent culture doesn't value religious poverty; neither does religious obedience seem to make sense among people who highly value personal freedom, especially when there is no questioning of what the freedom might be for (p 521).

Catechesis, therefore, plays a vital role in helping young people discern their vocation. In his message to mark the XXVIII Day of Prayer for Vocations, 21 April, 1991, Pope John Paul II appeals in particular to the catechist to cooperate with Christian parents, priests, religious and many lay people involved in education and in the work of fostering religious vocations.

> Dear catechists, how important and delicate your mission is! The children and young people entrusted to you depend on your service for their growth and development as Christians. In the Church, catechesis is needed so that the word of God, the sacraments, the liturgy and the duties proper to the Christian life may be properly known. But there is also a need, especially at certain moments of young people's development, for a catechesis which offers guidance in choosing a state of life. For only in the light of faith and of prayer can we grasp the meaning and power of the God's individual calls.

VOCATIONS

May your ministry as catechists be carried out in faith, nourished by prayer and sustained by genuine Christian living. May you become experts in speaking to today's young people, and may you be effective and credible teachers in presenting the Gospel ideal ... on the meaning and value of the various vocations to the consecrated life (*Osservatore Romano*, 10 December, 1990, p 9, Weekly Edition).

Within the local Church certain individuals and structures occupy a primary place in the promotion of vocations:

The Bishop:

The Bishop, by the very nature of his ministry, is the guide and co-ordinator of the total framework of pastoral care including the pastoral care of vocations. But he cannot act alone. He promotes vocations by his preaching and teaching; by keeping alive a spirit of prayer for vocations and by urging and encouraging those who have special responsibility for their promotion. In particular he sustains, guides and co-ordinates the work of the diocesan Director of Vocations and the team that assists him (cf *The Conclusive Document*, n 29).

The Priest:

In a very real sense every priest is a promoter and director of vocations. He fulfils this duty by his preaching and above all by his way of life. The Irish Bishops place special emphasis on the latter:

Questions about the credibility of priesthood and religious life arise from many people. Their lives may appear to the young to be rather remote from the everyday concerns of people whom they are to serve. On the other hand, the whole-hearted availability, as well as the simple lifestyle and sincere prayerfulness of priests and religious is a big influence in the way young people view them and think of joining them (*Come, Follow Me*, p 4).

Apostolic zeal, therefore, true charity and enthusiasm for one's ministry are the keys to promoting religious vocations. Enthusiasm of priests for their ministry is the strongest selling point for vocations. 'We simply need to love our priesthood, to give ourselves completely to it, so that the truth about the ministerial priesthood may become attractive to others' (Pope John Paul II, *Holy Thursday Letter to Priests*, 10/3/1991 n 2). Priests show this enthusiasm by the way in which they celebrate the liturgy and minister to people in their parish. The pastoral care of young people is one of the most effective ways of promoting vocations because 'the pastoral care of the young and the pastoral care of vocations are two complementary things' (*The Conclusive Document*, n 42). Finally, the priest must see it as his duty to personally approach a person whom he thinks might be open to the choice of a consecrated life and whom he thinks suitable (cf *ibid*, n 32 & 49). Pope John Paul II challenges priests and religious in the following words:

> God is always free to call whom he wishes and when he wishes. But usually he calls by means of us and our words, so do not be afraid to call. Go among your young people, go and meet them personally and call them. (*Message to mark the XVI World Day of Prayer for Vocations*, 29 April 1979, cf *Conclusive Document*, footnote 97, p 69).

The Family:
The Christian family, or the domestic Church, as the Second Vatican Council calls it, plays a vital role in the promotion of vocations. It is the school of faith and the first seminary where the seeds of a religious vocation are sown and nurtured. Family prayer and Christian formation of both parents and children as well as their involvement in apostolic activities are conducive to the growth and encouragement of vocations. 'The family, a community of faith, life and love is the normal place for the human, Christian, and vocational growth of children' (*ibid*, n 39). Parents should be encouraged to put the ideal of a religious vocation before their children. In our culture today parents are often reluctant to do so. The latent fear that their son or daughter may not persevere in the religious vocation chosen often constitutes a major deterrent for parents.

Male and female Religious:
Like priests, male and female Religious have the duty of promoting vocations in and through their witness of life and example. As spiritual guides they can play an invaluable role in helping candidates discern their particular vocation. Given their involvement in areas such as education, health care, social services, etc., they frequently work in close contact with people who may be open to contemplating a religious vocation. While at all times working in co-operation with the diocesan community Religious

Institutes have the right and duty to make known their own charism and promote their own vocations (cf ibid, n 34). By arrangement with *Response* (the national body responsible for co-ordinating Religious vocations promotion) each post-primary school in the diocese is visited yearly by representatives of three different Religious Institutes.

Seminarians:

Like the priest and Religious, the seminarian through his own commitment and lifestyle plays a vital role in fostering vocations. 'No one is more suitable to evangelise the young than the young themselves. The young students preparing themselves for the priesthood, and the young men and women on the path of religious and missionary formation, both as individuals and as community, are the 'prime and direct apostles' and witnesses of vocation in the midst of other young people' (*ibid* n 41).

Catechists, Teachers and Educators:

As the Pope emphasises, catechists, teachers and educators play an indispensable role in the promotion of vocations. Priests should work in close collaboration with catechists, religion teachers and School Principals. They deserve great encouragement, respect and gratitude for putting the ideals of a religious vocation before their pupils.

2. Practical Ways of Promoting Vocations

There are many practical steps that can be taken both at diocesan and parish level towards the promotion of religious vocations. Some of these are already in place, others in the process of taking shape:

i) Diocesan Vocations Team:

The Diocesan Vocations Team was established in 1990. Presently it consists of three priests, one religious sister and two lay people. Its work entails the pastoral care of prospective candidates thinking about priesthood, and the arrangement of vocations workshops, etc.. In addition, it relays to the diocese information about vocations promotion in other areas of the country and works in close collaboration with those responsible for promoting vocations to the Religious Life.

Concretely, the Vocations Team sees its role in terms of four distinct programmes or areas of promotion.

a) Awareness Programme:
This area of the programme seeks to heighten awareness about vocations to the priesthood in both the parish and the school - Primary, post-Primary and Third Level Colleges.

b) Accompaniment Programme:
The Team seeks to accompany those who are at a cross-roads in their lives and are considering priesthood as an option. Such a programme takes place in stages:
- Vocations Workshop and a follow-up programme for those who attended;
- Accompaniment Programme which entails meeting prospective candidates a number of times over a protracted period;
- Individual Guidance for those not yet ready to participate in either a Vocations Workshop or an Accompaniment Programme.

c) Discernment Programme:
This programme is aimed at those wishing to enter seminary and have applied or are about to apply to the Bishop. The programme involves a process of reflection for the candidate and a number of meetings with the Vocations Team. The aim of the programme is to discern what is best for the person making the application. While it is the Bishop alone who will make the final decision with regard to a particular candidate, he will normally consult with the Vocations Team for their assessment and recommendations in particular cases. It is earnestly hoped that candidates wishing to enter seminary in September should have made their application prior to June 30th of that year.

d) Link-in Programme:
The work of the Vocations Team is not complete as soon as the candidate has entered seminary. It is hoped that at least one member of the said Team would continue to accompany the candidate during his time in the seminary.

ii) St. Joseph's Young Priests Society:
For many years now a group of lay people called the St Joseph's Young Priests Society has been actively engaged in promoting vocations to the diocesan priesthood. Their apostolate is principally through praying for vocations and financial support of seminarians in paying part of their fees and personal expenses, etc.. At its meeting in May 1990, the Ossory Council of Priests,

having discussed the theme of vocations to the diocesan priesthood, highlighted the great work done by St Joseph's Young Priests Society and recommended establishing branches in parishes.

iii) Prayer:
Since the work of fostering vocations devolves on the whole Christian community, everybody has a duty to pray for vocations.'The prayer of the community leads to action on the part of the community. Personal prayer opens the soul to the will of God. The vocation takes shape as a 'call-response'.... Prayer is not a means of receiving the gift of the divine call, but the essential means, commanded by the Lord' (*ibid* n 23).

A prayer for vocations should be included regularly in the Prayer of the Faithful at Mass. Thought might be given to arranging occasionally a Service of Eucharistic Adoration in the parish or Religious House to pray for vocations. No effort must be spared when it comes to keeping the issue of religious vocations in the forefront of people's minds.

iv) Preaching:
Priests should preach regularly on the theme of vocations. 'The individual vocation and vocations in general must become a fundamental theme in preaching, prayer and catechesis. It is not enough for the theme to be treated solely in a direct manner: it must be present as an indirect element at other times of preaching, prayer and catechesis' (*ibid* n 18). In an age of rampant materialism and secularism parents need to be convinced about the place and value of the religious vocation. Priests and Religious are the first to acknowledge their indebtedness to the encouragement they received from their parents and family in pursuing their vocations.

v) Direct Contact:
Early in St John's Gospel there is reference to different disciples being introduced to Jesus through the mediation of another. Andrew took his brother Simon Peter to Jesus (1:42) while Philip introduces Nathaniel to him (1:47). The priest must see it as part of his ministry to introduce other people to Jesus so that they too may become his disciples. He does this by individual and personal contact. 'The awareness (of a vocation) can occur – and must ever more occur – following a direct call, a personal call,

VOCATIONS

addressed by a responsible person to a subject who is considered suitable. This call too is an act of Grace. There is a proper
moment for the call. The expert and prudent teacher knows how
to estimate it. When the conditions are right it is never too early
to address the call. The important thing is not to arrive too late'
(*ibid* n 49).

vi) Active Involvement of Young People in the Parish:

Young people often complain of feeling alienated from society
and the Church. The parish must try to be a place of welcome for
all its people, young and old. It is within the context of the parish
– the faith community – that vocations are nurtured and brought
to fruition. This is best achieved in and through small groups
with which the young people can identify. 'Faith development
and vocational growth in Ireland take place, apart from the family, largely with prayer groups, folk-groups, social justice groups.
The first two groups set much store by the immediacy of emotional, liturgical effect and feelings. They speak to the felt needs
and experience of young people ...' (D. Neary, *art cit* p 522).

Other areas that might be considered include the involvement of
young people in designing vocation literature to coincide with
Vocation Sunday and Mission Sunday. The Priest must try to
motivate and involve young people as readers, choir-members,
eucharistic ministers, etc..

vii) Vocations Sunday:

The Church sets aside a particular Sunday each year – the Fourth
Sunday of Easter – when she focuses attention on the theme of
vocation to the priesthood and religious life. Some parishes
mount a vocations exhibition on that day, highlighting the
names and apostolates of people from the parish serving in the
mission fields of the world. Such a venture affords the opportunity to involve young people in preparing it and a heightening
of parish awareness on the whole issue of religious vocation.

viii) Parish-based Ordinations:

For some years now it has been diocesan policy to hold ceremonies of ordination to the priesthood in the candidate's home
parish. 'The celebration of the sacrament of Holy Orders, particularly in the communities to which the ordinands belong, is a
providential occasion to re-awaken the sense of responsibility of
the People of God towards those who have been called.

Ordination is an event for the community. It reveals a great gift of God offered to the community itself and to the whole Church. It finds encouragement thereby to make itself more worthy to receive other gifts' (*Conclusive Document* n 21).

Recommended Reading:

The Conclusive Document, Polyglott Press, Vatican, 1982.
Irish Bishops' Conference, *Come, Follow Me*, Veritas, Dublin, 1989.
Neary, D., 'The Priest and Vocations to the Priesthood', in *The Furrow* 35 (1984), 519-524.
Neary, D., 'Vocational Accompaniment', in *Intercom*, April 1983, pp 5-7.
Dalton, W., 'The 1990 Synod of Bishops', in *The Furrow* 41 (1990), 92-100.

CHAPTER 12

Ecumenism

1. Introduction

The search for Christian Unity was one of the principal concerns of the Second Vatican Council. This search found official expression in the *Dogmatic Constitution on the Church, Lumen Gentium* and in the *Decree on Ecumenism, Unitatis Redintegratio*. The foundations for a genuine ecumenical spirit are to be found in the conciliar assertions that see the Church of Christ as 'subsisting in the Catholic Church, which is governed by the the successor of Peter and the bishops in communion with him' and that 'many elements of sanctification and of truth are found outside of its visible confines' (Vatican II, *Lumen Gentium*, n 8, Flannery, vol I, p 357). The Ecumenical Movement is the term given to those activities and initiatives aimed at exploring these common elements of holiness and truth shared by the different Christian traditions.

The impetus and inspiration for this movement derives from Christ himself. He prayed 'that all may be one ...' (Jn 17:21) but unfortunately many who profess to be followers of Christ differ in mind and go their separate ways as if Christ himself were divided. 'Such division openly contradicts the will of Christ, scandalises the world, and damages that most holy cause, the preaching of the Gospel to every creature' (Vatican II, *Decree on Ecumenism*, Flannery, vol I, p 452).

2. Directives on Ecumenism

The Second Vatican Council called for a *Directory on Ecumenism*. The said *Directory, Ad Totam Ecclesiam*, was published in two parts, one in 1967, the other in 1970 (cf Flannery, vol I, pp 483-501 & 515-532). Subsequent Roman documents and the 1976 *Directory on Ecumenism in Ireland* of the Irish Catholic Bishops' Conference spell out in detail the practical implications of the principles enunciated in the *Directory, Ad Totam Ecclesiam*, 1967 and 1970. In 1993 the Pontifical Council for the Promotion of Christian Unity, issued a new *Directory for the Application of Principles and Norms on Ecumenism,* amending and changing slightly existing discipline in particular areas. Reference is made to such changes throughout this *Directory.*

3. Divisions in the Church: An historical overview

After the outpouring of the Holy Spirit on Pentecost Sunday and the birth of the Church in Jerusalem the Apostles soon left that city to preach the gospel to other communities. These new communities soon aligned themselves to other communities, especially those associated with one or more of the twelve Apostles. Out of these grew the major liturgical families of Antioch, Alexandria and Rome. These families and the various liturgical sub-divisions are sometimes called rites. People belong to a particular rite and given certain conditions they may even change rites (cf cs 111 & 112).

The first major division between the Latin and Oriental Churches came with the Great Eastern Schism in the 11th century. The rift divided the hierarchies of the one Church of Christ. The Christian East involved in this rift came to be known as the Orthodox or Eastern Orthodox Church. The West was called the Catholic Church.

During the subsequent centuries various attempts at healing this division were made but all to no avail. From the 16th century onwards small groups of Eastern Christians returned to full communion with Rome, accepting papal primacy but maintaining their own spiritual and liturgical heritage. These came to be known as Uniates. Those who did not enter into full communion with Rome continued to be known as Eastern Orthodox. Their major point of division concerns the Primacy of the Pope of Rome and the interpretation of Revealed Truth.

The Roman Catholic Church recognises its special relationship with the Orthodox Church. 'These Churches, although separated from us, yet possess true sacraments, above all – by apostolic succession – the priesthood and the Eucharist, whereby they are still joined to us in closest intimacy. Therefore some worship in common, given suitable circumstances and the approval of Church authority, is not merely possible but encouraged'

(*Decree on Ecumenism*, n 15, Flannery, vol I, p 465). Hence, the norms governing sacramental sharing and common worship with Orthodox differ significantly from the corresponding norms governing separated churches in the West. This is evident in the section of this *Directory* dealing with the 'Practice of Ecumenism'.

The 16th century Reformation introduced further division into the Body of Christ, the Church. The Reformation Churches differ considerably not only from us but also among themselves, due to their different origins and convictions with regard to doctrine and spiritual life. They differ from us:
  - in their interpretation of revealed truth;
  - in their understanding of the mystery and ministry of the Church;
  - in their understanding of the role of Mary in work of salvation;
  - in the way in which they perceive the divine authority of the sacred books;
  - in matters pertaining to papal authority and the Church's Teaching Office or Magisterium;
  - in their understanding of several of the sacraments, Baptism excluded.

Despite these 'very weighty differences', there are significant elements that unite the churches – their common love and reverence for Holy Scripture and the sacramental bond of Baptism. Baptism, however, is but a beginning, a point of departure. It is not the culmination of our journey towards unity. For this reason 'this sacred Council urges the faithful to abstain from any frivolous or imprudent zeal, for these can cause harm to true progress toward unity' (*ibid*, p 470).

4. Attitude of Catholics towards Ecumenism
1) There can be no ecumenism worthy of the name without interior conversion. It is from change of attitude that the desire for unity flows.
2) In order to avoid doctrinal indifferentism and consequent abuses Catholics ought to be familiar with the fundamental truths of their own faith and tradition. 'Above all they should know their own Church and be able to give an account of its teaching, its discipline and its principles of ecumenism' (*Directory for the Application of Principles ... n 24*). In practice this

means 'that the entirety of revealed truth, of sacraments and of ministry that Christ gave for the building up of the Church and the carrying out of its mission is found within the Catholic communion of the Church' (*ibid* n 17). In addition they should be aware of those truths which they hold in common with other Christian Churches. No good purpose is served by ignoring areas of fundamental difference between the churches or pretending that they do not exist.

5. Ecumenism in Practice

It is the obligation of all of us to work towards the elimination of the remnants of intolerance and misunderstanding and unchristian forms of competition between the churches. The fact that our neighbour belongs to one of the churches separated from us does not make him any less Irish. What is above all necessary is a 'deepening and broadening of the sense of Irish identity' (*New Ireland Forum Report*, Dublin, 1984, par 4.13, p 23). Such is indispensable for the building of the new Ireland envisaged in the New Ireland Forum Report:

> The new Ireland must be a society within which subject only to public order, all cultural, public, political and religious belief can be freely expressed and practised. Fundamental to such a society are freedom of conscience, social and communal harmony, reconciliation and the cherishing of the diversity of all traditions (*ibid*).

These ideals and aspirations can be realised through the churches working together on various social issues such as the combating of poverty and the promotion of peace, social justice and mutual works of charity at both parish and diocesan level.

i) In the Parish:

'The parish, as an ecclesial unity gathered around the Eucharist, should be, and proclaim itself to be, the place of authentic ecumenical witness. Thus a great task for the parish is to educate its members in the ecumenical spirit. This calls for care with the content and form of preaching, especially of the homily and with catechesis. It calls too for a pastoral programme which involves someone charged with promoting and planning ecumenical activity ...' (*Directory for the Application of Principles* ... n 67). With a view to putting these aspirations into practice certain activities might be undertaken at parish level:

ECUMENISM

1) Parishes are encouraged to arrange an ecumenical prayer service during the Church Unity Octave. In areas where non-Catholics are few in number, a group of parishes might consider combining together for a fuller celebration.

2) At parish level people are encouraged to become aware of the values they hold in common and to search for practical ways of giving common witness to these values, e.g. issues pertaining to health, environment, drug and alcohol abuse, etc..

3) Members of other churches should feel welcome to join committees and organizations within the parish.

ii) In the School:

1) The school can serve as an important vehicle in breaking down barriers and promoting a true ecumenical spirit. It is desirable that teachers be correctly and adequately informed about the origins, history and doctrines of other Churches and ecclesial communities especially those that exist in the region (*ibid* n 68). In the diocese there is one Church of Ireland Post-Primary School and three Church of Ireland Primary Schools.

2) Final Year Students in the post-primary school should study ecumenism as part of their preparation-for-life programme. This study should be supplemented by direct contact with members of other churches.

iii) In the Diocese:

1) *The Directory on Ecumenism, Ad Totam Ecclesiam,* urges that there be established in each diocese or group of dioceses a council or commission for the promotion of ecumenical activity (cf Flannery, vol I, p 484). The 1993 *Directory* elaborates further on the structure and role of this council or commission. It 'should reflect the totality of the diocese and generally include among its members clergy, religious men and women and lay people of various competencies, and especially those with particular ecumenical expertise. It is desirable that representatives of the presbyteral council, the pastoral council, diocesan and regional seminaries be included among the members of the commission or secretariat' (n 43). The role of this Commission is set down in n 44 of the same document. It entails:

- putting into practice the decisions of the diocesan Bishop, the directives of the Second Vatican Council and subsequent documents as well as those of the Episcopal Conference concerning ecumenical matters;

ECUMENISM

- fostering spiritual ecumenism;
- organising workshops and seminars aimed at promoting the ecumenical formation of both clergy and laity;
- promoting friendliness and charity between Catholics and other Christians;

The activities of the said Commission are to be co-ordinated by the Diocesan Director of Ecumenism, who is appointed by the Bishop.

2) The high point of diocesan ecumenical activity is the celebration of the Church Unity Octave (Jan 18-25) each year. Shared prayer is a way to spiritual reconciliation. The diocesan celebration of this event may take place at different locations throughout the diocese. Such services are governed by particular norms as laid down in the *Directory on Ecumenism*, (ns 32-37, Flannery, vol I, pp 494-495). Members of the different traditions may proclaim the Word of God and preach the homily as desired (*Directory for the Application of Principles ...*, n 118).

3) A study of ecumenism should form an integral part of the seminary course and also of Adult Religious Education Courses being held in the diocese and should never be omitted from the post-ordination formation of the clergy (cf Irish Catholic Bishops' Conference, *Directory on Ecumenism in Ireland*, 1976, n 23).

4) 'A high priority in the work of the diocesan ecumenical commission should be the education of clergy and laity in ecumenism. Occasionally a clerical conference should be devoted to the study of some topic of ecumenical significance' (*ibid* n 22).

iv) In Worship and Sacraments:

Sunday Eucharist: Catholics who occasionally because of their public office or blood relationships or friendship attend Mass on a Sunday or holiday of obligation in the Orthodox Church are not bound to assist at Mass in the Catholic Church. Likewise Catholics who cannot attend Mass in their church are encouraged to attend the liturgy in the Orthodox Church, if this is possible (cf *Directory on Ecumenism*, ns 47 & 50, Flannery, vol I, pp 497-498).

Special Occasion Masses: Occasionally priests may be asked to celebrate Mass for baptised persons who are members of other churches or ecclesial communities. There is no difficulty about the celebration of private Mass for such persons (cf c 901). Public Mass, however, is only permitted if the following conditions are fulfilled:

a) it must be expressly requested by the relatives, friends or subjects of the deceased person for a genuine religious motive;

b) there must be, in the judgment of the Ordinary, no danger of scandal to the faithful;

c) the name of the deceased must not be mentioned in the eucharistic prayer;

d) the norms pertaining to intercommunion must be observed (cf S.C.D.F., *Decree on the Public Celebration of Mass in the Catholic Church for other Deceased Christians*, 11/6/1976, Flannery, vol II, pp 59-60).

Priests are forbidden to concelebrate the Eucharist with ministers of other churches not in full communion with the Catholic Church (cf c 908). In the Catholic Eucharistic Liturgy the homily is reserved to the priest or deacon since it is a presentation of the Christian way of life in accordance with Catholic teaching and tradition (cf *Directory for the Application of Principles ...*, n 134).

Proclaiming the Scriptures at Mass: 'The reading of Scripture during a Eucharistic celebration in the Catholic Church is to be done by members of that Church. On exceptional occasions and for a just cause the Bishop may permit a member of another Church or ecclesial Community to take on the task of reader' (*ibid*, n 133). The above principle applies to weddings, funerals, as well as other occasions.

Baptism: As a general rule Baptism is to be carried out by the minister of the church or rite to which the parents of the child, or those who take their place, belong, or in the case of an adult the church or rite into which he/she wishes to be baptised. Except in danger of death, it is unlawful for a Catholic minister to baptise a child of non-Catholic parents (cf c 868 # 2). It should be remembered that it is the intention of the parents and the rite to which they belong that determines the church and rite into a child is baptised and not the actual rite used. If parents belong to different rites and the parents cannot agree as to which rite the child should belong, he/she follows the rite of the father (cf c 111 #1).

Occasionally priests will be asked by parents in a mixed marriage to participate in an 'ecumenical Baptism', i.e. the priest and non-Catholic minister jointly performing the Baptism and

ECUMENISM

the child being registered in both churches. This is not permitted
(cf *Directory for the Application of Principles* ..., n 97). The integrity
of the rite of Baptism demands that its essentials (i.e. the pouring
of the water and the pronouncing of the Trinitarian formula) be
performed by one and the same person. Since a person cannot
belong to two different churches simultaneously, it is absurd to
register his/her Baptism in more than one church. Neither is it
permitted to repeat the sacrament in the church of the other
spouse.

A non-Catholic may in the company of a Catholic sponsor act as
a Christian witness at a Catholic baptism and vice versa (cf c 874
#2). Because of the close communion between the Catholic
Church and the Eastern Orthodox Churches, it is permissible for
a just cause for an Eastern faithful to act as a sponsor together
with a Catholic sponsor.

For the reception of a baptised non-Catholic into full communion with the Catholic Church cf p 70ff of this *Directory.*
Indiscriminate attempts to re-baptise infants or adults are theologically erroneous and ecumenically insensitive. They are also
forbidden. Only if a prudent doubt still persists after diligent investigation about either the fact or validity of the Baptism already administered, may conditional baptism be invoked (cf c
869 and *Directory for the Application of Principles* ..., n 99).

Confirmation: Oriental Churches confer the sacrament of Confirmation (Chrismation) on infants immediately after Baptism.
The Roman Catholic Church recognises both the validity of this
sacrament and the legitimacy of the practice. The fact that no
mention is made of Confirmation in the certificate of Baptism
does not give grounds for doubting that this sacrament was also
conferred (*ibid* 99a).

The Roman Catholic Church admits to Confirmation members of
non-Catholic churches when they are being received into full-
communion with it (cf p 70ff above).

Eucharist: The reception of the Eucharist by Eastern Catholics in
full communion with Rome from a Catholic minister and *vice
versa* presents no difficulty.

For the Orthodox, reception of Holy Communion in a particular
church signifies complete union with that community; on princi-

ple they oppose intercommunion. In case of necessity, however, and wherever a genuine spiritual advantage commends it (e.g. there is no Catholic Church or minister in the area), and provided the danger of error or indifferentism is avoided, a Roman Catholic is encouraged to fulfil his/her Sunday obligation by joining in the Orthodox liturgy and is permitted to receive Holy Communion also (cf c 844 #2). A reciprocal arrangement exists for those members of the Orthodox Church who spontaneously asks for the Eucharist and are properly disposed (cf c 844 #3).

Generally speaking intercommunion with non-Catholics, even in the context of a mixed marriage, is not permitted. Various documents on Ecumenism, the 1983 *Code of Canon Law* and the 1993 *Directory for the Application of Principles* ... (cf nn 129-131) admit exceptions to this norm. Eucharistic sharing is permitted:

a) if there is danger of death and the person cannot approach his/her own minister and he/she demonstrates a faith in the Eucharist in conformity that of the Catholic Church (cf c 844 #4);

b) if, in the judgment of the Bishop, there is a serious spiritual need to receive the Eucharist and the person is unable to have recourse to a minister of his/her own communion, and demonstrates a faith in the Eucharist in conformity with that of the Catholic Church (cf c 844 #4).

Priests who receive requests for eucharistic sharing should consult the Bishop, and in the event of such permission being granted ensure that adequate explanation be given to the Catholic congregation to avoid possible confusion. A more detailed discussion of the different circumstances where eucharistic sharing might be permitted is to be found in the document: S.P.U.C., *On Admitting Other Christians to Eucharistic Communion in the Catholic Church*, 1/6/1972, and *Note Interpreting the 'Instruction on Admitting Other Christians to Eucharistic Communion in the Catholic Church Under Certain Circumstances'* 17/10/1973, Flannery, vol I, p 554 ff.) Each particular case must be examined on its own merits. 'Nevertheless, the bishops can in the various situations decide what are the needs that make exceptions applicable, that is to say, what constitutes a special case, and they can determine the manner of verifying whether all the required conditions are fulfilled in such a particular case' (*Directory on Ecumenism in Ireland*, n 41).

ECUMENISM

Penance and Anointing of the Sick: Sometimes in the course of hospital or prison ministry a priest may be approached by a member of another church not in full communion with Rome for the sacrament of Reconciliation or Anointing of the Sick. If the person is a member of the Orthodox Church and the minister of his own church is not available, he may go to a Catholic confessor, and receive the Anointing of the Sick, should he so wish. Should a Roman Catholic find himself/herself in a parallel situation, a similar arrangement applies (cf *Directory on Ecumenism: Part I*, n 46, Flannery, vol I, p 497).

If the person requesting these sacraments is not a Catholic (e.g. Church of Ireland, Methodist, etc.) he/she is permitted to receive them if the following conditions are verified:
   a) danger of death or urgent need (it is for the Bishop to decide on what amounts to an urgent need);
   b) the person cannot approach his/her minister;
   c) the person spontaneously asks for the sacrament;
   d) the person is properly disposed and manifests faith in the sacrament consistent with that of the Church.

Should a Roman Catholic find himself/herself in similar circumstances, he/she may not ask for these sacraments except from a minister who has been validly ordained (cf *ibid*, n 55, p 499).

Marriage: All relevant information will be found under the heading of 'Mixed Marriages' in this *Directory* (cf pp 153-154) and in the *Directory on Mixed Marriages* (1983) of the Irish Episcopal Conference.

Burial Services in other Christian Traditions: When requested by the family, priests may officiate at the funeral services of people belonging to other traditions in funeral homes and at the graveside. Priests are not to officiate at church funerals of persons belonging to other communions. They may, however participate in accordance with the norms enunciated above.

Recommended Reading:
Vatican II, *Decree on Ecumenism, Unitatis Redintegratio*, Flannery, vol I, 452-470.
—*Decree on the Catholic Eastern Churches, Orientalium Ecclesiarum*, Flannery, vol I, 441-451.

Secretariat for the Promotion of the Unity of Christians, *Directory on Ecumenism, Ad Totam Ecclesiam,* 14/5/1967 & *Spiritus Domini,* 16/4/1970, Flannery, vol I, 483-501 & 515-532.

—'Declaration on the Position of the Catholic Church on the Celebration of the Eucharist in Common by the Christians of Different Confessions', 7/1/1972, Flannery, vol I, 502-507.

—'On Admitting Other Christians to Eucharistic Communion in the Catholic Church', 1/6/1972, Flannery, vol I, 554-559.

—Note Interpreting 'Instruction on Admitting other Christians to Eucharistic Communion under Certain Circumstances', 17/10/1973, Flannery, vol I, 560-563.

Pontifical Council for the Promotion Of Christian Unity *Directory for the Application of Principles and Norms on Ecumenism,* 25/3/1993.

Irish Catholic Bishops' Conference, *Directory on Ecumenism in Ireland,* 1976.

Yarnold, E., *In Search of Unity,* St Paul's Publications, Slough, England, 1988.

ECUMENISM

CHAPTER 13

Funerals

1. The Catholic Understanding of the Funeral Ritual

Of all the Catholic sacramentals that a priest or deacon will celebrate, none is more important than the funeral ritual. Here the
priest is at one and the same time a helper, a healer and a recon-
ciler. People turn to him spontaneously for advice in making the
funeral arrangements, for help in mending their broken and
shattered lives and very often as mediator of the Lord's forgiveness in the sacrament of Reconciliation. Priests and others
engaged in the ministry of consolation should be especially
sensitive to people's needs and feelings at this time.

In its *General Introduction to the Order of Christian Funerals*, (1991),
hereinafter *O.C.F.*, the Church spells out her understanding of
the funeral ritual and the theology of death and resurrection un-
derpinning it.

i) Nowhere in the funeral rites does the Church pass judgment
on the deceased – much less condone or condemn the kind of life
that the individual may have lived, or the manner in which
he/she may have died. Rather '... the Church intercedes on behalf of the deceased ... and ministers to the sorrowing and con-
soles them in the funeral rites with the comforting word of God
and the sacrament of the Eucharist' (*ibid* n 4). 'The Church
through its funeral rites commends the dead to God's merciful
love and pleads for the forgiveness of their sins ... Though separated from the living, the dead are still at one with the community
of believers on earth and benefit from their prayers and intercession. At the rite of final commendation and farewell, the community acknowledges the reality of separation and commends
the deceased to God. In this way it recognises the spiritual bond
that still exists between the living and the dead and proclaims its
belief that all the faithful will be raised up and reunited in the
new heavens and a new earth, where death will be no more' (*ibid*

n 6). Thus, what used to be known as the absolution which was pronounced over the coffin has disappeared from the post-conciliar text and is now replaced with a final commendation of the deceased to God. David N. Power sums up very succinctly the new way of thinking that has inspired the post-conciliar revisions of the *Order of Christian Funerals:*

> Before the liturgical revisions prompted by that Council, Christian burial was celebrated as an act of suffrage and absolution, having taken on that perspective in the Middle Ages. Ecclesiastical authority exercised much the same power over the souls of the dead that it had exercised over them during life. The absolution over the coffin paralleled the absolution of the confessional .... The use of this power and authority required that the Church's minister pass some judgment on the life and death of the deceased, just as the exercise of the power of absolution in the confessional could not be used without making some judgment on the sinner's worthiness ('The Funeral Rites for a Suicide and Liturgical Developments', in: *Concilium*, n 179 (1985) p 76).

ii) The funeral liturgy is not a eulogy of praise in honour of the deceased. Like every other liturgical celebration it is the worship of God that is in question and not the worship of the individual. 'Christians celebrate the funeral rites to offer worship, praise and, thanksgiving to God for the gift of a life which has now been returned to God, the author of life and the hope of the just' (*O. C. F.* n 5).

iii) While firmly professing faith in the next life and our communion with those who have died, our present funeral liturgy dwells heavily on the aspect of bidding farewell to a loved one rather than on a theology of the afterlife. The very prayers used at the different stages of the funeral rite suggest this, e.g. ' ... we believe that all the ties of friendship and affection which knit us as one throughout our lives do not unravel in death' (*O.C.F., Vigil for the Deceased*, n 88, and *Transfer of the Body to the Church*, n 142). These same sentiments are echoed again in the Prayers of Final Commendation, n 180: 'Before we go our separate ways ...', etc..

FUNERALS

2. The Ministry of Consolation

The ministry of the priest on the occasion of funerals is not confined to liturgical and sacramental ministrations. Together with other members of the believing community he shares in the very important task of consoling those who have lost their loved one. With other members of the community, especially relatives, neighbours and friends he brings a message of hope to the anguished and the bereaved. This ministry of consolation is anchored in Christian hope, i.e. that sin and death have been conquered through the passion, death and resurrection of Christ and that life will ultimately triumph over death.

> Members of the community should console the mourners with words of faith and support and acts of kindness, for example assisting them with the routine task of daily living. Such assistance may allow members of the family to devote time to planning the funeral rites with the priest and other ministers and may also give the family time for prayer and mutual comfort' (*O.C.F.* n 10).

The practice and custom of helping out a neighbour at a time of bereavement is deeply rooted in our Irish culture and traditions. Such customs and traditions are to be encouraged and consolidated.

3. Funeral Liturgy

The series of rites surrounding the death of a Christian, and which make up the funeral liturgy, consists of several parts. Each of these are constructed around the word of God and hence the latter may never be omitted or replaced by other prayers or readings. This is because the Lord is present *par excellence* in his word as comforter and consoler.

Particular attention is drawn to the 'Additional Texts' provided in Part III of the *O.C.F.* ns 314-323). These Prayers and Intercessions are tailored to particular circumstances and should always be used when appropriate.

i) Prayers after Death:
This rite provides a model of prayer that may be used when the minister first meets with the family following death (*O.C.F.* n 51). This first visit is a tangible expression of the community's support for the mourners and can be of invaluable help to the

FUNERALS

priest when it comes to planning the other stages of the funeral liturgy. Through it he gains new insights into the needs of the family in their time of loss.

ii) Prayers in the Home of the Deceased or Funeral Home:

It is customary for members of the family, together with relatives, neighbours and friends to gather for prayer in the home of the deceased. The *O.C.F.* provides two different rites, (*Gathering in the Presence of the Body* and *Vigil for the Deceased*) either of which may be used, depending on the circumstances. The recitation of the Rosary may be incorporated into either one. In the absence of a priest the faithful are urged to recite these prayers themselves. Parishes might consider establishing a small group of people (along the same lines as Special Ministers of the Eucharist, etc.) specialising in the ministry of consolation. Their ministry could entail:
- leading the funeral prayers in the home or funeral home, in the absence of a priest;
- helping relatives with funeral arrangements;
- helping relatives to prepare and celebrate the funeral liturgy;
- bereavement counselling, etc.

iii) Transfer of the Body to the Church:

This rite will normally be celebrated immediately before the sealing of the coffin and usually includes the Rosary, Litany of the Saints or Psalms. It may be led by a priest, deacon or lay person, i.e. either by a member of the family or somebody designated by the community. The moment of the sealing of the coffin is an emotional one for the immediate family. It should be approached with sensitivity and privacy should be ensured. The family may wish to say a final farewell, and to do so in its own personal way – a kiss, a touch, signing on the forehead or sprinkling with holy water *(O.C.F.*, n 102).

iv) Reception of Remains at the Church:

It is the prerogative of the parish priest or other priest of the parish to receive the remains of his deceased parishioner (cf c 530 #5). Priests are encouraged to make the most of this celebration through their use of the word of God, prayers and, if possible, hymns and music. A few well-chosen words of comfort and consolation from the priest are deeply appreciated at this time. Not infrequently relatives and friends who travel from a distance are disappointed by the brevity of this celebration. The entire funeral liturgy offers an unique pastoral opportunity for reaching out to people, especially to those who might feel estranged from the Church. It can be instrumental in helping them rediscover their path to full and active membership of the Church.

Of special concern is the congestion that frequently occurs at the door of the church on the arrival of a funeral. The entrances become jammed while the body of the church remains partially empty. Priests are encouraged to invoke the use of ushers on such occasions or perhaps have the people enter the church before the funeral procession itself.

Ordinarily the priest or deacon receives the funeral dressed in soutane, surplice and stole. A purple cope may also be worn. Other clergy in attendance wear appropriate clerical dress.

In some parishes the time of arrival of a funeral is arranged to coincide with the scheduled evening Mass in the parish. In this instance, the priest vested for evening Mass receives the funeral at the door, sprinkling the coffin with holy water. While the procession moves into the church, an entrance hymn or the responsories given in the Order of Christian Funerals may be sung or said. Mass then continues in the normal way. The liturgy of the word is never duplicated.

If on the other hand the arrival of the funeral is not planned to coincide with evening Mass, at least ten minutes should elapse between the conclusion of the rite of reception and the beginning of Mass. This is to allow people time to sympathise with the bereaved. In such instances the *Reception of the Body at the Church* stands on its own as an autonomous rite and must always include a liturgy of the word. 'The reading of the word of God is the high point and central focus of the reception rite' (*O.C.F.* n 124). A liturgy of the word is now an integral part of all postconciliar liturgies.

The Christian symbols of the funeral pall, the Book of the Gospels, and the Crucifix may be placed on coffin. The lighted Paschal Candle is placed near it.

v) Funeral Mass:

Central to the funeral liturgy is the Eucharist. Like any other

Eucharist this should be prepared for with care and sensitivity. Whenever possible, ministers should involve the family in planning the funeral rites: in the choice of texts and rites provided in the ritual, in the selection of music for the rites, and in the designation of liturgical ministers' (*O.C.F.* n 17). Normally, members of the family will want to do the readings and prayers of intercession.

Liturgy of the Word: In selecting the readings and prayers, ministers should keep in mind the life of the deceased and the circumstances of his/her death. Biblical readings must never be replaced by non-biblical ones. A brief homily based on the scripture readings is always given after the gospel. It must neither be a 'preached-biography' nor a moral-dogmatic dissertation on death and resurrection. Rather it must try to relate the Christian understanding of death and resurrection to the life of the deceased and the manner of his/her death. The preacher must endeavour to weave into one the personal story of the deceased and the Christian story. He does so through a careful selection of the scripture readings and other prayers. One is free to select any suitable scripture readings and hence is not limited to those given in the Lectionary for Funerals. Experience tells us that people are more open and attuned to listening to God's word at a funeral than on probably any other occasion. Those present are there because they have chosen to be there and because they too feel the need to be nourished and uplifted. Relatives of the deceased should be invited to compose a Prayer of the Faithful to suit the occasion. The priest might consider supplying them with a standard model or formula around which they might construct their own prayers. In this way the prayers will be more personal and meaningful. The thing to be avoided on such occasions is simply reading set formulae as prayers of intercession. Every person is unique and every funeral is different.

The funeral liturgy can be greatly enhanced by a tastefully arranged and executed offertory procession.

Music and singing: 'Music is integral to the funeral rites. It allows the community to express convictions and feelings that words alone may fail to convey. It has the power to console and uplift the mourners and to strengthen the assembly in faith and love' (*ibid*, n 30). The music chosen should be appropriate and suitable for use in the funeral liturgy. Secular songs or music have no place in the funeral liturgy. Marian hymns should not be used during Mass. They may, however, be used as a recessional or at the graveside, e.g. the *Salve Regina*. Indeed, it might well be possible in some parishes at least to establish a 'funeral choir' consisting of some regular, daily Mass-goers, retired people, etc. who would sing a few suitable hymns at funerals. When no choir or cantors are available, an organist or other instrumentalist might play some suitable music.

It is strongly recommended that insofar as possible the funeral Mass would coincide with the regular daily Mass in the parish. Apart from ensuring a more authentic liturgical celebration it also expresses better the community dimension of the occasion.

Having said the post-communion prayer, the priest proceeds immediately to the final commendation. He does not give the final blessing of the Mass. When a funeral liturgy coincides with a public Mass, those in attendance should be encouraged to remain for the final commendation. It only takes a few minutes at most. Apart from creating liturgical disorder and confusion, their premature departure can often be interpreted by the bereaved as a sign of disrespect and insensitivity.

If the funeral liturgy coincides with a solemnity, or a regular parish Mass on Sunday or holyday of obligation, one is obliged to use the Mass of the day together with its proper prayers and readings. For non-concelebrating clergy the appropriate dress is choral, i.e. soutane and surplice.

vi) At the Graveside:
The *O.C.F.* provides a combined *Rite of Committal with Final Commendation* or simply a *Rite of Committal* for celebration at the graveside. Due dignity and decorum should be observed by both priests and people as they process to the place of committal. Active participation by all present in the prayers and responses is encouraged. The use of some form of public address system facilitates both communication and community participation.

vii) Symbols:
The lighted Paschal Candle is placed at the head of the coffin and depending on local custom other candles may be placed near the coffin during the funeral liturgy. The Paschal Candle is not carried in procession.

A pall may be placed over the coffin. This is a simple white cloth devoid of any symbols as such because the pall is itself the symbol. It is a sign of the Christian dignity of the person and a reminder of the baptismal robe used at Baptism. In addition it signifies the basic equality of all people in the sight of God. It is draped over the coffin when it reaches its place before the altar by family members or friends. It is done with dignity and decorum and it is not a task that should be left to the servers or the undertakers. It is a practical but powerful way of involving the mourners in the liturgical action. Its link with Baptism becomes all the more evident if the folded pall is brought not from the sacristy or front pew but from the baptistery or the font itself, where it has been visibly prepared and waiting. Mourners should be given the option of using the pall or not.

Discretion and sensitivity is called for in regard to the use of other symbols such as the national flag, or flags or emblems of associations, etc.. If these are to be used, they should be placed on the coffin as it leaves the Church on its way to the place of committal. 'Only Christian symbols may rest on or be placed near the coffin during the funeral liturgy. Any other symbols, for example, national flags, or flags or insignia of associations, have no place in the funeral liturgy' (*ibid* n 38). The family of the deceased should first consult with the priest as regards the most appropriate time and manner for using such symbols, etc..

Fresh flowers and wreaths can enhance the setting for the funeral rites.

4. Particular Problems and Related Issues

i) Priest's Funeral:
The priest-executor of the will together with the priest(s) of the parish, in consultation with the Bishop and the diocesan Master of Ceremonies, arrange the funeral liturgy for a deceased priest. The remains are received at the church by the other priest of the parish or by the Dean or Vicar Forane of the area if there is none. This celebration is that given in the *Order of Christian Funerals*, celebrated with full solemnity, i.e. with readers, music and singing, etc..

The Bishop is normally the chief celebrant at the funeral Mass, assisted in the sanctuary by a suitable number of concelebrants such as the Vicar(s) General and Vicar Forane, classmates of the deceased, relations, and priests of the parish. Every effort should be made to involve the priest's relatives and parishioners both in the preparation and celebration of the funeral liturgy. The symbols of his priestly ministry – stole, chalice and Breviary – may be placed on the coffin in the Church. Finally, the priest executor is responsible for ensuring that the death is registered. One copy of the Death Certificate must be sent to the Diocesan Offices.

ii) The Funeral of a Child:
The *Roman Missal*, the *Lectionary* and the *Order of Christian Funerals* all made provision for the funeral of a child who dies either before or after Baptism. The *Roman Missal* and *Lectionary* have special Masses and readings for these circumstances. Alternatively, the family may opt for a liturgy of the word to be celebrated in the child's home, in the hospital or at the graveside. The priest should be especially sensitive to the needs of the grieving parents in these circumstances.

iii) Stillborn Children and Cot-deaths:
During the course of their ministry most priests will occasionally encounter the tragedy of stillbirth and cot-death. The pastoral care of bereaved parents calls for a special degree of sensitivity on the part of the priest. The mother especially experiences feelings of bewilderment and depression. For the role of the priest in these circumstances see section of this *Directory* dealing with Stillbirth pp 78-81.

iv) Funeral of Suicide Victim:
Self-inflicted death or suicide is an ever increasing phenomenon in our time. It is not limited to any particular age group or social class. The grief and pain that it causes to those left behind often spring from an older understanding and discipline. The 1917 *Code of Canon Law* forbade ecclesiastical burial and Requiem Mass to those who deliberately and with full use of their faculties took their own lives (cf cs 1240 & 1241). That discipline and the moral suppositions upon which it was based have changed radically in recent years. New insights in the fields of psychology and psychiatry have unseated old certainties and raised afresh the whole question of guilt and moral responsibility.

The Church's current teaching on this matter is touched on in the 1980 *Declaration on Euthanasia*:

... suicide is also often a refusal of love for self, the denial of the natural instinct to live, a flight from the duties of justice and charity owed to one's neighbour, to various communities or to the whole of society - although as is generally recognised, at times there are psychological factors present that can diminish responsibility or even completely remove it (*Congregation for Doctrine of the Faith*, in: Flannery, vol II, p 512).

The 1983 *Code* omits any mention of prohibition of ecclesiastical burial to suicide victims. 'This, of course, does not indicate moral justification of the act of suicide, but is more likely to express haziness about the psychological state and motivations for suicide' (David N. Power, 'The Funeral Rites for a Suicide and Liturgical Developments', in: *Concilium* 179 (1985) p 76).

Counselling those bereaved through suicide:
Of all bereavements, a death through suicide can be the one most difficult to bear.The burdens of guilt, anger and shame are great. Relatives often feel in some way responsible for not having heeded the warning signs. Unresolved quarrels with the deceased, loving words left unsaid and concern for the eternal salvation of the victim – all of these can give rise to deep anxiety and pain. The priest should try to put people at ease by explaining the Church's attitude to suicide. In addition, helping them to come to terms with their pain and grief will entail:
  - acknowledging the fact of suicide rather than trying to conceal it;
  - seeking help and support from somebody who has been down that road already. The individual must make the first move. People are at the best of times reluctant to intrude into the privacy of others. Those trying to come to terms with bereavement should avoid isolation at all costs.
  - seeking professional help when necessary.
Above all, the priest should visit and keep in contact with the bereaved.

iv) Funerals and the Reception of Holy Communion:
The socio-cultural changes of recent years coupled with a new ecumenical spirit have meant that those who attend funerals are less likely to be Catholic only. Even if they are, some are likely to be unchurched or lapsed or only irregular churchgoers at the

very best. While the Lord's house must always be a place of welcome for all the people, not all belong to it in the same visible
way. Hence, not all are entitled to receive the Eucharist. The
United States National Conference of Catholic Bishops has issued *Guidelines for Receiving Holy Communion*. A copy of these is
normally to be found printed on the back covers of missalettes
and other booklets in use in church. Some may find these guidelines useful. They run as follows:

For Catholics:
Catholics fully participate in the celebration of the Eucharist
when they receive Holy Communion in fulfilment of Christ's
command to eat His Body and drink His Blood. In order to be
properly disposed to receive Communion, communicants
should not be conscious of grave sin, have fasted for an hour,
and seek to live in charity and love with their neighbours.
Persons conscious of grave sin must be reconciled with God and
the Church through the sacrament of Penance. A frequent reception of the sacrament of Penance is encouraged for all.

For other Christians:
We welcome to this celebration of the Eucharist those Christians
who are not fully united with us. It is a consequence of the sad
divisions in Christianity that we cannot extend to them a general
invitation to receive Communion. Catholics believe that the
Eucharist is the action of the celebrating community signifying a
oneness in faith, life and worship of the community. Reception
of the Eucharist by Christians not fully united with us would
imply a oneness which does not yet exist, and for which we
must all pray.

For those not receiving Communion:
Those not receiving sacramental Communion are encouraged to
express in their hearts a prayerful desire for unity with the Lord
Jesus and with one another.

For non-Christians:
We also welcome to this celebration those who do not share our
faith in Jesus. While we cannot extend to them an invitation to
receive Communion, we do invite them to be united with us in
prayer (NCCB of U.S.A., Bishops' Committee on the Liturgy,
November 8, 1986).

Priests should endeavour to catechise their people at a suitable time and in an appropriate manner concerning these matters but preferably not during the funeral Mass.

v) Funerals of non-Catholics:

There is no prohibition against Catholics attending the funeral of a non-Catholic or vice versa. Generally speaking the exercising of a ministerial role at such functions is discouraged:

> A separated brother is not to act as a scripture reader or to preach during the celebration of the Eucharist. The same is said of a Catholic at the celebration of the Lords' Supper or at the principal liturgical service of the Word held by the Christians who are separated from us' (*Directory on Ecumenism:* Part 1, 14/5/1967, n 56, Flannery, vol I, p 499).

As this norm restricts the free exercise of rights, it is to be interpreted strictly (cf c 18). Hence, there exists no prohibition against a non-Catholic exercising the ministry of reader or preacher at a Catholic funeral liturgy outside of Mass. Even within the context of Mass he/she may do so 'on exceptional occasions and for a just cause' with the permission of the Bishop of the diocese (cf Pontifical Council for the Promotion of Christian Unity, *Directory for the Application of Principles and Norms on Ecumenism*, 25/3/1993, n 133). Eucharistic sharing is, however, always excluded.

A Priest may offer a public Mass for a deceased non-Catholic if the following conditions are verified:

> 1) the public celebration of the Eucharist must be expressly requested by the relatives, friends or subjects of the deceased person, for a genuine, religious motive;
> 2) there must, in the judgment of the Ordinary, be no risk of scandal to the faithful;
> 3) the name of the deceased must not be mentioned during the eucharistic prayer, as this would presuppose full communion with the Catholic Church;
> 4) the norms concerning eucharistic and spiritual sharing must be observed (cf *Congregation for the Doctrine of the Faith, Accidit in Diversis*, 11 June 1976, Flannery, vol II, pp 59-60).

vi) Cremation:

With growing frequency priests will be asked to assist at funerals where the remains have been cremated or are about to be.

'The Church ... does not forbid cremation, unless it is chosen for reasons that are contrary to Christian teaching (c 1176 #3). The latter will very rarely if ever be the case. If the remains have already been cremated, the ashes are not normally taken to the church for the funeral Mass (though they may be if the famly so wishes) but directly to the place of burial. The funeral Mass is celebrated in the usual manner, excluding the final commendation.

vii) Disposal of Amputated Limbs:

It is recommended that amputated limbs as well as other portions of bodies be buried in a blessed place. They may, however, be disposed of by some other hygienic means, but the preference of the person and the family must always be respected.

5.Guidelines for Funeral Directors
(Circulated to Funeral Directors at Diocesan Study Day on
'Order of Christian Funerals', 25 March 1992).

1. The funeral director fulfils a unique position in bringing hope and consolation to bereaved. He is the 'bearer of the tenderness of the Church'.

2. The relationship between the priest and his people is also unique. He is never a functionary. He represents the Church in mediating hope and consolation both through his words and his silent presence. The funeral director must not see himself as a kind of 'go-between'.

3. The Order of Christian Funerals (1991) places strong emphasis on the involvement of the local community in celebrating the funeral. This involvement lays the foundation for participation in the funeral liturgy. Hence, such involvement is strongly recommended, e.g.:
   - preparation of the body – friends and neighbours regard it as a privilege to be asked to do this;
   - carrying the coffin;
   - putting on and removing the pall;
   - opening and filling the grave.

4. On being contacted about a death the funeral director should notify the priest and parish immediately. The times for the various rites are arranged in consultation with the priest and family. The said times are adhered to punctually.

5. Significant changes from the rite in use up to now:
Between the occurrence of death and transfer of the remains the
Church proposes different services:

 i) *Prayers after death* (priest + family – home, hospital);

 ii) *Gathering in Presence of Body* (in family home, funeral
 home, etc. when all members of family can be present. A lay
 person may lead service).

 iii) *Vigil for Deceased* (wake, funeral home – community event;
 time should be advertised. A lay person may lead the service).

6. Transfer of body – note provision for family private farewell.
A lay person may lead this service.

7. Reception of Remains – the funeral pall is placed on coffin by
relatives, assisted by funeral director on arrival before altar. All
other symbols are removed before coffin is taken into the the
church. Only Christian symbols – Bible, Cross, Rosary, (for priest
– stole & chalice) – are placed on the coffin while in the church.
Flowers are placed near the coffin but not on it. Likewise Mass
cards are placed in a basket or suitable container beside the coffin. Directors might lend a hand in showing people to their
places so as to avoid crowding inside the door.

8. The Paschal Candle is placed near the coffin.

9. All Christian symbols including the pall are removed after
prayers of final commendation. People like to carry the remains
of their loved one to its final resting place. Whenever possible
the option of carrying the coffin is to be preferred to placing it
on a trolley.

10. The coffin is placed in the grave after the words of committal,
cf pp 101-102, par 221. Directors should give relatives the option
for waiting until the grave is filled in, should they so wish.
Funeral directors should provide a public address system for
the presiding minister (priest, deacon, lay person).

11. Funeral homes in their decor and appointment should por-
tray the Christian vision of death with a noble simplicity. The
Christian symbols such as lighted candles, holy water and cross
should hold pride of place. Each funeral home should have a
copy of the *Order of Christian Funerals* (Veritas, 1991).

12. Cremated remains or ashes may be brought into the church.

Recommended Reading:

Order of Christian Funerals, Veritas, Dublin, 1991.

Rutherford, R., *The Death of a Christian: the Rite of Funerals*, Pueblo, 1980, republished 1991.

Gogan, B., 'Still Birth: Care of Bereaved Parents', *Doctrine and Life*, Dec. 1984, 563-570

Quinlan, J., *Loved and Lost: The Journey through Dying, Death and Bereavement*, The Columba Press, Dublin, 1996.

Dean, S (ed.), *The Parish Funeral*, McCrimmon, Essex, 1991.

Calhoun, G.J., 'Ministry at the Time of Death', *The New Dictionary of Sacramental Worship*, P.E. Fink (ed.), Gill & Macmillan, 1990, 319-324.

Green, G., *Coping with Suicide*, The Columba Press, Dublin, 1992.

Worden, J.W., *Grief Counselling and Grief Therapy*, Routledge, London, 1991.

Appendix I

Marriage Preparation – Private Tuition

Sometimes particular couples either do not wish to or cannot attend a regular pre-marriage course. In such instances the priest must undertake to prepare them or enlist the help of some competent lay people. It is envisaged that such a course should consist of three separate meetings with the couple, each of about one hour duration. The priest himself (preferably the one who is due to officiate at the wedding) would take one of those sessions to talk about the sacramentality of marriage and help the couple prepare the wedding liturgy.

What follows are some notes and indicators to help the priests and lay people who may be called upon to exercise this very important ministry.

Session I

Aim: To help the couple understand each other better and plan their future together.

The priest (or counsellor) meets the couple in a welcoming and cordial manner when he can devote undivided attention to them, i.e. free from answering the telephone, the door, etc.. He endeavours to put them at their ease by establishing a comfortable rapport with them. The environment in which he meets them is important. It should be comfortable, hospitable and inviting.

For the couple themselves it may be their first time having individual and personal contact with a priest as adults. It is perfectly understandable, therefore, if they arrive filled with a certain amount of nervous anticipation and apprehension. Complications in their own personal situations will intensify their feelings of anxiety. It is important that they perceive the priest as having time for them and being genuinely interested in their marriage and their future.

To initiate contact and create a trusting atmosphere the priest
might have recourse to a series of non-threatening questions,
such as:

When and how did you first meet?

This question leads the couple almost imperceptibly into talking
about themselves in a more personal and intimate way.

Where do you work or what is your trade?

In the present climate of high unemployment this issue has to be
treated very delicately.

What were your first impressions of him? ... of her?

The exchange, while remaining on a rather surface and non-
threatening level, now goes deeper and can become more re-
vealing. This may be the first time that they have disclosed those
long past and immediate reactions to one another.

Why do you think you fell in love with each other?

The interview now plunges rather quickly and profoundly into
the nature of the the couple's relationship. The question will
normally leave them a little puzzled and groping for words to
articulate their feelings *vis-à-vis* each other. The priest/counsel-
lor avails of the opportunity to get across the Church's pastoral
concern for their marriage.

Your hopes and expectations from marriage?

This questions enables the priest to evaluate the couple's attitude to marriage from the viewpoint of fidelity, indissolubility,
children, etc.. He will be in a position to fill in answers to many
of the questions given in the Pre-Nuptial Enquiry Form without
actually interrogating the parties directly.

He leads them into discussing other areas which enhance their
understanding of each other:
- the different home backgrounds of each and their relationship with their families;
- their interests, talents, friendships and how marriage is going
to affect them;
- their work or lack of it;
- where they hope to live and who will mind the money and
pay the bills, etc.;
- the couple's attitude to money. Is there agreement?

Conclusion:
The priest concludes the session by summing up what has been discussed and outlining what will be done at their next meeting. He invites the couple to pray, with him for the success of their forthcoming marriage.

Session II

The Sacrament of Married Love: Partnership, Sexuality, Parenthood

Aim: To help the couple realise that they are the ministers of this sacrament not merely when they pronounce their marriage vows but through their daily sharing of the ups-and-downs of life.

Invite the couple to reflect on what it means to them to say that 'Christian marriage is a sacrament'. They may have difficulty in grappling with the concept of sacrament. Help them to understand that it is nothing more than God's love being made visible and tangible in the life of people. Their total and unconditional love which they already have for each other is what makes their marriage sacramental. Their love for each other is a sharing in God's own love. When they exchange marriage vows they celebrate and announce that love to the whole community and commit themselves to making that love grow deeper and more authentic.

The centrality of Communication in Marriage:
- talking and listening to each other;
- being with one another
- doing things together;
- body language – signs of affection, etc.;
- the sacrificial aspect of married love;
- coping with silence and misunderstandings;
- factors that damage communication – blaming; nagging; possessiveness; drinking to excess; gambling, etc..

The Crowning of Communication – Sexuality:
- the expression of love proper to marriage is the sexual relationship;
- it is an expression of total self-giving; being able to discuss this aspect of their marriage;

- it is a sharing in God's gift of creation; more physical for man, more emotional for woman;
- it must be open to new life.

Family Planning:
- love and fertility;
- planning one's family and different methods of family planning;
- the challenge of parenthood – parenting and Christian education of the children that God may send them.

The Couple's own Faith-Commitment:

This meeting will most likely raise the issue of the couple's own faith and level of religious commitment. If necessary the priest should consult the section of this *Directory* dealing with 'the uncommitted Catholic', p 149-152. He will encourage them to prepare themselves spiritually for this great occasion in their lives by receiving the sacrament of Reconciliation.

Conclusion:

The priest concludes the meeting by summing up what has been discussed and outlining what will be dealt with at their next meeting. He gives the couple a copy of:

a) the Celebration of Marriage, Veritas, 1984;

b) Readings for Your Wedding, Veritas, 1995;

c) Christian Marriage, preparation and celebration, 1990 (for the musician),

with a view to having the couple select their own wedding liturgy. At the next meeting the priest and couple will finalise the marriage liturgy.

Session III

Aim: To prepare the wedding liturgy and help the couple discuss their own religious beliefs and practices.

The priest has recourse to that section of this *Directory* dealing with the liturgical preparation and celebration of marriage, i.e. pp 142-144. He helps the couple to choose those scripture readings that appeal to them and discusses them with them. People usually make choices because something in the readings or prayers strike a chord with them in their own own life story and experience.

The priest and couple reflect on the readings together and pray about them. The aim is to get the couple to discuss God's place in their marriage. Questions such as:

    Why get married in Church?
    How can they be a vehicle of God's love to each other?
    How a married couple might pray together?

The priest helps the couple select the formularies for the exchange of consent, blessing of the rings, nuptial blessing, prayer of the newly married couple, etc. as well as the music and hymns. If the wedding is being celebrated within the context of Mass, the question of Holy Communion from the chalice is discussed and explained. The couple themselves will invariably want to raise other issues pertaining to their wedding arrangements.

Before concluding the priest checks that the pre-marriage documentation is in order or at least in the process of being sorted out.

The meeting concludes with the priest and couple praying together for the success of their forthcoming marriage.

Useful background reading for the priest:
Reidy, M., *Freedom to be Friends: Morals and Sexual Affection,* The Columba Press, Dublin, 1990.

APPENDICES

Ceremony of Engagement

Occasionally couples will ask a priest to bless their engagement. Any ceremony should be flexible, taking into account the background, temperament and wishes of the couple. It may be combined with a eucharistic celebration or be a ceremony in its own right. In which case it consists of a liturgy of the word followed by the exchange of promises, the blessing of the engagement ring, the Lord's Prayer and a final blessing.

Opening Greeting
Liturgy of Word:
> O.T. Reading
> Responsorial Psalm
> (Marriage readings) N.T. Reading
> Gospel

Homily

Exchange of Promises
Man: 'In the name of our Lord Jesus Christ, I N.N., promise that one day I will take you N.N., as my wife. I will love you as I love myself. I will be faithful and loyal to you as Christ is faithful and loyal to his Church. I will comfort and take care of you. I will become one with you in mind in heart and in body. All that a man ought to do for his fiancee I promise to do for you. If it be God's will I will through the sacrament of Marriage pledge myself to you and you alone and forever. May the Lord continue to pour out his blessings upon both of us as we prepare ourselves to be united to him and to one another in Christian marriage'.

Woman: 'In the name of our Lord Jesus Christ, I N.N., promise that one day I will take you N.N. as my husband. I will love you as I love myself. I will be faithful and loyal to you as Christ is faithful and loyal to his Church. I will comfort and take care of you. I promise to become one with you in mind, in heart and in body. All that a woman ought to do for his fiance I promise to do for you. If it be God's will, I will through the sacrament of Marriage pledge myself to you and you alone and forever. May the Lord continue to pour out his blessings upon both of us as we prepare ourselves to be united to him and to one another in Christian marriage'.

Blessing of Ring:

If a ring is being exchanged, the celebrant may bless it in these or similar words:

'God, author of love and source of life, so bless this ring which N. and N. are exchanging here today that it may be a true sign of their growing together. We ask this through Christ our Lord, Amen'.

The man then places the ring on his fiancee's finger, using these or similar words:

'N. wear this ring as a sign of our commitment to each other. May it be a constant reminder to us both or our calling to Christian marriage'.

The woman may respond:

'N. I love you and promise to grow in that love as we prepare for our marriage'.

Prayer of the Faithful

Lord's Prayer

Closing Prayer:

'Father this couple is soon to become one in Christian marriage. Bless that love which they have pledged here today. May it grow stronger as they journey towards their wedding day. May it be a constant reminder of your love for mankind. Help them grow in loving service of you, of one another and of all people. Support them and help them in their future life together. We make this our prayer through Jesus Christ our Lord, Amen'.

Final Blessing:

May the Lord bless you and keep you, Amen.
May the Lord make his face shine upon and be gracious to you, Amen.
May he look upon you and give you his peace, Amen.
May almighty God bless you, Father, Son and Holy Spirit, Amen.

Celebration of Silver Jubilee of a Marriage

Opening Greeting: *Celebrant greets couple and those assembled to celebrate the happy occasion.*

The prayers of the Mass are taken from the *Roman Missal* pp 777-778.

Liturgy of the Word:

> O.T. Reading
> Responsorial Psalm
> (Marriage readings)
> N.T. Reading
> Gospel

Homily

Renewal of Marriage Vows

Priest: N. and N. , you have proven your devotion to each other by your life together. I now ask you to join your right hands and renew your commitment to each other before God and his Church.

Couple: We having given ourselves totally to each other, renew our pledge of mutual fidelity, love and commitment. We will continue to love and honour each other all the days of our life both in sickness and in health. We ask you Lord to continue to shed your abundant blessings upon us and to bring us ever closer together in the years ahead. We thank you Lord (for the gift of our children and) for the support of our relatives, friends and neighbours. May the Lord continue to pour out his blessings upon all of them. We make this our prayer through Jesus Christ, your son who is Lord forever and ever, Amen.

Prayer of the Faithful

Prayer of Couple after Communion

> We thank you, Lord and we praise you for bringing us to this happy day, in which we celebrate our silver wedding anniversary.
> You have given us to each other.
> Now, together we give ourselves to you. We ask you, Lord: make us one in your love and keep us in your peace. Continue to protect our marriage. Bless our home and family. Make us gentle and kind.
> Keep us faithful.

And when life is over, unite us once again, where parting is no more, in the kingdom of your light and love. There we will praise you forever in the happiness and peace of our eternal home. We make this our prayer through Jesus Christ, your Son, who is Lord forever and ever, Amen.

Concluding Prayer

Final Blessing:
May the Lord bless you and keep you,
Amen.
May the Lord make his face shine upon you and be gracious to you,
Amen.
May he look upon you and give you his peace,
Amen.
May almighty God bless you, Father Son and Holy Spirit,
Amen.

Appendix II

Norms for Parish Finance Committees, 1993

Preamble

Material goods are a necessary part of the Church's mission. While these goods belong to the Church as such, their stewardship is entrusted to different people within the ecclesial community. These stewards depend very much on the expertise and advice of competent people within that community. Hence, diocesan and parish finance committees play a vital role in the administration of ecclesiastical goods and properties. Their administration and management must be in harmony with the Church's overall mission of bringing Christ's message of salvation to people.

Canon 537 of the *Code of Canon Law* requires each parish to have a Parish Finance Committee. The norms which follow are intended as guidelines towards the more effective functioning of Parish Finance Committees.

Norms

1. The Parish Finance Committee advises and assists the Parish Priest/Team Leader in the administration of the ecclesiastical goods of the parish.
2. The Parish Finance Committee shall advise the Parish Priest/Team Leader in all areas pertaining to the financial management and administration of parochial property and goods. The competence of the Parish Finance Committee pertains to the following areas:

    a) it shall assist the Parish Priest/Team Leader in compiling an up-to-date, comprehensive inventory of all parochial property and equipment. A copy of this is to be kept in the parish archives and another lodged in the diocesan archives (cf c 1283 #2 & 3);

    b) it shall with the assistance of a sub-committee, if desirable, assist the Parish Priest/Team Leader in drawing up an annual budget or making projections of income and expenditure for the parish. Throughout the year, the Parish Priest/Team Leader shall, with the help of the Parish Finance Committee, monitor the income and expenditure of the parish in the light of the agreed budget or projections.

    c) it shall assist the priests of the parish in preparing the Parish Account Books. The latter are to be brought to the Diocesan Office on the occasion of the visitation;

    d) through its prudent advice, Parish Priests /Team Leaders shall ensure that the ownership of ecclesiastical goods and properties are safeguarded in ways which are valid in civil law (c 1284 #2, 2);

e) it shall advise the Parish Priest/Team Leader on the acquisition, protection and sale of parish property and investments, without prejudice to the provisions of current diocesan, administrative guidelines;

f) it shall advise the Parish Priest/Team Leader with regard to adequate security and insurance of all Church property and goods;

g) the Parish Finance Committee shall also advise and assist the parish in its fundraising policy.

3. In accordance with Canon 532, the Parish Priest/Team Leader, not the Parish Finance Committee, represents the parish in all legal matters.

4. The Parish Finance Committee is distinct from any exclusively fundraising committee, even of a permanent or official nature, which may be in the parish. It should, however, under the direction of the Parish Priest/Team Leader, work closely with any such committee even by co-opting a member on to that committee, to ensure the proper execution of the agreed fundraising policy for the parish

a) The Parish Finance Committee is likewise distinct and separate from the Parish Pastoral Council (cf c 536).

5. Each parish is to have one Parish Finance Committee for the whole parish.

a) Where a parish has more than one church, each with its own 'area', each 'area' should be represented by at least one lay member on the Parish Finance Committee.

6. The Parish Priest/Team Leader and Curate(s)/ Team Member(s) in the parish are *ex officio* members of the Parish Finance Committee.

a) The Parish Priest/Team Leader, or his delegate, is to be the Chairman of the Parish Finance Committee.

b) Curate(s)/Team Members shall attend all meetings.

c) Priests shall continue as members of the Parish Finance Committee for the duration of their parish appointment.

7. The Parish Finance Committee, in addition to its priest member(s) must have at least four lay members, of whom at least two should be laymen and at least two lay women.

a) The Parish Priest/Team Leader, in consultation with the other priest(s) of the parish and with suitable lay advisers, as he may see fit, shall appoint the members of the Committee.

b) Lay members of the Parish Finance Committee, who should be parishioners of the highest integrity, should be competent in management and financial matters. It is highly desirable that at least some members be competent in the area of insurance.

c) The term of office of the lay members of the Parish Finance Committee is to be three years. Lay members, on completion of their third consecutive term of office, are ineligible for immediate re-appointment.

8. When a parish becomes vacant the Parish finance Committee remains in office for the remainder of its term.

   a) The Bishop appoints a Chairperson, who remains in office until a new Parish Priest/Team Leader is appointed. The appointment of the Chairperson during the vacancy must be made in writing.

   b) While the parish remains vacant, all decisions of the Parish Finance Committee must have the written approval of the Bishop before being implemented.

   c) Within the first year of accepting his appointment, the new Parish Priest/Team Leader, having consulted the other priest(s) of the parish and, if necessary lay parishioners, may appoint new lay members or, with the written permission of the Bishop, constitute a new Committee for the remainder of the present Committee's term of office.

9. The Parish Finance Committee is to meet at least three times a year.

10. At its first meeting the newly-appointed Parish Finance Committee shall appoint a Secretary, who shall keep the Minutes of all meetings.

    a) Likewise, at the first meeting also, the members shall be given an accurate picture of the current financial position of the parish.

    b) They shall also be informed of the policy of the Church and of the Diocese in respect of the administration of Church Goods (cs 1273-1279).

    In this diocese, its attention must be drawn to the Diocesan Investment Portfolio, the Diocesan Deposit and Loan Scheme, Diocesan Collections and Diocesan Committees.

    Attention must also be drawn to the regulation that all projects whose total cost exceeds a specific sum must have the Bishop's approval.

11. A quorum for meetings of the Parish Finance Committee is to be one half of the members and the Chairperson.

15. Members of the Parish Finance Committee are required to keep confidential matters discussed at meetings, unless otherwise advised by the Parish Finance Committee.

23rd November 1993

Draft Constitution for a Parish Pastoral Council

1. *Name:*
   1. 1 The Council shall be called 'The .... Pastoral Council'.

2. *Nature and Function:*
   2. 1 The Parish Pastoral Council is a representative body of Christ's faithful whose purpose it is to promote the mission of the Church in its entirety in this particular parish. It shall at all times work in close collaboration with the priest(s) of the parish, advising him/them in matters pertaining to Pastoral ministry (cf cs 528–529).
   The concern of the Pastoral Council is the entire pastoral mission of the Church, long-range and short-range goals and objectives, and to design those procedures and processes through which the pastoral work of the Church is to be accomplished.
   2. 2 In accordance with the mind of the Church, the Council shall have a consultative voice only. Through its insights, expertise and prudent advice, it will help the priest(s) identify, implement and evaluate those pastoral initiatives and policies best suited to the spread of the Gospel in its particular area (cf cs 536 #2; 127).

3. *Membership:*
   3. 1 The following shall be *ex officio* members: all priests of the parish (and the parish sister or Pastoral assistant, if there is one).
   3. 2 The priest(s) shall freely co-opt onto the Council not more than five members, noted for their charisms, skills or positions they already hold in the parish.
   3. 3 Insofar as possible, at least one person representing the different areas of pastoral ministry in the parish shall be elected or nominated to the Council. Care shall be taken to ensure that the different geographical areas, age-groups and social classes are represented.
   3. 4 The Council shall consist of fifteen to twenty members.

4. *Selection of Members:*
   4. 1 Some members of the Council shall be *ex officio* (cf 3.1 above).
   4. 2 Not less than half the members shall be freely elected by the people of the parish, taking into account the criteria laid down in nos 3.2 -3.3 above.
   4. 3 The parish priest shall freely appoint some others in accordance with no 3.2.

5. *Officers:*
   5. 1 The Parish Priest shall be President of the Pastoral Council.
   5. 2 The Chairperson, whose function is the effective running of meetings, is appointed annually by the members.
   5. 3 The Pastoral Council shall have a Secretary and a Treasurer,

who are elected by the members. They shall hold these positions
for not more than two consecutive years.

5.4 Each sub-committee shall elect from its members a Chairperson
and a Secretary.

6. *Meetings:*

6.1 Meetings shall take place each month except during the months
of June, July, August and December. The Parish Priest or another
priest designated by him, shall preside at all meetings. There can
be no meeting without the priest.

6. 2 The priest and secretary prepare the agenda for the meetings.
Other members may propose motions to be included in the
agenda. The agenda shall include matters pertaining to the mission of the Church, i.e. the full-range of pastoral activities which
will enable this particular faith-community to listen more attentively to God's word and put it into practice in their day-to-day
lives.

6. 3 Because of the unique nature of the Council, a short period of
each meeting shall be given over to prayer and reflection on an
appropriate passage of the word of God.

7. *Period of Membership:*

7. 1 The term of office for a Council shall be three years. No member
shall serve more than two consecutive terms but shall be eligible
for re-nomination subsequently.

7. 2 Any member failing to attend four consecutive meetings without reasonable explanation shall be deemed to have resigned.

7. 3 Vacancies shall be filled by co-option.

8. *Quorum:*

8. 1 A quorum shall consist of half the members of the Council.

9. *Cessation of Council:*

9. 1 Since the Council is, by its very nature, advisory to the Parish
Priest, it ceases to exist when the parish becomes vacant.

10. *Sub-Committees:*

10. 1 The Council may establish sub-committees to advise it on matters of special pastoral concern. Other people because of their
particular expertise and competence, may be co-opted onto
these sub-committees.

11. *Ongoing Formation of Members:*

11. 1 Study, reflection and inservice education on the nature and
mission of the Church is of paramount importance for every
member of the Council.

12. *Approval of the Constitution:*

12. 1 The norms of this Constitution are approved by the Bishop of
this Diocese.

Appendix III

A Procedure for Reconciliation in the Church (Dioceses of the Dublin Province)

1. This procedure is designed to lead to a equitable solution of disputes or differences which may arise within the Church as a result of administrative decisions.
2. The criteria to be used in applying the procedure shall be Christian love, justice and equity and the requirements of canon law.
3.1 The procedure does not derogate from procedures already in existence for the resolution of disputes.
   3.2 Where a matter is currently the subject of, or has been determined by, a formal juridical process within the Church, or by some other duly established procedure, it may not be reviewed by this procedure.
   3.3 The determination of doctrinal or theological matters is also excluded from this procedure. But administrative decisions made as a consequence of a dispute in such matters may be considered.
   3.4 Disputes arising from decrees appointing priests to different offices or positions in the Church are, unless the competent authority should decide otherwise excluded from this procedure.
4.1 The procedure is adopted when the parties in dispute have failed to arrive at an amicable resolution of the dispute on their own, and is in two stages.
   4.2 The first described as the 'conciliation stage', is the central and essential one, which may never be omitted.
   4.3 This second, or 'mediation stage', can take place only when the first has not succeeded in resolving the dispute, and provided the parties are willing to adopt this stage.
5.1 The essential aim of the procedure is that the dispute be resolved as quickly as possible.
   5.2 Unless in a particular case there are serious reasons for a more protracted determination, the conciliation stage shall be completed within not more than three months, and the mediation stage within not more than six months, each to be calculated from the initiation of the stage in accordance respectively with Article 8.1 and Article 10.1.
6. The conciliation stage shall be conducted in strict confidence, in accordance with Article 8.

7.1 In each diocese there shall be not fewer than three Conciliators.

    7.2 These Conciliators shall be selected on the basis of their good judgment and mediation ability, by the diocesan Council of Priests, and shall be submitted to the Bishop for approval and appointment.

    7.3 The appointment of each Conciliator shall be for a period of three years but any of them may be re-appointed in accordance with the procedure of paragraph 2 of this Article.

8.1 A party to a dispute which has not been resolved by the parties themselves may approach one of the Conciliators appointed in the diocese with a request for assistance in resolving the dispute. A party which is unwilling to approach a Conciliator of his/her own diocese may approach a Conciliator of another diocese in the province.

    8.2 The Conciliator thus approached shall (unless there be a serious personal reason for not doing so - in which case another of the Conciliators may be approached) get in touch with the other party and, if that party agrees to participate in the procedure, shall make every reasonable effort to resolve the problem, in accordance with Article 2. If this effort is successful, the matter shall be deemed closed.

9. If conciliation does not lead to a resolution of the dispute, the Conciliator shall invite the parties to participate in the mediation stage, which involves the intervention of two mediators and a Chairperson.

10.1 If both parties agree to mediation, each shall select one person to act as Mediator from among the Conciliators appointed in the Province.

    10.2 The two mediators thus selected shall choose another Conciliator from among those appointed in the Province or, should they fail to agree on one of these, another person of proven expertise and experience to act as Chairperson.

    10.3 The group designated in accordance with nn. 1 and 2 of this Article shall form a Mediation Board, the function of which is to investigate the dispute and issue a recommendation designed to resolve it.

    10.4 The Board shall determine its own procedure, taking account of the basic rights of the parties, in accordance with Article 2.

    10.5 The Board shall sympathetically consider, in the light of Article 2, the position of the persons who may claim privilege in respect of information received by them in confidence.

    10.6 The Board shall acknowledge, and the Chairperson shall instruct all who appear before it, that the proceedings are strictly confidential. The recommendation referred to in n 9 of this Article shall be issued to the parties only. No information regarding the recommendation may be given to a third party or made public without the approval of the Chairperson.

APPENDICES

Index

Prayer:
leading people in prayer 28-31
funeral prayers 235-237
prayer groups 28-29
prayer for church unity 227
prayer for vocations 219
pre-confirmation spiritual preparation 85
popular devotions 32-34

Priest:
caring for his own health 133-135
ongoing education and formation 129-132
priestly identity in the post-conciliar church 121-129
priestly morale 135-136
spiritual life of the priest 132-133
the priest and the alienated 50-53
the priest and the missions 137
the priest and vocations 215-216
the priest in his parish 24-27
the priest in the post-primary school 36-37
the priest in the primary school 35-36
the priest's relationship with the presbyterate 136-137

Reconciliation:
a procedure for reconciliation in the church 262-263
children's confessions 102
different rites of reconciliation 98-99
doing penance 100
faculties to hear confessions, diocesan priests and religious 99-100
first confession before first communion 102
formula of absolution to be used 100
parish celebration of reconciliation and healing 96
place and time of reconciliation 100-101
reconciliation and members of other churches 231
reconciliation and those living in irregular unions 102-103
relating reconciliation to life 96; 100
relationship to healing 96
relationship to eucharist 95-96
remission of censures 104-105

Religious:
collaboration between diocesan clergy and religious 209-210
faculties for religious to hear confessions 100
religious working in parishes 210-211

Sick:
bringing holy communion to the sick and housebound 110-111
sacrament of the sick 111-114